The EVERYTHING
Cover Letter Book

Dear Reader:

Here we are, starting a book on letter-writing with a letter. Ironic, maybe? Appropriate, definitely! Now more than ever, cover letters are a critical part of the job-search process. The ideas and samples presented here will help you get the job you want, no matter what your background, age, or circumstance.

Just a decade or so ago, job-search communication could only take place by mail and phone. Now, you can use e-mail, instant messages, voice mail, faxes, Web-based systems, and express mail. Transmission techniques have changed, so your communication strategies should as well.

Cover letters and resumes are the crucial dynamic duo of documents. Follow-ups are also essential, yet they are often forgotten. The power of words will definitely influence the effectiveness of your actions. Fortunately, all of the information you need is right here in this book, which has the power to make you a successful job-seeker. Read on, and then write right!

The EVERYTHING® Series

Editorial

Publishing Director	Gary M. Krebs
Managing Editor	Kate McBride
Copy Chief	Laura M. Daly
Acquisitions Editor	Gina Chaimanis
Development Editor	Julie Gutin
Production Editors	Jamie Wielgus
	Bridget Brace

Production

Production Director	Susan Beale
Production Manager	Michelle Roy Kelly
Series Designers	Daria Perreault
	Colleen Cunningham
	John Paulhus
Cover Design	Paul Beatrice
	Matt LeBlanc
Layout and Graphics	Colleen Cunningham
	John Paulhus
	Daria Perreault
Series Cover Artist	Barry Littmann

Visit the entire Everything® Series at *www.everything.com*

THE
EVERYTHING®
COVER LETTER
BOOK

2nd Edition

Winning cover letters for everybody
from student to executive

Burton Jay Nadler

Adams Media
Avon, Massachusetts

An Everything® Series Book.
Everything® and everything.com® are registered trademarks of F+W Publications, Inc.

Published by Adams Media, an F+W Publications Company
57 Littlefield Street, Avon, MA 02322 U.S.A.
www.adamsmedia.com

ISBN: 1-59337-335-X
Printed in the United States of America.

J I H G F E D C B A

Library of Congress Cataloging-in-Publication Data
Nadler, Burton Jay
The everything cover letter book / Burton Jay Nadler.-- 2nd ed.
p.   cm.
(An everything series book)
Rev. ed. of: The Everything cover letter book : great cover letters
for everybody from student to executive / Steven Graber.
ISBN 1-59337-335-X
1. Cover letters. I. Graber, Steven. Everything cover letter book. II. Title. III. Series: Everything series

HF5383.G636 2005
650.14'2--dc22
                        2004026915

This publication is designed to provide accurate and authoritative information with regard to the subject matter covered. It is sold with the understanding that the publisher is not engaged in rendering legal, accounting, or other professional advice. If legal advice or other expert assistance is required, the services of a competent professional person should be sought.

—From a *Declaration of Principles* jointly adopted by a Committee of the American Bar Association and a Committee of Publishers and Associations

Many of the designations used by manufacturers and sellers to distinguish their products are claimed as trademarks. Where those designations appear in this book and Adams Media was aware of a trademark claim, the designations have been printed with initial capital letters.

This book is available at quantity discounts for bulk purchases.
For information, please call 1-800-872-5627.

Contents

Cover Letters for Special Situations / 77

In Response to Employer-Identified Postings / 105

In Response to Confidential Postings / 177

"Cold" Contact Letters to Employers / 187

Other Letters / 273

Acknowledgments

To students and alumni of Southern Methodist University, Dartmouth College, University of the Pacific, University of Rochester, and University of Dreams. Each letter of yours that I critiqued taught me much. Now I share these lessons through this book and the samples within. Thanks for all that you have taught me, for allowing me to teach others, and for the continued honor of working with you.

To Justin and Jordan. You two will always be the focus of my love and pride. I hope that whenever you wish, you will able to share your unique talents with others through cover letters, resumes, and interviews. And I pray that all of your career and life dreams will come true. While books are gifts I share with many, you are the legacy that your mother, grandmothers, grandfathers, aunts, uncles, great-aunts, great-uncles, and I give to all.

Top Ten Cover Letter
Do's and Don'ts

1. Do always accompany your resume with a cover letter or cover notes.

2. Don't use multipurpose resumes and cover letters that lack focus.

3. Do highlight qualifications in a well-crafted and targeted cover letter.

4. Don't use vague phrases like "To whom it may concern" or "Dear Sir/Madam" as a salutation.

5. Do be a proactive job-seeker and respond to opportunities quickly.

6. Don't assume no one will read your cover letter.

7. Do take the time to edit and revise your cover letter before you send it out.

8. Don't simply copy sample cover letters, changing only the employer's name.

9. Do take advantage of new technologies, particularly e-mail and Web-based resume and cover-letter uploading systems.

10. Don't forget to follow up—a great thank-you letter can be as effective as your initial letter.

Introduction

▶ Some claim that the art of letter writing is dead. I contend that it's alive and well and that all job-seekers can create viable and effective letters to suit their needs. Together with a resume, a cover letter is a very special job-search correspondence. Anyone—high school students, college students, internship candidates, entry-level candidates, and experienced candidates—can take specific steps that will lead to the ability to write successful cover letters.

This book details the steps required to write right and informs readers of how cover letters fit into the overall job-search process. It inspires readers to blend actions and words—to write great cover letters but also to follow up with all the actions required in a successful job search.

Resumes and cover letters are the dynamic duo of job-search documents. They really can get your foot in the door for a job interview. Both must be targeted, contain key words, and reveal to readers that you know the skills required for particular jobs. Together, the sum of these job-search parts is greater than the whole, but each must independently present qualifications and yield interview invitations. In this book, you'll learn about the power of targeted resumes and how to create one of your own.

In addition to writing great cover letters, you'll learn about other letters that are useful during the job search: letters of application, letters of introduction, and networking notes. Well-crafted and focused correspondence generates interest in your resume and candidacy and, ultimately, inspires readers to invite you to interview.

This book also addresses questions regarding format and content, special circumstances, and the use of the Internet. Typical queries may reveal unique, creative, and inspirational responses, designed to make you think outside the metaphorical box and act assertively, appropriately, and effectively. Step by step by step, you will be guided through the process of writing your cover letter, developing your resume, surviving the interview, and accepting the job.

If imitation is the sincerest form of flattery, it can also be the best cover-letter strategy. In the more than 200 samples included here, job-seekers of varied goals and backgrounds can have their questions answered and find some guidance and inspiration during the writing process. Before-and-after samples reveal how following the guidelines in this book will maximize the impact of your efforts. Timely and timeless content of cover letters for positions ranging from Administrative Assistant to Writing Instructor will provide useful information as well. All the letter samples are presented to diminish confusion and eliminate procrastination. They are not meant to be copied, but to inspire you in writing right.

As the title implies, this book offers *everything* you need to succeed. Read on, write right, and get the job you want!

Chapter 1

Let the Job Search Begin

Thomas Edison, one of history's most inspired and productive inventors, is credited with saying "Genius is one percent inspiration, ninety-nine percent perspiration." While a job search also involves inspiration and perspiration—and a bit of consternation—to be successful you need to have a plan and know what you're doing. This chapter reviews how the cover letter fits into the job-search process and what else is required to get the desired outcome.

It's About Communication

Who would have thought the phrase, "I'm applying for a job," would reveal a flaw in the strategy of many job-seekers? They assume that the job search is an application process, so they look for ads and apply to them. But a better approach is to view job searching as a process of communication.

ESSENTIAL

Even if it's your first time to write a cover letter, don't be nervous. A job search is nothing more than a series of steps toward a particular goal. Following the advice in this book, you too can complete these steps, one at a time, until you achieve your goal.

The Everything® Resume Book, 2nd Edition, introduced the concepts of heartfelt versus head-thought motivations and actions. Simply, the heart wishes things will come true and believes the more postings you answer, the more open and vague your cover letters, and the more passionate your feelings about a job, the more likely a potential employer will find you qualified and react favorably to your application efforts. The head, on the other hand, conducts field, function, and firm oriented pRe-search (research before job search), identifies and presents key qualifications via targeted resumes and cover letters, conducts follow-up efforts, and prepares for interviews. That is, the head thinks strategically about "What's next."

Which is the right approach? In truth, you need to have a combination of both heart and head and to be inspired by emotions and logic, personifying the best of both doer and dreamer.

Similarly, the application part of the job-search process is important. But effectively communicating your sense of focus and qualifications through well-crafted letters and notes and appropriately enthusiastic discussions will yield success.

Simple Steps for Success

Searching for a job isn't easy, but the process itself is a simple one. It is best thought of as composed of eight clearly achievable steps:

1. Figure out your job-search goals—what kind of a job are you looking for?
2. Create or update your resume, and draft a general cover letter.
3. Develop a "target list" of potential employers and a "network" of advocates.
4. Respond to posted openings with a cover letter targeted and revised for each posting.
5. If there are options for how to submit your cover letter and resume, the best approach is faxing, followed by e-mail, and finally mail.
6. Follow up with each submission.
7. Use your resume and cover letter for guidance during the interview.
8. Receive offers, and accept one.

ALERT!

"I'm looking for anything" is not a goal. You should know what kind of a job you're looking for and concentrate in that field. A job search built upon unclear or unrealistic goals is likely to be frustrating, prolonged, or even unsuccessful. The inability to articulate goals can be overcome by doing adequate job market research before you begin answering job ads.

Targeting the Job You Want

Cover letters and resumes do not have to state lifelong dreams, but they must express your immediate job-search goals. Ideally, they will help the potential employer imagine your future performance with the new company. This can be done with two kinds of information: your past academic and employment achievements, and your skills and capabilities. Good cover letters and resumes demonstrate understanding of the job and its specific functions, as well as self-knowledge and confidence.

It is easy to be focused when responding to postings because you can target the requirements of the specific job described in the announcement. When conducting a broader proactive search, focus comes from "pResearch" (research before job search). Research into careers and job functions teaches you to use the appropriate language needed to create great resumes and cover letters.

From Resume to Cover Letter

Once you've developed and updated your resume to reflect your job goals, you'll feel more comfortable about writing a dynamic and focused cover letter. (Chapter 3 details the relationship between resumes and cover letters.) You can use this letter as your starting point for each targeted cover letter. All you need to do is fine-tune the letter, projecting your qualifications for a specific job.

QUESTION?

What if I don't know what kind of job I want?
Try to focus on specific employment fields and functions, as well as the kinds of companies you'd like to work for. If you truly don't know what you want, you can try reviewing the postings and flagging the ones you're interested in. Eventually, your interest should reveal a pattern of strong focus on particular types of jobs.

The Power of Networking

To whom will you send your resume and cover letter? To those on your target list of potential employers and people who can support your efforts! Develop this list using professional directories, reference materials, and online resources. (Appendix B lists valuable printed and online materials.)

Networking is perhaps the most effective yet most often misunderstood and poorly implemented approach to finding a job. You can use networking to learn about fields of particular interest and to learn to articulate your goals in those fields. Talking to people in the professional industry without the pressure of a formal interview will make it easier for you once you start responding to job postings. Additionally, the more your name and qualifications become known in the industry, the more likely you are to be granted an interview.

Professional colleagues, friends, family, faculty, and fellow graduates can be very helpful with networking and job-search undertakings. As you read on, you will learn how to create effective networking notes to accompany a targeted resume.

Once you compose your list, it's time to use the phone to confirm the information. You must make sure you have the right contact persons and, if possible, their fax number and e-mail address. Always update your list, and keep track of all interactions with those you contact. Know who you talked to, e-mailed, or faxed, and the nature of your communications. This information will be critical when it's time for following up with your contacts.

Networking can be initiated with a phone call or, more effectively, via e-mail. In a brief networking note, introduce yourself and state clearly and concisely your need for consideration, referrals, or information. End by stating that you will follow up with a call. Either in your note or during your follow-up call, ask the contact person for names of other contacts or to set up an informal "information conversation," so you can learn more about your network member and identify those who can help you in your job search.

ESSENTIAL

"Hit lists" of employers can be generated using printed or online directories. Membership directories, employee directories, top–twenty-five firm listings, and alumni listings are great sources of information. Identify and use these resources by using an Internet search engine or with the help of a reference librarian.

As you continue your networking efforts, remember that networking is about sharing your goals and asking for support. Vague requests or unstated hidden agendas are ineffective and inappropriate. Know what you want, don't be afraid to ask politely for help, and be straightforward and sincere.

Responding to Postings

It's a good idea to post your resume and general cover letter on various job sites and maybe also on your personal Web site, but don't be passive in limiting yourself to this strategy. Too many job-seekers foolishly believe that posting resumes on job sites is a good way to do a comprehensive job search. To perform a good reactive job search, you must also respond to actual job announcements.

The resumes and letters you use to respond directly to postings must be focused and targeted. Generic drafts should be "specialized and finalized," that is, adapted so that the content matches requirements stated on job announcements. Remember, you should "apply to" and "be inspired by" postings.

Keep It Going

Remember, a job search is all about communication, not simply application! Your goal is to communicate appropriately. For instance, when you respond to a job listing, be sure to do so in the manner requested in the posting. If the ad states "No phone calls," do not attempt to find out the phone number of the hiring manager and call anyway. (You can still call the organization's general number to confirm the correct contact person.)

QUESTION?

How does the cover letter get me a job?
A cover letters complements and supplements the resume. Together, these documents inspire employers to interview you for a particular position. If you interview effectively, you will likely earn a job offer.

To be sure you start off on the right foot, double-check your information before you fax or e-mail your resume and cover letter. Typical first phone contacts are easy. They might sound like the following:

"Hello. I would like to speak with the person who does the hiring for your firm. Specifically, I am looking for a position as a [*type of job desired*].

Can you tell me the name of the person I should talk with about such a position, and his or her title, and then forward my call? Thank you so much."

"Hello. I would like to fax or e-mail a cover letter and resume to the right person. If I am looking for a position as a [*type of job desired*], is there a particular person I should contact? Can you tell me to whom I should send a cover letter and resume, and provide me his or her e-mail address or fax number? Thanks."

Follow Up!

There is always an appropriate and effective way to follow up initial contacts. Just as you did the first time around, e-mail whenever possible, clearly and concisely stating your reason for communicating. Faxing is a good second option; snail mail is somewhat less effective. Thank-you notes are the most common form of following up, but you can also confirm receipt of initial communications, express continued interest in seeking an interview, and regularly inform others of any changes in your search status. You can use follow-ups in networking by keeping those you've already contacted updated with your job-seeking progress.

Each follow-up is a small step toward an interview and, ultimately, an offer. Regularly assess your approaches, and don't be afraid to contact someone or some organization again and again or to refocus your efforts. You can even follow up on a posting that seems outdated or one that has been filled. Be polite yet persistent. Call to confirm that your documentation was received. Ask when you should follow up again. Be patient, not a pest. Strategically use network members and advocates to follow up as well. These individuals can send an e-mail or make a call on your behalf.

It is your responsibility to communicate through all stages of the job search. Don't wait for prospective employers or others to follow up with you, and don't expect resumes and cover letters to magically get you an interview as you sit back and relax. Job-search documents are critical, but following up ensures that they will be read and that you will be successful. Remember, it's communication, not just application!

Surviving the Interview

You may have heard that "the resume and cover letter get the interview, but the interview gets the offer." Chapter 4 contains detailed advice and exercises needed to effectively use your resume and cover letter during this critical conversation. The most important thing to remember about interviewing is that someone has already read your resume and cover letter and identified your qualifications. Your competence is assumed, so you should feel confident and focus your discussion on the already read correspondence.

To enhance your confidence and show off your strengths, be prepared. Your resume and cover letter can be focal points for interview preparation. But preparation also involves additional communication. By phone or e-mail, ask in advance about what to expect: how many people you will be meeting, how long the interviews might take, and whether there are "particular issues or questions I should think about or materials I should read?"

It's okay to ask about proper attire. Know whether you should be business formal (a suit for both men and women) or casual khaki (pressed slacks, ironed shirt, tie, and blazer for men; pressed slacks or skirt, ironed shirt or sweater for women).

Generally, interviewers may be grouped into three categories. Conversational interviewers like to chat about almost anything. Traditional interviewers tend to ask typical questions and query resume entries top to bottom. Behavioral interviewers delve deeply into past accomplishments and details regarding behaviors that yielded achievements.

The Job Offer

Ultimately, you will receive a job offer, and you will have to determine whether to accept or reject it. Be enthusiastic and appreciative at first, but put some thought into what you're getting. Prepare a list of critical questions and issues, and arrange for a post-offer visit or detailed phone conversation. Communicate honestly at this stage. Before you accept that first offer, you should (confidently) call other prospective employers and ask if they can accelerate their consideration process or give you any feedback regarding your candidacy. This is a courteous move that gives your other prospects a heads-up that you are about to come off the job market. If they plan to make you an offer, they can do so without delay, and you can judge and weigh all your options without that haunting feeling that something better might be out there somewhere. Do not ever accept an offer, continue your job search, and then renege on your first commitment.

Proactive and Reactive Strategies

As you can see, the eight steps to getting a job you want require both proactive and reactive strategies. Reactive strategies involve your reactions to the job ads posted by companies that are looking to hire employees. Proactive strategies are those that involve efforts like networking and self-initiated contact with organizations.

Most survey data reveal that at best about 30 percent of all job-seekers find positions through job ads. Unfortunately, many job-seekers focus 100 percent of their efforts on responding to printed and online announcements. To become an effective job-seeker, don't ignore proactive strategies and techniques. Self-initiated contact is effective, especially when using a well-written cover letter.

The information and exercises within this book should inspire your head as well as heart, making you a confident and competent job-search communicator. The cover letters you will create will be suited for all circumstances and will help you maximize the number of interviews.

Three Ps in Perspective

Another way to break down your task of searching for a job is to consider it as a combination of three Ps: Your efforts must be a dynamic series of communications with postings, people, and places.

Postings

Almost everyone knows where to look for postings. You can search through the help-wanted ads in the newspaper, check online job ad sources like *www.hotjobs.com* or *www.monster.com*, or browse individual company job-opening pages.

You can use the postings in two effective ways. The more obvious approach is to use the postings to apply for the jobs. A secondary approach is to use the information you glean from the postings to communicate with the employer about other, unlisted job possibilities.

People

Ultimately, even if you use Web-based resources, you must communicate with people. When you respond to postings, you should address your letter to a particular person. When networking to seek consideration, referrals, or advice, you are communicating with specific individuals. After you apply for postings, you inform advocates and seek their support to gain an interview. When you interview, it's face-to-face communications that ultimately yield an offer. In short, people-work is as important as paperwork.

Places

You can and should identify the employers that you want to work for and focus on cities or states where you want to work. Looking for "any job anywhere" is not a strategy that enhances your potential for success. In truth, being so open limits your chances. Focusing on a field, function, and firm is best.

The Fourth P: pRe-search

For those who cannot articulate goals, pRe-search begins with reading books and other resources on careers in different fields, especially the "What-can-I-do-with-a-major-in [*your major here*]" variety. Those with clear goals should begin with pRe-search, in which you identify employers and potential network members. Employer directories, professional association membership lists, alumni directories, college or university Web sites containing faculty biographies, and employer Web sites are great getting-started resources. Do your homework, make lists, identify appropriate individuals, and then use great cover letters to make initial contact.

FACT

The inability to articulate goals is most commonly cited by career counselors, placement professionals, and career coaches as the factor most likely to prolong a job search and as the source of most job-search frustration. Self-assessment and active research will enhance your abilities to clearly and concisely express job-search goals in your cover letters.

Do It RIGHT

"Do the RIGHT thing!" can be your cover-letter rallying cry. The acronym RIGHT stands for the five-step process of cover-letter writing:

Review (cover-letter samples, job ads, and other relevant documentation)
Identify resume "keys"
Generate a draft
Hone a finished product
Transmit to employer

Following these five steps will help you make your correspondence come alive!

Do Your Research

To get going, review sample letters—there are more than 200 in this book!—and job ads. Pay attention to the phrases or special language used in letters as well as postings. You must transform key phrases in job postings into the best paragraphs in your cover letters. Remember, imitation is a great cover-letter writing strategy.

Identify Resume "Keys"

Look at your resume with the job you are applying for in mind. Identify key points that you wish to highlight in your cover letter. These should be field-focused qualities as well as directly related academic, employment, or co-curricular achievements. What is it about your resume that you think most strategically links you to the job or the employer? What two resume entries do you want the cover-letter reader to examine in detail?

Generate a Draft

Keep your first draft to a page if possible, but don't worry too much about length—you can edit it later. Make sure you follow some of the format and content suggestions appearing in Chapter 2, but don't copy any of the samples that inspire you. Just get some ideas down on paper or on screen. Don't feel pressured to come up with the final draft right away.

One size, shape, or content does not fit all! Do not write one cover letter and then use it for all your job searches. You should be using proactive and reactive documents—letters of application, letters of introduction, and networking notes—and each letter should be tailored for a specific job or firm you're interested in.

Hone a Finished Version

You'll find some before-and-after examples of how you should edit your cover letter drafts in Chapter 5 and a critiquing checklist and last-minute tips to ensure that your final document is as close to perfect as possible in Appendix A. Remember, this is your first writing assignment for your prospective employer. It should not contain typos or any major grammatical or style errors.

Send It Off

Once done, don't delay sending your letter and resume out. There truly is no reason to wait. Never procrastinate.

Chapter 2

The Letter-Writing Process

Chapter 1 introduced the basics of how to write "right." Writing right means doing research, identifying what it is you want to say, writing a first draft, polishing it, and sending it off. This chapter will give you something else—more specific information about appropriate cover-letter format, wording, and issues related to electronic communication.

Putting Your Best Foot Forward

Your cover letter is the first writing assignment you will complete for a prospective employer. It's a preview of your work. To demonstrate your future performance, it only makes sense for you to stay on task and focused, presenting relevant information in an easy-to-read format. In your cover letter, you should be specific, focusing on the job you're applying for or a function you're interested in. You have to impress the readers in a subtle way, by presenting the information they need and suggesting what you think the next step should be. A cover letter must be independently strong yet complementary to your resume. Together, these two documents motivate readers to invite you to interview.

QUESTION?

Which comes first, the resume or cover letter?
You present the cover letter to an employer as an introduction to your resume—remember, it "covers" the resume. But when it comes to writing, you should complete the resume first. In fact, many cover letters appearing here have been inspired by the resumes listed in *The Everything® Resume Book, 2nd Edition.*

Cover-Letter Formats

There are three types of cover letters: letters of application, letters of introduction, and networking notes. Each is written with a particular purpose and to target specific readers, yet all three types share common content and format. As you review samples in this book, you will see obvious differences in some cases and more subtle ones in others.

Letters of application and letters of introduction should be written in either traditional or memo style. Networking notes, on the other hand, can use an informal tone and style. A traditional business letter begins with your name, address, phone number, and e-mail address appearing letterhead-style across the top of the page. Underneath and in left-justified block form goes the date (for example, June 1, 200–), followed by extra line breaks, and the name, title, and address of the letter's recipient. Following a few more line breaks, include the salutation, such as "Dear Ms. Cummings:".

Here's an example of the beginning of a letter in traditional business style:

Chris Smith
123 Any Street • City, ST 12345 • (555) 555-5555 • csmith@email.com

June 1, 200–

Pat Cummings
Account Supervisor
Any Advertising Agency
456 Any Street
City, ST 12345
FAX (555) 555-5557

Dear Ms. Cummings:

You can also choose to use memo style for your letter. Memos present DATE:, FROM: [*your name*], and SUBJECT: or RE: after capitalized headers on the left of the page. You will also in most cases want to include a TO: line to address the letter to the attention of a particular person or department.

The memo style is a good choice if you do not know the name of a contact person at an organization, and you need to send a letter to a department ("Human Resources Department") or unspecified person ("Hiring Manager").

Here's an example of the beginning of a letter in memo format:

Chris Smith
123 Any Street • City, ST 12345 • (555) 555-5555 • csmith@email.com

DATE: June 1, 200–
FROM: Chris Smith
TO: Human Resources Department
RE: Marketing Director Position

You don't include a salutation ("Dear . . .") in a memo-style letter; instead, the body of the letter begins directly (after one blank line) below the RE: or SUBJECT: line. This lack of a salutation enables you to avoid writing such dated and impersonal constructions as "Dear Sir/Madam" or "To Whom It May Concern."

You may choose to use the memo style even when you do in fact know the name of the person you are writing to. For one thing, this format can help to give your letter a serious, businesslike tone. Also, if you are unable to determine whether the person you are writing to is a man or woman, using the memo style is an effective (if slightly sneaky) way of avoiding the entire problem of choosing "Dear Mr." or "Dear Ms." In other circumstances, you might actually know the person you are writing to, but only slightly, leaving you unsure whether "Dear Pat" or "Dear Ms. Cummings" is more appropriate. The memo style can help you to sidestep that choice as well.

One more word on formats: When you send an e-mail, your e-mail program will likely automatically include "Date:", "From:", "To:" and "Subject" lines in a box at the top of the e-mail. This leaves you the choice of beginning the body of the e-mail cover letter directly with a salutation ("Dear Ms. Cummings:" or "Dear Pat:") or with several lines of text in the memo style. One important difference between regular letters and e-mails is that in e-mails your contact information (street address, phone number, and e-mail address) will usually be placed at the end of the e-mail after your name, and not in a header at the beginning.

Letters of Application

The most common cover letter is a letter of application, used to respond to postings. Letters of application should contain job-specific phrasing and match qualifications with those listed in the posting.

This type of letter is the easiest to write because you have the job ad to help you figure out what you need to say. An effective letter of application should focus on two or three key requirements and corresponding resume entries. The goal of this letter is to show the employer that you have the skills and qualifications they are looking for in filling their job opening.

The following situations call for a letter of application:

- **Employer postings**—These postings include the company name and may or may not provide a contact name. In this case, make sure you do some research on the company and incorporate it into your cover letter. If you don't have a contact name, use the memo format to write the letter.
- **Confidential postings**—These postings don't identify the employer. A letter in response to a confidential posting must focus on the job description and on your analysis of the skills required to succeed, which you should demonstrate that you possess.
- **Employment agencies**—When you are contacting a headhunter or other professional who specializes in job placement, you may use phrases such as "should you judge my candidacy worthy of an interview for this position with your client firm . . ."
- **Executive search firms**—These firms deal with filling senior and executive positions. Again, focus your letter on motivating the reader to support your candidacy and to forward your information to the client (the hiring organization) with a recommendation to interview.

FACT

Most cover letters are about 200 to 400 words long, and networking notes are fewer than 200 words. Communication done via e-mail should be shorter, but you can attach additional files like your resume and a more official cover letter. In any case, it's not really the length that's most important. It's the content used to support your candidacy that is crucial and that has the most impact on your being offered an interview.

Letters of Introduction

These are proactive letters that introduce your candidacy to potential employers or allies. The challenge is to be strategically focused, even though you'll be tempted to be general and cast as wide a net as possible. Even though this letter isn't written in application for a specific job, you must communicate functions you are most interested in and qualified for.

You may want to write a letter of introduction in the following situations:

- **Contacting a targeted employer**—If you're interested in a specific company, you can send a letter of introduction to a particular person (if you can get a contact name) or at least to human resources.
- **Before an on-campus interview**—Employers will be impressed if you send a letter of introduction after being selected to meet.
- **Before a career fair**—This is a way to better your chances of being granted an interview for post-baccalaureate jobs or internships.
- **Broadcast letters**—This popular method is ineffective if a generic, unfocused letter is sent to hundreds of employers. Not to worry! You can make it work as long as you stay focused, identifying functional areas of interest and addressing the employer directly.
- **Initial contact**—You can use letters of introduction to make contact for the first time. You might, for example, send letters to people listed in directories for professional associations or specialized fields. Whatever the case, don't be shy about contacting someone and introducing yourself and your goals.

Networking Notes

These are brief, informal statements, usually e-mailed. They concisely request consideration, advice, or referrals from advocates and potential network members. Because e-mail has become the medium of choice for these messages, brevity and clarity are crucial. Also be sure to attach your resume and mention that you will send a cover letter later.

Content Is Crucial

You probably already know that a cover letter and a resume should each be one page in length. But how are you supposed to fill that page? Choose the information about you and your skills and achievements that is pertinent to the particular job or field. This information goes in a certain order.

Introductory Focus Paragraph

The initial paragraph cites the job title or functional area you are interested in and requests an interview. This first section can identify the foundations upon which you will rest your candidacy. Is it education? Is it work experience in general, or can you claim one or two specific accomplishments? Is it a specific project that matches stated requirements?

Remember what you once learned about the five-paragraph essay? Begin your essay with a clear thesis statement that is supported by three paragraphs and then end with a conclusion. Cover letters are pretty similar—think of each letter as having an introduction, supporting paragraphs, and a conclusion.

Qualification and Motivation Paragraphs

These two paragraphs, which may be presented as a series of bullet-point lists, discuss your qualifications and motivation. They identify examples from your past that project abilities to perform in the future. This is where you apply the "R-I" of RIGHT: review cover-letter samples and job ads, and identify resume "keys." What key resume points will you present here? How can you connect previous achievements to the listed job requirements? Be specific! The more you use the language of the field you wish to enter (special phrases and key words), the better. Use appropriate language to ensure that you will soon walk into an interview with confidence.

Closing Paragraph

Restate your desire for an interview, perhaps suggesting a phone interview as a convenient next communication. State that you will follow up to confirm the contact's receipt of the letter and accompanying resume. If you wish, you can close with the most critical point you wish to cover during the interview. Of course, also say thank-you. While you must sign any cover letter you fax or mail, when using e-mail (more and more the case), you can use a script font to represent your signature, if you like.

Special Circumstance Statements

These can be added in the last paragraph or as postscripts. You may want to note that you anticipate being in a particular city at a particular date, that you have an offer in hand and limited time to conduct interviews, or that you also have enclosed supporting documents like writing samples, letters of recommendation, or other materials.

FACT

Basically, cover letters have three components—an introductory paragraph, qualification and motivation summaries, and a closing paragraph. Effective letters focus on particular titles or functions, and they present specific traits and abilities that match those required to do the job.

Myths and Realities

As soon as you start your job search, it's likely that you'll start getting all kinds of advice from those around you. Unfortunately, there seem to be a lot of misconceptions about the most effective and ineffective ways of looking for a job. Let's identify some job-searching myths in order to prevent misguided action and achieve positive outcomes faster.

Myth #1: No One Reads Cover Letters

Some employers who screen candidates prefer resumes. Others read both resume and cover letter. A lot depends upon the job and the field, but it's safe to say that in many cases cover letters are very carefully reviewed. If writing talents are critical to job performance, this document will be scrutinized with particular attention. Also, electronic key-word search capabilities include cover letters. So someone almost always reads your correspondence.

Myth #2: Getting Attention by Being "Different"

If creative talents are associated with job requirements, you can be as creative as you wish in formatting your cover letter. However, direct, concise, and skill-focused cover letters will still get more attention. Matching desired capabilities and achievements is more important than being different. Cover letters stand out when they express qualifications effectively and when letters and resumes together project interview-worthiness.

Myth #3: You Can't Upload a Cover Letter

When using online job sites, you can post your cover letter along with the resume. Some posting and resume submission sites seem to allow you to upload only resumes, but in most cases you can transmit your cover letter as well. Just create and upload a two-page document, with the first being the cover letter and the second the resume.

Myth #4: Individualized Cover Letters Are Impossible

On the contrary, individualized cover letters are easy (and a must). Always refer to the name of the company and, when possible, use the actual job title in the first and last paragraphs. Ideally, also reveal to readers that you have reviewed the job posting and the mission statement of the firm. You are a unique individual and candidate. Your letter should be, too.

QUESTION?

What if I don't have a name to address a cover letter to?
Try to get a name by calling or exploring a company's Web site. If you can't find a name, don't fret. Use memo format and focus on the content of the letter, not on the recipient. The most important person is you—the writer, the candidate.

Common Mistakes

While it is always best to see the metaphorical glass as half full, remaining optimistic and positive, sometimes we can learn from common mistakes. In all cases, it's okay to fill strategic plans with good ideas and best steps to success. Some of the before-and-after samples appearing in Chapter 5 will reveal how you can transform mistakes into masterpieces.

Mistake #1: Too Much Creativity

Unless the job you are applying for involves copywriting, scriptwriting, or artistic and graphic creativity, it's best to avoid too much creativity. Instead, just be direct, enthusiastic, and clear. Stories about someone sending a cover letter and resume in a shoebox, and stating, "Let me put my best foot forward with your organization" are urban myths. Effective job-seekers don't deliver resumes in shoeboxes, nor do they print cover letters and resumes on T-shirts or huge posters. You can be effective with a traditional approach, allowing your skill-focused writing style and follow-up techniques to support your request for an interview.

Mistake #2: No Job Stated

This sin of omission can be costly. If readers have no clue about the job you want, serious consideration is impossible. Be sure you state the job when writing letters of application and your functional areas of interest when writing letters of introduction. Your networking notes should also clearly identify your chosen positions. Always make your goal clear, and you'll be more likely to get a positive response.

Mistake #3: No Reference to Employer

Include the name of the organization you are applying to somewhere in your cover letter. Broad requests that do not state your desire to interview with and work for a particular firm are significantly less effective. First and last paragraphs are best for stating the name of the firm, while all paragraphs are appropriate for citing job titles and functions.

Mistake #4: Lack of Focus

Those who fear focus are most prone to send open letters, stating an eclectic mix of talents and a wish for the reader to identify a best fit. It's ironic that trying to be open ends up getting the door closed on you for serious consideration. Your cover letter is there for you to project goals and qualifications. It is not the responsibility of readers to analyze your candidacy and determine what jobs are right for you. You are the one who must state what you want and what you are qualified to perform.

New Issues for the E-Generation

Only a decade or so ago, job-seekers were limited to mailing resumes and cover letters. Then came express mail, which speeded the process and magnified the importance of messages delivered by a next-day carrier. Next, faxing introduced immediate communication and allowed for follow-ups minutes after resumes and cover letters were faxed. Now, almost all job-seekers must become "e-fficient": able to effectively use the Internet and electronic communications in their job search.

ALERT!

Access to the World Wide Web is essential for job-seekers today. You must use the Web to identify and respond to postings, to explore potential employer Web sites, and to e-mail your resume and cover letter (plus other supporting documents) as attachments. If you don't have your own computer and a way to connect to the Web, use the free resources at your local public library.

E-mail Etiquette

Today, e-mail is an acceptable way of sending cover letters and resumes, but you should follow proper strategies when doing so. When e-mailing, include the name of the job in the subject heading whenever possible. Keep your e-mail text concise, or adapt what would be the initial paragraph and refer to the "attached cover letter and resume." Spell-check your e-mail—typos characterize you as someone who does not pay attention to detail. A good feature of most e-mail programs is the ability to send yourself a secret copy of your messages. Another option is to save all the messages you send. This will allow you to review those messages at a later date, just like saving a paper copy.

Voice Mail

Voice mail is also appropriate for transmitting messages to potential employers and advocates, but try to stick with brief statements and don't expect responses immediately. Keep messages brief and to the point, always ending with a question, like "Should I call again or will you e-mail me your response?" If possible, alternate between e-mail and voice mail, so you won't appear to be a nuisance. And be patient regarding responses. A day or two may seem like forever, but it's perfectly normal.

Resume Uploading Systems and Sites

Unrealistic expectations associated with online job-search services are endless. On sites like *www.monster.com* and *www.hotjobs.com*, you have the option of uploading your resume so that potential employers may browse through it. Although this is a passive approach to searching for a job, it does occasionally work and is probably worth your while. Plus, when you do find good postings, you may be able to simply forward your uploaded resume in application for those positions.

ESSENTIAL

You can upload cover letters into Web-based systems, even if they appear to only allow resumes. Create and then upload a multiple-page document. Make the first page the cover letter and subsequent pages the resume. Always supplement resumes with cover letters, even when using Internet resources.

Key Words

Often, before any actual person reviews your cover letter and resume, the documents are electronically scanned by key word. Potential employers identify and read only those documents that contain predetermined words and phrases. Knowing this will surely make you appreciate the importance of using key words appropriate to your chosen field and, if applicable, in the job description.

E-mail Won't Fail

Some postings offer the option of e-mailing, faxing, or mailing cover letters and resumes. Whenever you can, e-mail first, but if you want to be sure, follow up with a mailing. Your e-mail message will be the "cover note," and your resume and lengthier "cover letter" will probably be attached as Microsoft Word files. The first line of the e-mail message should state your purpose: "I would like to interview for the Account Executive position." Subsequent lines state qualifications concisely and clearly. E-mails should be quick, direct, and informal. Lengthy and overly formal e-mails are hard to read. The attached letter can be more business-like.

E-mail is the transmission method of choice for most initial contacts and follow-up communications. Of course, you may have to use the phone to identify the e-mail address of your desired contact person. A quick search of an organization's online directory (if one is available) might give you this information as well.

FACT

Microsoft Word is used by more than half of all business professionals. To ensure your documents will be accessible when you attach them to e-mails, use Word when drafting and editing cover letters and resumes. Here's a word of warning, though: Do not use the templates provided. They limit your ability to personalize documents and to present the most important content first.

Crucial Challenges to Overcome

As you read this book, you will realize that cover-letter writing can be simple. Too many job-seekers find reasons for putting off this critical job-search task. Now that you know about letters of application, letters of introduction, and networking notes, and you are ready to communicate via electronic and traditional means, nothing should stop you from taking all steps required of job-search success. To motivate the best attitude and actions during trying times, President Franklin Roosevelt said: "The only thing we have to fear is fear itself." To motivate your efforts, you must overcome psychological and logistical concerns.

Fear of Focus

Some job-seekers mistakenly fear that stating goals in a cover letter limits the scope of consideration. These candidates send off broad and ineffective letters, hoping that employers will find something of interest—or they don't act at all. They wait for inspiration to strike, when they should be conducting active research into fields of interest, functional areas that match their qualifications, and firms that they may be interested in contacting. Remember, being "open to anything" often leads to nothing. Get focused and stay focused.

Follow-up Phobia

Use the phone, fax machine, and e-mail to follow up. Don't be afraid of being too pushy. If you treat others the way you would like to be treated, you will be following the golden rule of follow-up.

Follow-ups can always be politely posed as a query, like so:

- "Did you receive the resume and cover letter?"
- "Would it be appropriate to arrange an interview?"
- "Am I among the candidates receiving continued consideration?"
- "Should I send additional documentation?"
- "When should I call back?"

All of these are proper questions to ask. Don't be afraid of following up, hoping to avoid rejection. As you will see later in this chapter, you can and should also follow up rejections.

Over-Analysis Paralysis

Too often, too much thinking delays action. Don't overanalyze what your cover letter should contain or fret over every word, comma, or period. Have confidence in your abilities. Be optimistic that your candidacy will be granted appropriate consideration. As long as you start with a first draft and then edit it to the final version, you've done enough. Don't try to over-think the format or content, delaying transmission. If your well-crafted documents lead to interviews, wonderful. If not, following up can rekindle consideration or yield referrals to other persons, places, or postings. Also, you can send revised documents, getting second and third chances to make good impressions.

If you find a posting that is close to but not exactly what you are looking for, send a letter of introduction, rather than a letter of application. Tell the employer, "I was inspired to contact you regarding similar opportunities when I reviewed a posting that appeared on your Web site," then state your goals and refocus the reader on the job you want and on the attached resume.

Follow Up on Your Letter

You may have finished your final draft and mailed it off, but this doesn't mean you're done. An important but often forgotten part of writing cover letters is following up on them. Waiting passively for employer responses is not strategically sound. You are not done after you have been granted an interview, and extended an offer. You are done after you accept a position. Once you have transmitted a formal acceptance letter, all job-search efforts must stop. While you could (and should) send updates to all on your networking hit list, thanking them for help and informing them of your decision, no direct requests for consideration should be made.

Strategies and Subtleties

Everyone knows you should send a thank-you note after an interview, but other ways of following up may be less obvious. You can respond to a confirmation of resume receipt. Send a very positive, job-focused thank-you letter with a renewed request for an interview. Even if you don't receive confirmation, follow up a week or two after your first contact. Via voice mail, e-mail, or fax, state, "My interest in this position remains sincere and my desire to interview strong," and attach another resume "to remind you of my background and for your files." Don't assume they remember your name or have easy access to the documents submitted earlier.

Also try to get your advocates involved in the follow-up. Ask them to send brief e-mails to specific employers, stating, "I strongly encourage you to grant this candidate an interview." And, advocates can also send post-interview recommendations to further enhance your chances of receiving an offer.

ALERT!

Remember, advocates can be professional peers, faculty, or other individuals who can attest to your abilities to do a great job. Passively, they are "references," but actively and strategically, they are advocates.

Follow-up Faux Pas

Even those who try to be polite and persistent—not pesky—sometimes make mistakes. While these errors of judgment may be avoidable, they will not cost you a chance for an interview. Trust prospective employers to understand how enthusiasm may lead to less-than-perfect communication. Don't fear follow-up, but do try to avoid making any faux pas by following these simple do's and don'ts:

- Don't follow up every day for a week or more.
- Do leave voice-mail messages whenever you call, briefly stating why you called and leaving a phone number or e-mail where you can be reached.
- Don't overuse voice mail, calling more than once a day or, frankly, more than twice a week, unless you have been told to do so. (Phone tag should only be played by mutually agreed-upon contestants.)
- Do vary your mode of communication, including phone, e-mail, and fax.
- Don't pressure the employer by appearing impatient.
- Do use someone within the company as an advocate, especially if they are in a position of power, and let them communicate on your behalf with decision-makers.
- Don't ask for feedback regarding how to improve your cover letter, resume, or interview skills.

- Do ask for reconsideration or referrals to other departments or organizations after receiving "We'll keep you on file" or "Sorry, we've selected another candidate" messages.
- Don't use deceptive techniques to bypass "gatekeepers," such as using "information conversations" as ruses to gain interviews.
- Do be assertive, confident, and communicative when stating and restating sincere requests.

Responding to Rejection

It's human nature to ignore those who reject you, so this is the most underused follow-up technique. But you are definitely encouraged to follow-up rejection messages, or communicate anew with an employer after you are told you won't get an interview. If you do get a "No thank-you" note from an employer, or if several weeks have passed, follow up by seeking reconsideration or referrals to other departments or organizations.

Chapter 3
Resume Review

More often than not, you will send out your cover letter together with a copy of your resume. *The Everything® Resume Book* contains all you need to know about writing a successful resume. This chapter is a quick review on how to create and update your resume. In addition, it explores the relationship between the resume and its cover letter.

Seven Steps to Resume Success

You already know how to use the five-step RIGHT process to write an excellent cover letter. A similar process also exists for writing resumes. This one has seven easy steps:

1. Review samples. This includes your old resumes, examples in this chapter, and those in *The Everything® Resume Book, 2nd Edition.* Pay attention to those that might relate to your goals and those with appealing formats. Don't hesitate to circle or highlight sections you think effectively project qualifications, capabilities, and achievements.
2. Determine format, content, and order of information. When it comes to choosing a format, imitation is a good approach. Consider using the Everything Resume format, described in this chapter. Also determine your categories, like "Experience" and "Education," and their order on the page.
3. Identify objectives and target your audience.
4. Inventory your qualifications and achievements.
5. Analyze competencies and capabilities.
6. Draft and critique your resume.
7. Duplicate and distribute your resumes. (More than one targeted version is okay.)

FACT

Many of the sample cover letters that appear in this book correspond to resumes in its companion publication, *The Everything® Resume Book, 2nd Edition.* The review of resume writing in this chapter is a condensed version of what you'll find in that book.

Each step of the resume-writing process is dependent upon your ability to figure out and communicate your goals. For many job-seekers, that is the missing link to resume writing, cover-letter writing, interview skills, and job-search success. When you focus on your goals, you can create targeted letters that demonstrate your confidence in knowing what you want and what you're capable of doing.

The Everything Resume

A great resume presents past achievements as well as capabilities that qualify you for a new job. Before you start writing your resume, it is a good idea to understand the different types of resumes and the purposes they serve. Note that the recommended format is the Everything Resume. It is a targeted document that is focused on qualification and capabilities, and it projects the future while reviewing the past.

Chronological Versus Functional

Chronological resumes present information in reverse chronological order. They typically use one-word headers to identify sections. In most cases, these resumes are one page in length. Functional resumes present skill discussions independent from job descriptions, if descriptions are included at all. Combined resumes include a skill profile, and they present work history, educational background, and other content under typical headers in reverse chronological order. Targeted versions include an objective or some clear presentation of goals and qualifications. Multipurpose resumes are intended to broadly present one's candidacy. The Everything Resume is a blending of all these formats.

Format That Maximizes Focus and Success

The Everything Resume begins with a clear and concise objective statement or a detailed qualification summary with a headline that reveals goals. If a statement of objectives is first, the qualification summary is second. The qualification summary is very focused on a specific job or functional area of interest. Throughout the resume, and particularly in the qualification summary, language and phrases specific to fields of interest should be used.

Next, presented under descriptive headlines, comes either an education or an experience section. You determine the order of presentation, with most significant and goal-directed information presented first. Be sure to present courses, seminars, or certifications relevant to the job. These may be classified under education or in a separate professional-training section. Other pertinent headlines and information may also appear here.

The more targeted your resume (and all job-search documents), the better. Word-processing software makes it possible to create razor-sharp documents for each targeted communication. Do not fear focus, worrying that reviewers won't see you as well rounded and qualified for various opportunities. The Everything Resume presents goals articulately and clearly, focusing on your vision of the future. Employers will definitely broaden their perspectives and consider you for other options if you and your documents are focused.

Cover letters and resumes created "the Everything way" are the most powerful. These documents are targeted, rather than multipurpose, and reveal knowledge of your candidacy, of the job desired, and of the employer contacted.

Headlines, Not Headers

The Everything Resume uses multiple-word headlines, not one-word headers. As in a newspaper, headlines reveal much about what will appear in "the story below." Typical headers are "Education," "Experience," and "Training." More effective headlines read like so:

- Business and Economics Education
- Finance and Accounting Experience
- Business and Project-Management Experience
- Specialized Financial Training and Seminars
- Professional Finance and Accounting Training

Headlines reveal self-knowledge. They enhance focus and inspire reviewers to read content and schedule interviews.

Sample Everything Resumes

The before-and-after resume samples on pages 38–41 illustrate how an Everything Resume is drafted.

Helpful Tips to Get Started

Too often, candidates ask, "Is this what employers want to see?" Frankly, you should ask "Is this what I want employers to see?" They are your documents, not theirs! You cannot read the collective minds of potential employers, but you can demonstrate that you did your research and are prepared. Documents are most powerful when they are targeted and clearly present your performance potential.

Here are a few more tips to help you create or update your resume:

- Be sure the format you choose matches your goals and is appropriate for the industry.
- Sections of your resume should be arranged from most important at the top to least important on the bottom. If you're a new graduate, place your education first (unless you have valuable internship experience). If you have particular skills that require attention, place the skills section in the upper half of the page.
- State your objective clearly and concisely. You may wish to modify it slightly every time you send it out to a particular company or person.
- Keep a collection of key words associated with the field or position you are interested in. Then, make sure you use them in your resume (and your cover letter).
- Do your best to keep your resume to one page in length. There's always a way to say the same information more briefly and directly.
- Run a spelling and grammar check, and ask someone you trust to proofread your resume.

Side by Side or Solo

Can your resume succeed solo? If just the resume were reviewed, would readers clearly and quickly see your objective, qualifications, and potential for success? Would descriptions of past behaviors predict future performance potential? While your resume should be powerful independently, it should mesh well with your cover letter to give an impression of a complete set.

Advertising Account Executive (Before)

CHRIS SMITH

123 Main Street
Hometown, NY 00000
(555) 555-1234

csmith@company.com

987 Centre Avenue
Hometown, NY 10001
(555) 555-5678

EDUCATION

1999-2002   UNIVERSITY OF ROCHESTER, Rochester, NY
Bachelor of Arts, French, with a major GPA of 3.5, May 2002.
Bachelor of Arts, Psychology, with a major GPA of 3.3, May 2001.
Minor: **Economics,** with a minor GPA of 3.4.
- **Management Studies Certificate,** for completion of courses taught by faculty of college and the William E. Simon School of Business Administration.
- Economics Council, Activity Board, and Campus Times Staff Writer.

1998-1999   HOBART AND WILLIAM SMITH COLLEGES, Geneva, NY

EXPERIENCE

Spring 2001   THE FINANCIAL GROUP DISCOUNT BROKERAGE, Pittsford, NY
Intern/Assistant to Operations Manager: Used computerized financial transactions and market tracking systems. Updated customer databases using Excel. Interacted with and completed administrative projects for licensed representatives and addressed client inquiries from throughout the United States.

Summer 2001   DAYS ADVERTISING, INC., Pittsford, NY
Intern/Assistant to an Account Manager: Assisted with design of television and radio ads and proposals for varied products and clients, including Wegmans and Bausch & Lomb. Developed customer database.

2000-2001   ADEFFECTS, Rochester, NY
Intern/Assistant to an Account Manager: Researched and developed promotional materials for local retail, manufacturing, and restaurant clients. Gained knowledge of small business marketing. Recommended changes in client advertising materials, consumer outreach strategies, and marketing literature.

Summer 2001   PEARLE VISION CENTER, Pittsford, NY
Sales Representative: Implemented strategy targeting upscale markets.

Summer 1999   IT HAPPENS, Antwerp, Belgium
Marketing Intern: Determined target markets and developed ad budget for concert, event planning, and entertainment agency. Conducted market penetration surveys. Assisted graphic artists producing ads, posters, brochures, and reports.

Before

CHRIS SMITH

123 Main Street • Hometown, NY 00000 • (555) 555-1234 • csmith@company.com
987 Centre Avenue • Hometown, NY 10001 • (555) 555-5678

ADVERTISING ACCOUNT MANAGEMENT QUALIFICATIONS

- Marketing research, strategic planning, promotions, customer service, and sales talents nurtured by diverse advertising, promotions, and retail internships and employment.
- Skills gained via courses including: Marketing, Marketing Projects and Cases, Motivation, Public Relations Writing, Advertising, and Consumer Behavior.
- German, French, Dutch, and Farsi fluency, and conversational Spanish capabilities.
- UNIX, HTML, Word, WordPerfect, Excel, PageMaker, PhotoShop, and Internet skills.

ADVERTISING AND MARKETING EXPERIENCE

DAYS ADVERTISING, INC., Pittsford, NY
Account Management Intern: Assisted with design of TV and radio ads and proposals for clients, including Wegmans and Bausch & Lomb. Developed client database. Summer 2001

ADEFFECTS, Rochester, NY
Account Management Intern: Researched and developed promotional materials for retail, manufacturing, and restaurant clients, using knowledge of small business marketing. Suggested client changes in outreach strategies, and marketing literature. 2000-2001

PEARLE VISION CENTER, Pittsford, NY
Sales Representative: Implemented strategy targeting upscale markets. Summer 2001

IT HAPPENS, Antwerp, Belgium
Marketing Intern: Determined target markets and developed advertisement budget for concert, event planning, and entertainment agency. Conducted surveys to determine market penetration. Assisted graphic artists with ads, posters, brochures, and reports. Summer 1998

BUSINESS, ECONOMICS, AND LANGUAGE STUDIES

UNIVERSITY OF ROCHESTER, Rochester, NY
Bachelor of Arts, French, with a major GPA of 3.5, May 2002.
Bachelor of Arts, Psychology, with a major GPA of 3.3, May 2002.
Minor: **Economics,** with a minor GPA of 3.4.

WILLIAM E. SIMON SCHOOL OF BUSINESS ADMINISTRATION, Rochester, NY
Management Studies Certificate, Marketing and Finance/Accounting Tracks, May 2002.

FINANCE EXPERIENCE

THE FINANCIAL GROUP, INC. DISCOUNT BROKERAGE FIRM, Pittsford, NY
Intern/Assistant to Operations Manager, Spring 2001

- Identifying information uses only two lines.
- Left-justified block text format is e-friendly; it can be uploaded to Web sites and copied and pasted into e-mail.
- Experience presented first, under a targeted headline.
- Education is presented under a targeted headline to highlight specialized studies.
- Courses are presented in the qualification summary to highlight their significance.

Chris Smith

123 Main St., Hometown, CA 00000, (555)555-1234, cs@company.com

CAREER OBJECTIVE

Challenging pharmaceutical sales position with a progressive organization seeking dynamic and driven sales professional.

EXPERIENCE

Pearls and Gemstones Corporation, San Francisco, California 6/01-Present
Sales Associate: Sell and market polished gemstones for the San Francisco office of international gemstone and pearl distributor and jewelry manufacturer.

Bank of Hong Kong, Hong Kong   6/00-8/00
Trader: International Securities Dealing Room: Responded to customers' executing orders in the areas of American and foreign equities, bonds, and options. Received training in and gained working knowledge of Bloomberg and Reuters information systems.

Bank of Hong Kong, San Francisco, California   11/97-10/99
Credit Analyst: International Lending Department: Prepared proposals on prospective customers and renewals and reaffirmations of existing facilities for credit committee. Performed financial statement, cash flow, and projection analysis. Conducted research using Bloomberg, Moody's, and S&P analysts and publications.

Computer Associates International, San Jose, California 1/97-9/97
Quality Assurance Analyst: Implemented quality assurance for inter/intranet-enabled, multiplatform, enterprise management solution used worldwide.

EDUCATION

University of California, Berkeley, California
Bachelor of Arts   Class of 1997
Major: Political Science. Minor: Economics.
Dean's List Fall 1996 and Spring 1995 and Overall GPA: 3.34/4.0

University of New South Wales, Sydney, Australia   Spring 1996

HONORS

International Internships, London, England
Gordon McMaster, MP: British Parliament   9/95-12/95
Performed research, assisted in speech writing, aided constituents.

IPA Political Internships, Washington, DC
Senator Barbara Boxer: U.S. Senate   6/95-8/95
Wrote research briefs on pending legislation.

Before

Chris Smith

123 Main Street • Hometown, California 00000 • (555) 555-1234 • csmith@company.com

OBJECTIVE

Pharmaceutical Sales Position using and expanding upon ...
- Record of success within direct marketing and information-driven sales roles.
- Confidence nurturing relationships via direct calls using information dissemination strategies.
- Capacity to understand and share knowledge of pharmaceutical products and protocols.
- Abilities to set goals, document efforts and outcomes, and maximize achievements.
- Bilingual English-Mandarin abilities and cross-cultural sensitivities.

SALES AND SALES SUPPORT ACHIEVEMENTS

PEARLS AND GEMSTONES CORPORATION, San Francisco, California   2001-Present
Sales Associate for Loose Diamond Division: Sell gemstones for international distributor and manufacturer. Sales methods include appointments onsite, telemarketing, trade show exhibiting, and Internet. Customers include manufacturers, retail and department stores, and catalogues.
- *Directly involved in sales to house accounts totaling $2.5 million in 2001.*
- *Indirectly involved in sales to salespersons accounts totaling $3 million in 2001.*

COMPUTER ASSOCIATES INTERNATIONAL, San Jose, California   1997
Quality Assurance Analyst: Analyzed business applications for functionality and marketability. Reviewed RFPs (Request For Proposal) and identified key marketing leverage points. Implemented quality assurance for worldwide projects and software products.
- *Supported customer service and sales representatives in refining product to match customer needs.*

BUSINESS AND FINANCE EXPERIENCE

BANK OF HONG KONG, Hong Kong   Spring 2000
Securities Trader: Executed American and foreign equities, bonds, and option orders.

BANK OF HONG KONG, San Francisco, California   1997-2000
Department Credit Analyst: Prepared proposals on prospective customers and renewals for credit committee. Researched using Bloomberg, Moody's, and S&P analysts and publications.

BUSINESS, ECONOMICS, AND LIBERAL ARTS EDUCATION

UNIVERSITY OF CALIFORNIA, BERKELEY, Berkeley, California   1993-1997
Bachelor of Arts Political Science, with minor in Economics
- Intern for Member of British Parliament, Fall 1995, and Senator Boxer, Summer 1995.

HAAS SCHOOL OF BUSINESS ADMINISTRATION, Berkeley, California   1993-1997
- Management Certificate for completion of Marketing and Business courses.

- Garamond font is professional and space efficient.
- Qualification summary describing assets and demonstrating field knowledge is blended with brief objective.
- Experience uses two headlines with the first matching objective.
- Education uses headline related to objective.
- Courses are presented to highlight their significance.
- Sales experience is presented first, using a format that highlights achievements.
- Education, using a targeted headline, is near the bottom.

Goal-Directed Documents

The best resumes are targeted to a specific job or area of interest. It is not the reviewer's job to analyze and determine where you best fit. It is your responsibility to project your goals. The more you reveal through these documents that you have analyzed your strengths and the responsibilities in particular jobs, the better!

QUESTION?

Isn't it redundant to use the same qualification summary on both resume and cover letter?
Yes, it is, but that's what makes it reinforcing and effective. Redundancy used as an engineering term means that backup systems are in place in case of structural, mechanical, or electronic failure. Using the same qualification summaries in cover letters and resumes reveals your focus as well as your self-knowledge and understanding of jobs and career fields. If it is well crafted, it should appear in both documents.

Strategic Analysis of Qualifications

The qualification summary can be thought of as a "resume that fits on a three-by-five card." If you had this limited amount of space, what five to seven brief retrospective and projective bulleted statements would you make? What qualification statements appearing in the samples seemed effective? A qualification summary is the key element to an Everything Resume.

ALERT!

Don't just change objectives when seeking to target resumes for particular jobs or career fields. You should revise and reorder entries in your qualification summary as well. In truth, this section of the resume is most critical.

Keep Your Audience in Mind

When drafting resumes and cover letters, think about who reads these documents. Employers start with a job description, then they prioritize qualification criteria sought in candidates. Some are determined essential, some optional, and other optimal. Candidates are sourced (via postings or search firms), screened (via resume and cover-letter reviews), and then selected (to interview and, finally, to receive an offer after interviews). All this is done based on predetermined traits and characteristics. Your potential employer will use your resume and supporting documents to determine if you meet these criteria. Thinking about the job, you can identify the key qualities these individuals look for in candidates worthy of interviews and make sure they appear in your resume and cover letter.

Human Resources Versus Line Managers

While resumes and cover letters sent to human resource (HR) professionals and a line manager should be the same, it is most often the managers who choose candidates to interview and, ultimately, to hire. Whenever possible, in addition to addressing correspondence to an HR professional or "recruiter," also send copies to someone who heads the department in question. When sending a resume and cover letter to two individuals in the same organization, do let them know (by "cc-ing" or with statements in the letters) you have done so.

Network Member Notification

Also let network members and job-search advocates know the status of your efforts. Send a brief e-mail stating, "I have just contacted [*name person*], applying for the [*name job*] position. Any advice or support you might provide would be welcomed. Should I send copies of my resume and cover letter (attached) to others in the organization? Would you be able to send a brief e-mail in support of my candidacy?" Individuals you contact second (or third) can have greater impact than those you contacted first.

Top-Down and All-Around Reinforcement

Sometimes it is effective to start at the top and let your cover letter and resume filter down. In this case, letters of application should be sent to is the individual identified in the posting. Never use "to whom it may concern" salutations. Initial correspondence can be sent in memo format if no contact name is identified, but follow-up notes can be sent to individuals you identify as senior managers. In this case, follow-up correspondence would have content similar to that discussed in Chapter 2. Letters of introduction can be sent to human resources and recruiting professionals, and they can also be sent to heads of departments or, in some cases, to the company CEOs themselves.

Key Word Focus and Function

As illustrated in resume samples, objective statements should be simple and stated in as few words as possible, ideally as a job title. They are best presented as a few nouns, not as flowery and lengthy adjective- and verb-filled statements. "If you can describe a job, you can get that job" is a simple statement that underscores the importance of goal articulation. If you can state your goal, you are focusing the reviewer's analysis on jobs in a particular field. If you can describe the job, you understand the skills required to perform effectively, and you can present these skills in all documents. Conversation is easiest when you have something in common with those you are talking to. Show you have something in common to yield that critical conversation we call "an interview."

Talk the Talk to Walk the Walk

You must use the language common to your fields of interest. Employers use special phrasing in job descriptions and postings and in information appearing on their Web sites. Your resume must reflect your ability to understand and use this language. It's important to demonstrate in all written and verbal communications that you understand the job you want and that you are career-literate.

Careers as a Second Language

You've heard of ESL, English as a Second Language. But do you know about CSL, Careers as a Second Language? If you are an experienced candidate, you are fluent and able to converse eloquently in field-specific vernacular. If you are a soon-to-be or recent college grad, you should complete some intensive self-instruction in your chosen CSL. The best ways to become familiar with a field-appropriate lexicon is to review Web sites, articles, and professional publications.

After a few Web searches or articles, you will notice common factors and phrases. Look for interviews or profiles of successful people in particular fields. What backgrounds did they bring to their jobs? Articles about trends and innovations within your field of interest are also very helpful. What issues should someone entering this field know about? What do persons within this field read about and talk about? Knowledge of these topics and concepts are most likely on an employer's list of qualification criteria. This knowledge must be communicated using key words, field-focused phrases, and the language of the job you want. Resumes and cover letters must contain these words and phrases.

Resumes the E-way

In today's technologically advanced world, it's important to be sure your resume is e-friendly and can be e-mailed easily. Many potential employers list opportunities on corporate Web sites. Others use large headhunting links, online job banks, and resume collection sites like *www.monster. com.* E-mail is a common way to send and receive job-search documents. Uploading is now easier then ever, and you don't have to worry too much about formatting and fonts.

E-resumes do not have to be limited to one page in length, but make sure yours is concise and contains as many key words as possible. Use phrases commonly used in your field of interest, as well as those in the posting or job description. Remember, while electronic screening is done first, ultimately a real person will review resumes and conduct final selections of candidates to interview.

Electronic Everything Resumes are best formatted as block text, with copy set flush left, not using intents or left-margin timelines. While bullets, bolding, and italics were once a concern, now with the use of PDF files or copy-and-paste resume submission systems, highlighting techniques are no longer an issue. As with all other resumes, don't get too creative with the graphics associated with headlines, copy, or entries. It's the words that truly count, not the attractiveness of the document when dealing with e-resumes.

FACT

Estimates vary, but most agree that there are now millions of job announcements and at least ten times as many resumes in cyberspace. Internet resume collection and posting systems were once difficult to use and required following some complicated directions. Now, however, they are quite user-friendly (for job-seeker and employer). Use general ones as well as those appearing on specific employer sites.

Chapter 4

Off to the Interview

Resumes and cover letters do get interviews, but as a candidate, you will get offers only if the interview goes well and you have the opportunity to demonstrate your conversational talents. Whether you snag a phone or in-person interview, this chapter shows how you can rely on your resume and cover letter to prepare for your interview and make it a success.

Your Prep- and Cheat-Sheets

You can use your cover letter and resume in two major ways. First, use these documents to prepare for your interview. Remember, your interviewer will probably have copies and will ask you questions based on the things that catch his or her attention. What do you think these questions might be? Once you formulate these questions, you can come up with well-polished answers that will make you sound like a great candidate.

Secondly, you can use your resume and cover letter to your advantage at the interview by referring to them during the conversation. A key connection between something on your resume and the job under discussion may just be all it takes to land you the job.

ALERT!

You can show that you have what it takes to succeed in the position you're interviewing for by referring to how well you've handled similar experiences in the past and sharing pertinent details that could not fit onto a one-page resume.

Highlighting Your Qualifications

Make a list of qualifications that appear on both the job description and on your cover letter and/or resume. Highlight the most significant experiences on your cover letter and resume. Identify at least three things from your resume or cover letter that you must discuss during the interview. Select the bullet points you should cover from your qualification summary, accomplishments cited under experience headings, or educational achievements. Your past has been documented and your future projected on these pages. You've been invited to support written statements over the phone or in person. What has been read must now be heard, presented enthusiastically and confidently.

Resumes and cover letters can nurture confidence and diminish anxiety, guiding you through interviews. You can have copies in front of you during the interview. To maximize your performance, use the resume and cover letter both before and during the interview to identify and link qualities and achievements to the job you are interviewing for. Use these documents to guide the conversation and to ensure that key points are covered and understood.

Soon you will clearly see how easy it is to identify key words used in your resume and cover letter, to understand the concepts associated with interview skill-building, and how to make the conversational connections needed to succeed. Like so many situations in life, planning and preparation are crucial.

Research and Preparation

Before each interview, be sure to confirm all the details with the person who has contacted you for an interview, and ask any and all pertinent questions that might assist with your preparation. Pre-interview communication with employers builds confidence, provides focus, and most assuredly enhances your chances for success.

Too many job-seekers spend hours researching historical and most likely irrelevant facts associated with a potential employer, often increasing their anxiety because memorizing this information seems impossible. These candidates research employers too much and their own backgrounds and prospective jobs too little. They don't accentuate the obvious, and they don't review their own resumes, cover letters, and job descriptions well enough. Most significantly, they *don't* ask questions *prior* to the interview.

Direct Questions

Call or e-mail a few days in advance to confirm your meeting or scheduled phone conversation, and whenever possible ask some very pointed questions about the job. Clarify the logistics of the day, particularly for on-site visits arranged after initial phone screenings. Know how many people you will be seeing and what to expect of your visit. You may ask any of the following questions:

- Are there particular questions I should be thinking about prior to the interview?

- In addition to the job announcement, is there a more detailed job description I can review?
- Is there a person I can speak to informally about the job before I interview?
- Are there key points you would like me to cover during our meeting/conversation?

Imagine how well prepared you will be if you received a list of potential questions or critical issues to address. You may be surprised how often interviewers provide this information when asked.

Definitely continue networking, and ask others within the organization for interview support. Again, people are more likely to serve as your advocate once you have been invited for an interview.

Queries can be made by phone or e-mail. If you cannot get through to the desired persons, leave a voice-mail message, followed by an e-mail or faxed note. If you start a few days in advance of the scheduled interview, you have a greater chance of getting a timely response.

Do Some Smart Research

Conduct a Web-based search, and visit with a reference librarian before phone or in-person interviews. Via the Internet or with the assistance of the librarian, seek information about the firm as well as information on general trends, issues, and current events related to the occupational field in question. You should, of course, spend some time reviewing the firm's Web site and get the basic information down, but don't dwell too long on researching the prospective employer. Basic field information is often much more valuable. Who are the firm's biggest competitors? What factors most likely influence profits or other success criteria? What are industry trends? Who are the key players, and what's new in the field? These are all queries your research should answer.

While it may seem somewhat old-fashioned, do seek the assistance of reference librarians. These professional problem-solvers can locate hard-to-find information efficiently and quickly. Plus, photocopied pages with sections highlighted in bold colors are easy to review prior to interviews. You may even bring these pages with you to send a subtle message about your ability to do smart research.

Know the Job

It's amazing that some candidates enter interviews with little understanding of the job or without ever having seen a job description. Do yourself a favor and request a printed description prior to the meeting, or ask if someone can explain the job over the phone. Pre-interview preparation is essential. Know the job and yourself, and then share your confident assessment of your candidacy.

The more you know about the job, the better. You are interviewing for a specific job with the company, not simply presenting broad potential and hoping someone deems you qualified. The more details you have at your disposal, the easier it's going to be to connect your past to your current candidacy and desired outcome.

ALERT!

Never interview without reviewing a copy of a job description or, at the very least, without holding an informal discussion regarding the job with some knowledgeable individual. Open-ended discussions of potential are not strategically sound. Focused discussions regarding your ability to serve within specific roles of the job will yield offers.

Typical Interviewer Styles

Another way to prepare for your interview is to learn how to recognize the interviewer's style. (As you'll see as you begin to go to interviews, some interviewers exhibit one style, while others may demonstrate two or more.) Being aware of these styles and recognizing them during the interview will help you diminish anxieties and remain confident.

Also keep in mind that different styles are presented during screening interviews, when candidates are judged for additional consideration and during selection interviews, when it is determined which candidate should receive an offer. No matter what the interview type or style, you should be prepared.

Conversational Interviewers

These interviewers have already learned all they technically need to know, by reviewing your resume and cover letter, so they use the interview to get to know you conversationally. Talking about general topics, your career interests, and what may appear as unrelated issues, this interviewer judges your communication skills and style. This interviewer is looking for "a fit," and you should be sincere in content, natural in approach, and anecdotal in your style.

Traditional Interviewers

These interviewers rely on common interview questions (discussed in the next section). These are typical questions that may follow the content of the resume and ask for clarification of some of the points as the interviewer moves down the page. This approach is the most common, yet it still requires that you be prepared, focused on the job, and ready to share stories reflecting your potential to serve in specific job roles.

Behavioral Interviewers

While interviewers have a personal style, there are some identifiable interview techniques, too. The behavioral interview allows interviewers to quantify what truly is a subjective process. It is based upon the principle that past behaviors are predictors of future behaviors and that trends in behaviors are better predictors than isolated incidents.

The behavioral interviewer asks questions that begin with phrases like "What did you do when . . ." or "What would you do if . . ." It's important to understand that when it comes to these questions, the interviewer already has the "correct" answers in mind and is investigating whether you have the qualities with which such answers are associated.

Be prepared for, and don't become rattled by, scenario-presenting questions. Note-taking by interviewers is not unusual, and they may seek clarification or contradicting evidence by continually probing, so don't get frustrated. Be ready to tell success stories, chronologically and behaviorally describing step-by-step what led to your most significant achievements.

You may never encounter a true behavioral interviewer, but the concepts associated with this approach can make you a very well-prepared candidate. If interviewers can create a pre-interview behavioral checklist, so can you.

Case Study or Technical Interviewers

In some fields, interviewers present cases or ask for specific technical information. Consulting, engineering, teaching, and counseling candidates should be prepared to analyze a case or address specific technical topics. A quick phone call or e-mail before the interview should reveal whether you will be expected to conduct case analysis or be conversant in technical terms. Avoid surprise by asking in advance.

Recruiters estimate that they review about 100 resumes and cover letters to identify one, two, or three candidates to interview. Often, at least three to five candidates are interviewed before one is extended an offer. Obviously, ratios vary based upon selectivity of the firm, the nature of the job, and availability of qualified candidates.

When called upon to do so, don't jump to the answer(s) too quickly. Clearly explain what you are thinking, how you approach the case, and ask questions to seek clarification or additional data. Interviewers want to learn about your thought processes, not necessarily your abilities to quickly share the correct answers.

Common Questions

No matter what the style of the interview, you should be prepared. Here are some questions you should practice answering in advance. Although it may sound like too much trouble, just consider how much easier it is going to be to answer a question you've had time to consider in the privacy of your home.

Traditional Interview Questions

Here is a sample of questions you might expect to be asked in a traditional interview:

- Why are you interested in this particular job and field of employment?
- What academic or career achievements are you most proud of?
- What are your greatest strengths and weaknesses?
- How would you describe yourself? How would others describe you?
- How do you characterize career success, and what motivates you to succeed?
- Why should we hire you?
- How have academic or training experiences to date prepared you for this job?
- What are your future academic goals?
- What have you learned from your mistakes?
- What might you have done differently with regard to your past career-related experiences?
- What do you think it takes to succeed in the job you are being interviewed for?
- What motivated you to first contact us?

Behavioral Interview Questions

The following questions are representative of those you might be asked to answer in a behavioral interview:

- Describe when you faced a problem at work that tested your coping skills. What did you do?

- Give an example of when you had to make a quick decision. What were the results?
- Describe a time you used communication skills to get a key point across. What were the outcomes?
- Describe a job circumstance when you had to speak up or be critical of others? How did they respond?
- Give examples of when you best motivated peers or subordinates. How could you tell it worked?
- Share an example of when you used fact-finding skills to gain information needed to solve a problem, describing how you analyzed the information and came to a decision.

ALERT!

Don't memorize answers! While you should prepare and practice answering these kinds of questions—and, more importantly, really consider your response to each one—do not attempt to commit these answers to memory word-for-word. Planned spontaneity is your goal. Interviews should be conversations with a purpose, not planned soliloquies.

- Describe an important goal you set and how you progressed to reach that goal.
- Describe the most significant written document, report, proposal, or presentation you've completed.
- Specify what you did on your last job to plan effectively and stay organized.
- Give an example of when you dealt with a very upset customer, coworker, or supervisor.
- Describe your most recent group effort.
- What would you do if I told you to create an impromptu presentation in the next ten minutes?
- How would you decide which of your subordinates should be laid off?
- How would you deal with a sensitive personnel issue, like harassment?

To maximize the impact of these possible queries, identify a list of the top five questions related to a specific job you will interview for. Then ask a friend, family member, or professional peer to do a practice interview using these five. Don't try to memorize or overanalyze answers. Remember, there are no right or wrong responses, and interviews must appear spontaneous—they are conversations, not interrogations. Practicing, however, can make your conversations more focused and you will appear more relaxed and thoughtful.

QUESTION?

Should I bring extra resumes, cover letters, or other documents to an interview?
Yes, most definitely do! You can offer copies to those who might not have them. And you can use one of these copies as your notes to inspire great communication. You can also bring supplemental documents with you to support your candidacy. These can include reports, presentations, or letters of recommendation.

Additional Tips

Don't overanalyze your performance or be a chameleon, changing who you are for particular circumstances. If your strategies and style remain sincere, no matter the interviewer's style, technique, or temperament, you will ultimately find a true match with a prospective employer. If you don't receive an offer, never seek feedback from the interviewer or ask why you were passed over. You could and should seek "consideration for other opportunities that better match my skills." Remain confident and focused.

Pre-Interview Prep Exercise

In addition to practicing answering interview questions, you can use your resume and cover letter as special preparation tools. The following is a simple activity that will maximize your potential to receive an offer.

To begin, print a copy of your resume and cover letter and, if possible, a job description. On the back of your cover letter, write the following four headlines:

- Three Key Requirements or Job Descriptors
- Three Qualification Connections
- Three Achievement Anecdotes
- Three Questions to Ask

Next, follow the instructions to create your checklist of twelve interview points to cover. Each interview will be somewhat different, but you should use one technique to prepare for all!

Three Key Requirements or Job Descriptors

Review the job description, focusing on the big picture, and identify what you believe are the three most significant requirements of the job. What are stated as requirements of the job? Which three are most important? What are the most important tasks you will be asked to perform, and what skills are needed to do so? For this exercise, don't state why. Just write down the top three requirements or key elements of the job you will be interviewing for.

Three Qualification Connections

Next, look at your cover letter and resume. Thinking about the already cited requirements of the job, what are three matching qualifications you possess? One could be that you held a similar position in the past or that you completed related projects. Another could be education and training or a special seminar you attended. Or it may have to do with career progression and future goals. Your qualification connections should be obvious, because something cited in these documents made you qualified to interview. What three things do you want to address during the interview? Connect your past to your desired future, your achievements to the requirements of this job.

Three Achievement Anecdotes

After identifying three qualifications connected to significant job requirements, be prepared to present anecdotal evidence that you possess skills that match requirements. These stories must be told in behavioral ways, actively describing what you did and when, and what the results of these efforts are. In fact, the acronym STAR (Situations, Tasks, Actions, Results) may prove useful when describing achievement anecdotes during the interview. For each anecdote, briefly jot down on the back of your cover letter the situations, tasks, actions, and results associated with that particular achievement. As you tell of your *star*ring roles in these tales, interviewers will be able to see how your past behaviors can predict your future performance.

QUESTION?

Is it appropriate to ask for feedback, particularly if I don't get the job?

Do not ask for interview feedback, but do express continued interest in working for that employer. Send a follow-up note and a revised resume, requesting consideration for "future opportunities or similar positions to the one I interviewed for." You can also ask for referrals to other contact persons or other firms.

Three Questions to Ask

Next, list three questions you want to ask during the interview. Ask one in the first five minutes of the interview, so you can use responses as key points as the discussion progresses. You can ask the other two (or more) during and at the end of the interview sessions. Here are some examples to get you started:

- How would you describe the job in terms of day-to-day roles and responsibilities?
- What qualities or strengths are you seeking in a candidate?
- What advice would you give me if I were starting the job next week?

- What should I expect of myself over the first few months on the job? After the first year?
- Who would have the highest expectations of me, and what might those be?
- Who should I use as a role model or mentor for this position, and why?

After you've done this exercise you can say, "My cover letter and resume got me the interview, and they will guide me during the interview." Use your checklist in appropriate ways, and have extra copies of your resume and cover letter with you during the interview.

Take the time to complete this exercise before each interview. It will provide you with a structured way for preparing and will help you formalize your ideas into quickly stated points.

Four Valuable Phrases

There are certain phrases that can help you guide the interview along and make the points you wish to make. Whether you say these out loud or just think them in your head, they'll help you navigate the interview and make the best impression you can.

Thinking About the Job

These four words will inspire you to connect past achievements and related qualities to job-specific requirements. Too often, candidates answer generally and vaguely, gloriously sharing their general qualities. The more focused you can be, the better. If you are thinking about the job, and speaking in focused ways, interviewers will think of you as if you already have the job. This image will be transformed from interview to offer.

As You Can See on My Resume

Interviewers use your resume as a point of reference when formulating particular questions. You can and must do the same when responding. Statements like, "As you can see on my resume," "As cited in the Qualifications section of my resume," or "As detailed in the 'Experience' section" will focus your listener, as well as you. Let your interviewer's eyes focus on specific sections of your resume and cover letter, and don't be surprised if they highlight these documents or take notes when you speak. This phrase perks interest and invites focused attention.

As Cited in My Cover Letter

When appropriate, precede answers to queries by referring to your cover letter. Reveal that you have been thinking about this job since you wrote this meaningful document and that it remains pertinent even during the interview. You might even say, "Since I read the job description and wrote what I hope is an effective letter, I have been thinking about that question." Or, "In writing what I believe to be a job-specific cover letter, I wanted to highlight particular qualifications."

QUESTION?

Should I take notes during an interview?
You should be an active listener and enthusiastic communicator, not a note-taker. Taking notes is often distracting to those seeking to gain information. Also, by doing so you become a passive participant, not a confident presenter of information. You will remember the important information discussed, and you should find verbal and nonverbal ways to show interest in important points.

I Definitely Want This Job

Be sure you show your enthusiasm and state during and at the end of the interview that you want the job: "I most definitely would like to be invited back for selection interviews." You are not committing to accepting an offer, but you are enthusiastically saying that you can envision yourself succeeding. If you can share that vision, the interviewer might make the desired decision. Don't be shy about stating sincerely how much you want the job or, more subtly, answering questions by stating, "If I am lucky enough and qualified enough to get this job, I would . . ."

After the Interview

Remember how important follow-up can be? Post-interview actions are significant, so do write thank-you notes and take significant follow-up actions. How well did you do in the interview? Did you determine the one or two persons who will actually make the decision? Did you learn what would be the critical decision-making criteria? What one factor do you want to reinforce in your thank-you note? Who can help you now? Answers to these queries can inspire effective post-interview efforts.

Say Thank You

You should send thank-you messages to everyone who talked to you (when possible) but at least to the one person who was your initial screener and who coordinated your on-site visit. While handwritten, snail-mailed notes may appeal to Ms. Manners's sense of proper etiquette, this approach is way too slow. You'd do better to use e-mail or voice mail. (Sample thank-you messages and notes appear in Chapter 15). For now, it is important to know that letters should contain an expression of appreciation, reference to the most significant qualification you possess, what you now clearly know is required of the job, and a definitive "I want this job" statement.

Advocate Contacts

While it is always appropriate to inform advocates about interviews and how well you did, in some cases you may request some additional support. When you really, really want an offer, ask an advocate to send an unsolicited recommendation. This would be a quick e-mail or voice-mail message directed to a person you have identified as a decision-maker. Basically, the advocate can say, "I understand that you interviewed [*name of candidate*] for the [*position*], and I am strongly encouraging you to hire him/her. If you want a detailed analysis of his/her candidacy, please do not hesitate to contact me."

Supplemental Documents

Sometimes after an interview, you may wish to send supplemental documents. These may include sample reports, proposals, or presentations; performance reviews; letters of recommendation; a draft brochure or correspondence associated with a hypothetical (but job-related) project you may be asked to do if you got the job. During the interview you will be able to determine whether writing is a critical qualification, and if it is, you will be able to provide evidence of your talents. However, do not overwhelm interviewers with a large number of documents. Quality and relevance are far more important here.

Chapter 5

Before-and-After Versions

Cover-letter writing is all about the before (first draft) and after (final version). This chapter reveals six cover-letter makeovers that illustrate how to improve new drafts or older versions of your job-search correspondence. Each "before" version has a brief do's and don'ts comment section noting strengths and weaknesses. Each "after" sample includes a detailed analysis of how changes yielded a more dynamic and goal-focused document. Note that some of these cover letters have corresponding resumes in Chapter 3.

Advertising Account Executive (Before)

- Don't use "Mr./Ms." Call to check the contact person's title and gender. If possible, get an e-mail address.

- Do your homework, but focus on your past successes and potential achievements in advertising.

- Don't assume one must start in "administrative" capacities.

- Don't list general skills alphabetically according to functional headings.

June 1, 200–

Pat Cummings
Account Supervisor
Any Advertising Agency
456 Any Street
City, ST 12345

Dear Mr./Ms. Cummings:

I am very interested in pursuing my career in the advertising industry at Any Advertising. While researching firms, I read an exciting piece in *Ad Age* about your recent campaign for Campbell Soups. Congratulations on receiving a Cleo Award for your efforts!

I would love to join your winning team in an entry-level, administrative position. I can offer administration, promotion, and communication experience as well as my broad academic background. The following achievements would be especially beneficial to your firm:

Administration: Recordkeeping and file maintenance. Data processing and computer operations, order fulfillment, inventory control, and customer relations. Scheduling, office management, and telephone reception.

Advertising and Promotion: Composing, editing, and proofreading correspondence and PR materials as well as developing advertising campaign components.

Communication: Interactions with existing and potential clients.

Computer Skills: Proficient in Microsoft Word, Lotus 1-2-3, Excel, Filemaker Pro, and Internet.

I would like to request a personal interview to further outline my skills and how they could be immediately applicable to an administrative position at Any Advertising. I will call your office on July 2nd to schedule a convenient meeting time. Thank you, Mr./Ms. Cummings. I look forward to our conversation.

Sincerely,

Chris Smith

Chris Smith
123 Any Street
City, ST 12345
(555) 555-5555

Before

Advertising Account Executive (After)

Chris Smith
123 Any Street • City, ST 12345 • (555) 555-5555 • *csmith@email.com*

June 1, 200–

Pat Cummings
Account Supervisor
Any Advertising Agency
456 Any Street
City, ST 12345
FAX (555) 555-5557

Dear Ms. Cummings:

I would like to interview for an Assistant Account Executive position. Relevant courses in Marketing, Finance, and Accounting, as well as independent marketing projects, required that I develop applicable skills and perspectives. Knowledge of strategic planning, marketing research, budgeting, advertising techniques and related report writing, and presentation skills have been fine-tuned in varied settings, all described on the attached resume. Qualifications that match those cited on your website include:

- Marketing research, strategic planning, promotions, customer service, and sales talents nurtured in advertising and promotions internships.
- Blend of quantitative, analytical, and creative problem-solving talents.
- Capacities to conduct research and transform data into persuasive proposals, reports, and graphics.
- Curiosity regarding consumer behavior, varied products and industries, and market segmentation.

Summarizing key points appearing on my resume, additional assets I offer include:

- Technical skills gained via coursework, including Principles of Marketing, Marketing Projects and Cases, Psychology of Human Motivation and Emotion, Business Administration, Public Relations Writing, Advertising, Mass Media, Persuasion and Consumer Behavior.
- Confidence serving on account team and interacting with clients and colleagues.
- Blend of research, analysis, writing, and presentation talents.

Recently, I graduated from University of Rochester with dual majors, a minor in Economics, as well as a Certificate in Management Studies in Marketing. In addition to academics, I have had a number of advertising-related internships with local as well as international firms. I would welcome the chance to discuss my qualifications for an Assistant Account Executive position or internship opportunities. I will call to confirm your receipt of this fax (originals to follow by mail) and to discuss next steps.

Sincerely,

Chris Smith

Chris Smith

After

- The actual contact person was learned via the Web site and confirmed through telephone conversation.

- The first bullet list rephrases qualifications in the announcement, and the second list summarizes the candidate's profile.

65

Paralegal (Before)

Chris Smith
123 Any Street
City, ST 12345

June 1, 200–

Paralegal Recruiter
456 Any Street
City, ST 12345

Dear Sir/Madam:

18 years of experience within paralegal and office management roles make me uniquely qualified for your recently posted position. I am looking for the opportunity to join the legal support staff of a large firm or corporation where I can put my experience to practical use and further develop my paralegal capabilities.

My expertise is in the supervision of support legal staff in all phases of research, document preparation, and coordination as required for all legal issues. I am well-organized, accurate, and conscientious, interface well with individuals and groups, and feel confident that I can be a contributing asset to your firm.

I am most anxious to become a part of your firm and would appreciate meeting with you at your convenience. The enclosed resume is a brief summary of my professional accomplishments and related experience.

I look forward to your response.

Sincerely,

Chris Smith

Chris Smith

Before

Paralegal (After)

Memo from Chris Smith
123 Any Street
City, ST 12345
(555) 555-5555
csmith@email.com

DATE: June 1, 200–
TO: 456 Any Street, City, ST 12345
SUBJECT: Paralegal Supervisor Position

Eighteen years of experience in paralegal and office management positions have allowed me to develop many qualifications for your recently posted Paralegal Supervisor position. Having recently relocated to the Santa Clara area, I am very motivated to find an opportunity to lead the legal support staff of a firm composed of individuals who aspire to personify excellence for clients and professional peers. In my case, I trust that past achievements in varied legal settings, including Brendan Ellis, where I contributed to annual growth in billings and reputation, will predict future performance at your firm.

Detailed on the attached resume, my expertise is in the supervision of legal support staff and in all phases of research, document preparation, and case coordination as required for diverse legal issues. In summary, I possess outstanding research, client relations, document management, and writing skills; expertise as a law-office manager, compiling training documents, and supervising personnel; as well as interview, negotiation, and mediation talents.

I am most anxious to learn more information regarding your firm and the expectations associated with the Paralegal Supervisor position. I do hope you will find my candidacy worthy of consideration and an interview. Because I am available to start as soon as needed, perhaps we could meet soon to discuss my professional accomplishments, related experience, and qualifications.

I look forward to your response.

Sincerely,

Chris Smith

Chris Smith

- Memo format is effective and professional when you are responding to a blind ad.

- Middle paragraph contains a strong summary of qualifications.

- Networking can identify a firm in need of a Paralegal Supervisor, facilitating personal follow-up.

Teacher (Before)

- Do identify position and source of announcement or referral early in letter.

- Don't refer to a "school system" when applying for a private school position.

- Don't simply restate resume entries or offer irrelevant information.

- Don't use "Dear" as a salutation for a committee.

123 Any Street
City, ST 12345

June 1, 200–

ABC School
456 Any Street
City, ST 12345

RE: Earth Science and Biology Teaching Position

Dear Search Committee:

I have enclosed my resume in response to your advertisement through Carney Sandoe and Associates. During the past several years, I have been preparing myself for a position as a teacher in an established school system, where I can apply my teaching experience to manage and motivate a classroom of students toward higher education.

As Teacher at Edison Technical and Vocational High School, I successfully taught 9th Grade General Science. Detailed on my resume, I received my bachelor's degree from Drew University in Madison, New Jersey, and, most recently, my master's degree and certification at Fairleigh Dickinson University, also in Madison. Also, I have acted as a Substitute Teacher in several school districts and I designed, organized, and taught my own tutorials for a special-needs student.

Currently, I am seeking an opportunity that offers continued professional development and the opportunity for advancement in the field of education. I would welcome a personal interview to discuss in detail my ability to handle the teaching position and my compatibility with the rest of your staff.

In the interim, should you require additional information, please contact me at the above address or by phone at (555) 555-5555.

Yours sincerely,

Chris Smith

Chris Smith

Before

Teacher (After)

Chris Smith
123 Any Street • City, ST 12345 • (555) 555-5555 • *csmith@email.com*

June 1, 200–

Pat Cummings
Headmaster
ABC School
456 Any Street
City, ST 12345
FAX (555) 555-5557

Headmaster Cummings and Members of the Search Committee:

When I earned my graduate and undergraduate degrees, commencement signified "a beginning," a time to start new experiences, yet never stop learning. Being a teacher requires self-motivation for ongoing learning and the ability to inspire others to do the same. As an Earth Science and Biology teacher, I will empower students to progress enthusiastically towards secondary commencement. Teaching at ABC will call upon me to diminish anxieties and misconceptions associated with memorization, with theory, and with cookbook-style labs. Instructional techniques learned through experience, creativity, and vivid memories of successful teachers will inspire me to motivate and educate students.

Currently, I teach various science and biology classes at an area public school. When earning certification, I served as a permanent substitute and student teacher. Clearly, I have learned that creativity and student involvement maximize learning. For example, when exploring classification, students show each other self-created flashcards and ask and respond to questions. In this way they learn the power of mnemonics as well as subject-specific knowledge of unit and lesson plans. Yes, I have more lesson plans to share!

A position at ABC will allow me to continue teaching, provide intrinsic rewards associated with inspiring young diverse students, and offer the continued learning environment I crave. I am pleased Carney Sandoe informed you of my candidacy, and I am eager to discuss qualifications by phone or in person. The attached resume, sample lesson plan, and statement of philosophy will, I hope, support my candidacy and, like this letter, reveal my motivations as well as qualifications. Thank you.

Sincerely,

Chris Smith

Chris Smith

- Response to a search firm's referral of materials is addressed to headmaster and committee.

- Presented as a presentation of philosophy and style, not just a synopsis of the resume.

- Includes specifics of one lesson plan and refers to many others as well as to supplemental materials.

- Acknowledges distinction between private and public schools.

Engineer (Before)

- Do use mail merge word-processing features to send broadcast mass mailings to a number of firms.

- Don't identify geographic goals as more significant than company.

- Don't close the letter with an open and vague hope to hear from the employer.

- Do search Web sites to identify one or more positions of interest.

123 Any Street
City, ST 12345
(555) 555-5555
csmith@email.com

<date>

<contact name>
<company name>
<department>
<street address>
<city>, <state> <zip>

My objective is a full-time optical laboratory position in southeastern New England building on my 10 years of experience in all stages of optical engineering from the optical fabrication process through prototype assembly and alignment. After viewing the positions description for <company name> I believe a number match my qualifications. Thus, I seek to interview for an immediately available position.

Substantial optical experiences at Kodak Pixel Physics and Melles Griot have provided me with the necessary skills to be successful in the industry, including project management experience. Outstanding research and development abilities have been nurtured through academic and industrial laboratory work, including prototype design and testing. Technical knowledge augments my optical background, including experience with optical system alignment, process engineering, Code V, and MatLab. Finally, written and verbal communication abilities complete my qualifications, including experience creating technical reports and maintaining laboratory notebooks.

As my attached resume indicates, I possess the optical engineering knowledge, research background, and communication abilities to be successful at <company name>. Quick trips to <city> are easy to arrange, and I would love to further discuss opportunities and my qualifications. I would be pleased to provide any additional information you may require, and I look forward to hearing more about current opportunities.

Cordially,

Chris Smith

Chris Smith

Before

Engineer (After)

Chris Smith
123 Any Street • City, ST 12345 • (555) 555-5555 • *csmith@email.com*

June 1, 200–

<contact name>
<company name>
<department>
<street address>
<city>, <state> <zip>

My immediate professional objective is a full-time optical laboratory position with <company name>. Over 10 years of experience in all stages of optical engineering, including optical fabrication processing, prototype assembly, and alignment, have allowed me to develop a skill set that is both broad and deep. After viewing the position descriptions on <company name>'s website, I believe a number of those match my qualifications. Therefore, I respectfully seek to interview for an immediately available position.

Substantial optical experiences at Kodak Pixel Physics and Melles Griot have provided me with the necessary skills to be successful in the industry, including project management experience. Proven research and development abilities have been nurtured through comprehensive academic and industrial laboratory activities, including prototype design and testing. Technical knowledge and computer skills augment my optical background. These complementary qualifications and experiences include optical system alignment, process engineering, Code V, and MatLab programming. Finally, written and verbal communication abilities, associated with creating technical reports, overseeing project teams, and maintaining laboratory notebooks, complete the basic qualifications I now offer.

As the attached resume indicates, I possess the optical engineering knowledge, research background, and overall abilities required to be successful at <company name>. Please review the Professional Engineering Accomplishment section for details pertaining my abilities. Quick trips to <city> are easy to arrange, and I would very much like to discuss opportunities and my qualifications. I will call soon to learn about the steps involved in <company name>'s recruiting and interviewing. I would be pleased to provide any additional information you may require, and I look forward to hearing more about current opportunities.

Cordially,

Chris Smith

Chris Smith

- Letter of introduction for transmission to many firms, for a number of positions, identified via Web search.
- Identifies goals, qualifications, and next steps succinctly and clearly.
- Reader is asked to review a specific section of the resume.

Marketing Intern (Before)

123 Any Street
City, ST 12345

June 1, 200–

Any Name and Associates
456 Any Street
City, ST 12345

Attn: Internship Coordinator

Dear Sir/Madam:

I would love to serve as a Public Relations Intern this summer!

Over the past three years I have studied business and marketing at the Ohio State University in Columbus, Ohio. Now, as my junior year ends, I wish to explore public relations as a career field and learn as much as I can before I graduate.

I have been very, very active in campus life at Ohio State, and I have held numerous leadership and committee positions. All of these positions involved working with people of diverse backgrounds as a team focusing on a particular goal. The attached resume details all of my academic and co-curricular achievements.

From a practical perspective, I have already been an intern for a travel abroad program; for a web-based advertising company; and for Abercrombie and Fitch. Now, I so very much want to be an intern at your firm. Marketing has been a part of my life for so long, but I now want to be involved in and learn about public relations. Please review my resume for information on these three internship experiences. I know you will find that they qualify me for your position.

To arrange an interview please contact me at the above address or by phone at (555) 555-5555.

Yours sincerely,

Chris Smith

Chris Smith

Before

Marketing Intern (After)

Date: June 1, 200–
From: *csmith@email.com*
To: *pcummings@email.com*
Subject: Marketing Intern

TO: Pat Cummings
RE: Summer Internship

I definitely want to interview for and, ideally, serve as a Public Relations Intern in your Any City office this summer. Over the past three years, I have taken academic, co-curricular, and practical steps towards a career in public relations. As an intern at Any Name and Associates, I will take a giant leap toward my professional goals.

As described on the attached resume, I am a business and marketing student. My marketing courses have overviewed concepts related to promotions, media relations, as well as marketing research. For these classes, I contributed to a comprehensive marketing and promotions campaign that included planning and budgeting a grand opening event, developing media releases and promotional materials, writing a detailed proposal, and creating and delivering a PowerPoint presentation.

To develop event planning, outreach, fundraising, and publicity skills, I have been active in campus life. All positions held involved planning, negotiating, motivating, working with diverse individuals, and serving as a goal-driven member of a team focusing on outcomes. Most significant, outside of academia, I have completed various internships. Each required that I develop the skills you state as desired of a successful intern. To date, I have served as a Recruiting and Marketing Intern for a travel-abroad program; as an intern completing sales and marketing projects for a web-based advertising company; and as a marketing intern for Abercrombie and Fitch. Now, I want to be an accomplishment-oriented intern at Any Name and Associates.

I hope you will determine my candidacy worthy of a telephone interview. Please be assured that I have made living arrangements in the city for the summer. Thank you for your consideration.

Yours sincerely,
Chris Smith
(555) 555-5555
csmith@email.com

After

- This letter of application is e-mailed, for a specific internship in a specific location.
- A phone call revealed the name of the internship coordinator.
- Career focus is projected, and qualifications are presented in increasing order of importance.
- Special reference is made to what could be a crucial "hidden obstacle," housing in the city.

Administrative Assistant (Before)

- Do identify your referral source early in the letter.

- Don't refer to a reference unless you also provide contact information.

- Do summarize and high-light all qualifications and related experience.

- Don't end with a vague hope for a call.

123 Any Street
City, ST 12345

June 1, 200–

Pat Cummings
Office Manager
Any Company
456 Any Street
City, ST 12345

Dear Mr. Cummings:

Stephanie Smith, a colleague and fellow member of the Chicago Area Office Man-agers Association, gave me your name. Stephanie suggested that you might be looking for an administrative assistant with a background that has included a variety of administrative experiences.

I am an extraordinarily organized and detail-oriented individual with three years, experience in office administration. I believe my qualifications would match your requirements. My strengths included independent working habits and superb computer skills. As an Administrative Assistant at Boston University Hospital, I completed receptionist, word processing, database management, budgeting, and computer support tasks. There, I was responsible for supporting three physicians, and I worked closely with a very pleasant and professional Office Manager, Mary Marks. In fact, Ms. Marks has offered to serve as a reference as I seek new oppor-tunities in the Chicago area.

I would appreciate the opportunity to discuss any positions in your office at your convenience. If you have any questions, do not hesitate to contact me in care of the phone number appearing on my resume.

Yours sincerely,

Chris Smith

Chris Smith

Before

Chris Smith
123 Any Street • City, ST 12345 • (555) 555-5555 • *csmith@er*

June 1, 200–

Pat Cummings
Office Manager
Any Company
456 Any Street
City, ST 12345

Dear Mr. Cummings:

Because I will soon be relocating to the Chicago area, I have spoken with Jones, a colleague and a member of the Chicago Area Office Managers Association, regarding my search for an administrative assistant position. She suggested you might be looking for an administrative assistant or that you might refer me to other hiring managers or search professionals.

As cited on the resume attached, I have over three years' experience in office administration. As an Administrative Assistant at Boston University Hospital (BUH), I completed receptionist, word processing, database management, budgeting, and computer support tasks enthusiastically and professionally. Prior, I held numerous part-time and summer positions, including those involving administrative and customer service roles. Summarizing, the qualifications I offer include:

- Ability to prioritize and complete tasks accurately and on time.
- Professionalism required to address concerns of patients and clients while maintaining office efficiently and following standardized procedures and policies.
- Flexibility and creativity to transform instructions and feedback of supervisors into projects completed independently and thoroughly.
- Capacities to use, support, and train others to use Word, WordPerfect, Excel, Access, FileMaker Pro, QuickBooks, and Internet applications.

I would appreciate the opportunity to discuss my qualifications for positions in your office and, if appropriate, any referrals. Please, do not hesitate to contact me in care of the phone number or email appearing above and on the resume. I anticipated being in Chicago and ready to work within the next three weeks. I will call immediately upon my relocation to discuss your reactions to this note. Thank you for your consideration and assistance.

Yours sincerely,

Chris Smith

Chris Smith

referral
tiative for follow-up.

Chapter 6

Cover Letters for Special Situations

The samples in this chapter are associated with diverse job-seekers and varied job-search circumstances, but the lessons learned as you review them will be common to all cover-letter writers. Always remember, RIGHT cover-letter writing begins with a review of sample letters and job announcements. The samples here and in the rest of this book can help you do just that, no matter what your job-search situation.

Special Strategies for Special Situations

Are you a recent college grad, looking for your first job or internship? Are you interested in returning to the job market after some time at home? Are you trying to overcome "traumatic job circumstances," that is, being fired or laid off? Or are you simply motivated to get that next big opportunity?

Almost every job-seeker perceives his/her situation as special, involving unique circumstances and challenges. In reality, your situation may not be so unusual, and you should find inspiration from the samples in this chapter. As you read on, you will see you are not alone and that you can identify job-search role models in the pages that follow.

As you review the samples in this and other chapters, keep in mind that the word count and the physical sizes of letters were reduced here in order to fit into this book. When you draft and finalize correspondence, you will use regular letter-size paper or e-mail. While each word should be carefully chosen, you need not limit yourself to the number of words in these samples.

Read and think about comments appearing at the end of the samples in this chapter. They identify key strategies associated with each special circumstance. Bulleted comments are offered as glimpses into their job-search circumstances and cover-letter strategies. Are they pertinent to your situation?

Over Age Fifty: Product Manager

Chris Smith

123 Any Street • City, ST 12345 • (555) 555-5555 • *csmith@email.com*

June 1, 200–

Pat Cummings
Vice President of Marketing
Any Corporation
456 Any Street
City, ST 12345

Dear Mr. Cummings:

Are you and your colleagues in need of a motivated professional with comprehensive product-management experience spanning decades? I would like to continue my achievement-filled career with Any Corporation. Through this letter, the attached resumes, and, ideally, an interview, I can present my qualifications for your consideration.

Past experience has provided me many opportunities to implement profitable product-management strategies, including those associated with pricing, production, distribution, as well as advertising for existing and new products. Specifically in reference to pharmaceutical and food products, I have been involved in all aspects of product/protocol development and management to obtain FDA product approval. As a Product Manager for Estrade, Inc., I coordinate all product development for a medical supply corporation with annual sales in excess of $400 million. Prior, I served in similar capacities for Vita Thirst, the manufacturer of healthful drink products. My product designs, production planning, and marketing techniques have been recognized as consistently innovative and, most important, profitable. Over the years, every product I have been associated with met or exceeded annual profit goals.

I would appreciate your consideration and look forward to speaking with you, with Sam Smith, or others you deem appropriate regarding how I might best contribute to Any Corporation, as you continue to work on the development of your new healthy snack line. I will call to discuss your thoughts regarding my candidacy.

Sincerely,

Chris Smith

Chris Smith

- Focuses on achievements and accomplishments for an "experienced" candidate.

- Refers confidently to tenure in field—hiding dates on cover letter and resume doesn't work.

- Closes with a mature and confident reference to marketing colleagues.

- Clearly did her research regarding this company's future products.

Experience at Only One Place: Materials Manager

- Boldly, with pride, refers to achievements within in one organization.

- Cites job functions and general achievements in the letter, referring to actual amounts cited on resume.

- Shows knowledge of the hospital's recent acquisition.

Chris Smith

123 Any Street • City, ST 12345 • (555) 555-5555 • *csmith@email.com*

June 1, 200–

Pat Cummings
Vice-President, Fiscal Affairs
Any Hospital
456 Any Street
City, ST 12345

Dear Ms. Cummings:

I am in search of exciting new challenges and achievements in health-care materials management. With this goal in mind, I would like to inquire about the possibility of joining Any Hospital's management team. As described with great pride on the attached resume, during the past eighteen years I have progressed rapidly in positions of responsibility at Current Hospital. As the supervisor of patient transportation, manager of warehousing/distribution, and in my current position as senior buyer and manager of inventory control, I have met budgetary goals and provided efficient and mission-driven services.

Most recently, I have been able to reduce the expenditures of all in-house medical and nonmedical supplies substantially each year through cost-effective negotiations, purchasing, and control. I also played a key role in automating inventories and providing a functional layout for warehouse locations that reduced the selection-and-distribution process for warehoused materials. This also enabled me to provide more stringent controls, reducing shrinkage, damage, and obsolescence—common problems in the health-care field. Estimated costs and savings are cited on the resume.

Past achievements within one organization prove my professional competencies and potential to succeed in new roles at Any Hospital. As your health-care operations grow with the acquisition of several local HMOs, I know that materials-management issues will become crucial. Please, let's discuss how I might help link growth with efficiency. I will call to confirm your receipt of this letter and to clarify the next steps.

Sincerely,

Chris Smith

Chris Smith

In-House Application: District Supervisor

Date: June 1, 200–
From: *csmith@email.com*
To: *pcummings@email.com*
Subject: District Supervisor Position

TO: Pat Cummings, Personnel Director
RE: Candidacy for District Supervisor (Grade 25)

In support of my candidacy for the management job posting for the above position, I present my resume and this memo, summarizing my experience with Any Gas Company and other employers in the gas distribution industry.

As you know, these positions required the ability to provide technical support, retain personnel, supervise outside contractors, and work with developers and public officials during the joint work programs and projects. My performance reviews during my tenure at Any Gas have all been above average, and my current supervisor, Kelly Stevens, has offered to support my desire for this promotion.

As reflected in all past reviews and training evaluations, I have the technical capability to work with and direct company and contractor personnel in all phases of gas distribution systems, from new construction to replacement and operation. Previous accomplishments with Any Gas indicate my strong communication skills and my ability to work with people at all levels of responsibility, including those who would report to and interact with a District Supervisor. Clearly, I feel professionally and personally ready to handle the challenges of the district supervisor position. During an interview, I can confidently yet objectively share these qualifications with you and others involved in the selection process.

I look forward to meeting with you to discuss my candidacy. Thank you for your consideration.

Sincerely,
Chris

- Uses e-mailed memo format for internal communication.
- Refers to performance review and support of current supervisor.
- Demonstrates understanding of the new job and new responsibilities.

Homemaker Re-entering the Work Force: Graphic Designer

Chris Smith
123 Any Street • City, ST 12345 • (555) 555-5555 • *csmith@email.com*

- Requests an interview in the first sentence; appropriate when portfolio must be presented.

- Focuses on targeted goals and specific achievements, not on special circumstance.

- Subtly and appropriately raises status as candidate seeking to return to workforce.

June 1, 200–

Pat Cummings
Creative Director
Any Advertising Agency
456 Any Street
City, ST 12345

Dear Mr. Cummings:

I would like to meet to discuss freelance assignments or a part-time position in graphic design or production. During this meeting, I can show you my portfolio and discuss how excited I am to continue my career within an industry that is for me a professional passion. Past achievements, all illustrated in my portfolio, should reveal my readiness to succeed at AAA.

In an effort to enhance my talents and nurture high-tech design talents, I am currently enrolled in the Massachusetts College of Art's Graphic Design Certificate Program. Prior, I earned a Bachelor of Arts degree in Art History, providing a broad foundation of research, analysis, and presentation talents upon which to build specialized training.

Professionally, I offer more that seven years of experience in production and traffic areas of print and graphic design and in related fields, including fundraising and direct and mass mailings. All of my professional accomplishments are highlighted on the attached resume. After a three-year hiatus, with my family well established, I am highly motivated to return to the workforce and contribute to the growth of Any Advertising Agency. In addition to my resume and portfolio, excellent references do support my candidacy.

Please, let's talk about how I can contribute to the Any Advertising team. You can respond via e-mail or call via the phone number above.

Sincerely,

Chris Smith

Chris Smith

Chris Smith

123 Any Street • City, ST 12345 • (555) 555-5555 • *csmith@email.com*

June 1, 200–

Pat Cummings
Hiring Manager
Any Advertising Agency
456 Any Street
City, ST 12345

Dear Mr. Cummings:

I would like to inquire about and, ideally, interview for a position at Any Advertising Agency. As detailed on the attached resume, I have over eight years of experience in promotion, communications, and administration. Now, it is with great focus and enthusiasm that I seek to contribute as an assistant, supporting client services, traffic, or media planning activities.

As owner of a successful and profitable housecleaning service for four years, I designed and wrote all promotional materials, including direct-mail coupons. Immediately after my first promotional campaign, the volume of business tripled, resulting in my hiring and overseeing six people. In addition to supervising employees, I completed all administrative and budgetary tasks, which entailed handling calls, scheduling, billing, recordkeeping, ordering supplies, and customer relations. Now, having just sold the business, I am seeking a position in advertising. Reality-based career exploration and past accomplishments support my desire to enter the field of advertising and begin an accomplishment-focused career in my industry of choice.

I also have strong planning, proofreading, and presentation skills from prior experience as a teacher. I procured donations of computers and software from a local business and successfully planned, implemented, and promoted school fundraising events.

I hope we will have the opportunity to discuss current or future opportunities during an interview. If no positions are available or anticipated, any referrals to other agencies would be welcomed.

Thank you for your consideration.

Sincerely,

Chris Smith

Chris Smith

- Requests an interview in the first sentence and identifies potential positions in first paragraph.

- Focuses on key qualifications in second paragraph, highlighting specific experience related to goals.

Chris Smith

123 Any Street • City, ST 12345 • (555) 555-5555 • *csmith@email.com*

June 1, 200–

Pat Cummings
Human Resources Director
Any Corporation
456 Any Street
City, ST 12345

Dear Ms. Cummings:

Via this letter and accompanying resume I wish to formalize my candidacy for the business consultant position recently posted in the Arkansas *Democratic-Gazette*. In summary, some of the qualifications I would like to discuss in detail during an interview include:

- Experience within consulting and instructional roles, specifically associated with marketing, management information systems, and strategic planning.
- Specialized knowledge of and experience conducting marketing research, SWOT analyses, and customer-service audits and recommendations.
- Confidence in report writing, presentation, and program implementation roles.

Currently, I am a faculty member in the Department of Management and Aviation Science at Henderson State University. I am also engaged in several consulting assignments involving troubleshooting, training, and installation, conversion, and maintenance of automated accounting systems. I have taught clients as well as students how to use several applications and operating systems, including spreadsheets, word processing, and accounting programs for Windows and Mac environments.

In strategic market development, the ability to assess customer needs in an e-commerce, web-based marketing environment, to relate them to overall market conditions, and then to determine a response is critical for successful business development. By first conducting appropriate quantitative research and analysis, then presenting findings and strategic implementation, I can provide you with innovative approaches to getting the job done. I look forward to speaking with you regarding value-added services and profitability enhancements. I have conducted some preliminary research already and would welcome the opportunity to share some ideas with you whenever appropriate.

Sincerely,

Chris Smith

Chris Smith

- Focuses on key qualifications in paragraph after bullet points, highlighting experiences related to position.
- Teases reader with references to preliminary research when requesting interview.

Career Change: Marketing Executive

Date: June 1, 200–
From: *csmith@net.com*
To: *pcummings@email.com*
Subject: Dealer Representative Position

Dear Ms. Cummings:

Please accept this e-mail and attached resume as evidence of my desire to interview for the marketing department position advertised on Jobs.com. As Any Corp's Dealer Representative, I will utilize my thorough knowledge of boating as well as sales, marketing, and communication skills to inspire those who sell your products, educate salespersons, and promote product lines directly to consumers. As a semiprofessional sailboat racer, I am very familiar with the Any Corp line. The pride I have in twice winning national honors and participation in the Cape Cod races will only be matched by accomplishments as a member of your marketing team.

The product knowledge I have gained as an avid recreational boater, who with great equipment and hard work evolved to become a successful competitor, will allow me to promote Any Corp with passion and confidence. Contacts with owners, officials, and dealers will also facilitate my efforts.

A career change that will involve a transition from a successful management career to a marketing, promotions, and consumer-relations career is most desired. I am confident that my business and boating background will ensure that I have favorable impact on sales, image, and continued growth. Please allow me the opportunity to make a great impression via an interview. Thank you for your attention. I do hope that I will have the chance to soon present my qualifications and motivations in person. Please, do not hesitate to email or call to arrange a meeting. And, I have asked some of my boating colleagues to contact you regarding their views of my potential. The more you know about me, the easier your decision regarding the search process!

Sincerely,
Chris Smith
123 Any Street
City, ST 12345
(555) 555-5555
csmith@email.com

- Requests an interview in the first sentence and again in the closing paragraph.

- Confidently and persuasively reveals desire to connect interest and career.

- Interesting reference to asking colleagues to support candidacy; reflects how large a circle of contacts the candidate possesses.

Career Change: Product and Services Developer

Chris Smith

123 Any Street • City, ST 12345 • (555) 555-5555 • *csmith@email.com*

- Immediately focuses on desired goal.
- Cites sales achievements and broad set of qualities in first paragraph.
- Reveals field research by stating functional titles.

June 1, 200–

Pat Cummings
Vice-President
Any Bank
456 Any Street
City, ST 12345

Dear Ms. Cummings:

Currently, I am seeking a career change and the opportunity to associate with a progressive bank where I can effectively apply my creative and innovative talents and capability for developing or increasing and successfully marketing new service products. During the past eight years, I have served as vice president and director of operations of an ever-expanding, quality-driven, function-and-recreation complex. In these capacities I had total responsibility for creating effective sales programs and assuring the quality of services provided. Last year, we exceeded our goals by 150% and grossed over $1.4 million in sales. Increased business resulted from an aggressive marketing effort targeting local businesses.

As I will share personally, if you grant me the opportunity to interview for a client services, loan officer, or marketing position, I am adept at making business-to-business contacts, at creating and utilizing promotional advertising and marketing programs, and at making effective presentations. All these talents have to date stimulated growth and profits. Quantitative documentation of my achievements appears on the enclosed resume. Reviewing that document, you will also find that I have undergraduate business coursework and that within my current capacities I am directly responsible for all banking relationships.

Research into the banking field has identified the above-cited titles, but I would welcome your thoughts regarding where I might best contribute to Any Bank. I will call to confirm your receipt of this note, to clarify next steps, and, I most sincerely hope, to arrange a brief meeting. Thank you for your consideration.

Yours sincerely,

Chris Smith

Chris Smith

Displaced Homemaker: Administrator

Chris Smith
123 Any Street • City, ST 12345 • (555) 555-5555 • *csmith@email.com*

June 1, 200–

Pat Cummings
Human Resources Director
Any Corporation
456 Any Street
City, ST 12345

Dear Mr. Cummings:

I am highly motivated and qualified to serve in an administrative position at Any Corporation. As is detailed on my resume, I offer extensive and varied experience in administrative roles in employment as well as community services roles. In summary, I offer Any Corporation:

- Experience with staff supervision and motivation.
- A record of success in meeting planning and direction and activities scheduling.
- Confidence in public-speaking situations.
- Excellent phone and correspondence skills.
- Bookkeeping, fundraising, and promotions talents.

If you are looking for someone with these skills, I hope you will give me the opportunity to speak to you. During a telephone conversation and, ideally, a meeting, I can expand upon the above bullet items and personalize my candidacy. A resume and cover letter can reveal a great deal, but in-person communications are, I believe, best.

Thank you for your time.

Sincerely,

Chris Smith

Chris Smith

- Focuses on desired goal and on resume in first paragraph.
- Summarizes qualifications via bullet points.
- Identifies phone and in-person interview as next possible steps.

Chris Smith

123 Any Street • City, ST 12345 • (555) 555-5555 • *csmith@email.com*

June 1, 200–

Pat Cummings
President
Any Executive Search Firm
456 Any Street
City, ST 12345
FAX (555) 555-5557

Dear Ms. Cummings:

Attached is a copy of my resume, a list of professional achievements, and letters of recommendation written by my colleagues and clients. I trust that these documents will convince you that I am worthy of an interview and that, after you have had the opportunity to evaluate my candidacy, I could soon become a strong member of the Any Executive Search Firm team.

As detailed in my resume, my recruiting skills and accomplishments were nurtured over seven years while recruiting high-technology managers, support staff, and marketing personnel. Much of this experience involved extensive travel, training program development, and networking prospective clients. In addition to a record of success and a well-earned reputation, I possess valuable contacts within the management information systems, software development, and engineering industries that would prove valuable to Any Firm's client base.

Of course, review of a candidate's supporting materials is the first step of an effective search process. Ideally, you and I could meet soon, whenever mutually convenient. My interest is so strong, and my enthusiasm so great, that I will call to confirm your receipt of this fax and to discuss your reactions to my request for an interview. In advance, thank you for your consideration.

Sincerely,

Chris Smith

Chris Smith

- Immediately focuses reader on three documents that support candidacy.

- Includes letter of recommendation written by colleague at previous firm; technique a fired or laid-off candidate should use.

- Demonstrates confidence and highlights all key qualifications, including potential contacts that can be brought to new firm.

Former Small-Business Owner: Environmental Advocate

Recycling Renegades

123 Any Street • City, ST 12345 • (555) 555-5555 • *csmith@email.com*

Chris Smith, President

June 1, 200–

Pat Cummings
Director
Any Environmental Agency
456 Any Street
City, ST 12345
FAX (555) 555-5557

Dear Director Cummings:

Your article in the May edition of *Save Our Earth* was impressive. In fact, the article and the mission and offerings of Any Environmental Agency, as dynamically presented on your Web site, have inspired me to seek employment with your agency. Do you currently have an opening for an environmental advocate, public relations person, volunteer coordinator, researcher, or lobbyist?

Described on my resume, and revealed through the annual report also attached, I have a passion for environmental concerns and practical experiences in all of the above areas. For the past four years, I have been operating an entrepreneurial venture, Recycling Renegades. I successfully acquired the first recycling permit in Cambridge for ferrous and nonferrous metal, aluminum, high-grade paper, and plastic. As owner and manager, I conducted research, developed pilot programs, formulated networks for voluntary recycling, picked up and processed materials, and distributed proceeds to community associations. While my motives were altruistic, my accomplishments proved profitable as well.

Now, I wish to use the skills I gained from this venture, and as an undergraduate environmental engineering major, in any of the above cited roles at Any Environmental Agency. It is time to shift to a wider focus, impacting a broader constituency. Would it be possible to meet for an interview? I have several ideas I'd like to share. Will you be attending the environmental affairs conference in New York City? If we haven't connected by phone, e-mail, or in person prior, perhaps we can meet at the conference. Your consideration and past, present, and future inspiration is much appreciated.

Sincerely,

Chris Smith

Chris Smith

- Identifies inspiration for contact immediately.

- Reveals technical knowledge as well as achievements in second paragraph.

- Reminds of the five possible roles, and reinforces knowledge of the field, desire to interview, and creative options for interacting in closing paragraph.

Former Freelancer: Production Assistant

- Reveals knowledge of field-specific Web site and dual source of posting immediately.

- Presents greatest strengths and qualifications as bullet points.

- Demonstrates idiosyncratic knowledge of field in closing paragraph.

- Will ask reference to make direct contact with cover letter and resume reviewer.

Date: June 1, 200–
From: *csmith@email.com*
To: *pcummings@email.com*
Subject: Experienced PA Seeks Position

Chris Smith
123 Any Street
City, ST 12345
(555) 555-5555

Dear Mr. Cummings:

I would like to apply for the production assistant position advertised on the PA.com Web site and in the *Herald*. While the attached resume reveals an extensive list of experiences in all aspects of video production, including positions as writer, researcher, director, and editor, only through an interview can you determine if I have what it takes to transform your vision into day-to-day production realities. In summary, the personal and professional qualities I possess include:

- 3 years as a freelance production assistant working on several commercial and documentary pieces.
- Skills and perspectives gained as chief assistant on *Milk Carton Kids: An American Crisis,* supporting preliminary research and writing, scheduling location shooting, and screening potential interview candidates.
- Breadth of administrative and logistical talents gained completing two public-service announcements for Miami Child Services, which included camera operation and heavy script and video editing.
- Patience, flexibility, creativity, and active listening skills required to thrive under the pressure of deadlines and to work within the demands of pre-production, shooting, and production stages.

I've admired Any Production Company's work for some time and attended your screening of *Silent Victims* at the Crime Awareness Convention last month. I now politely ask that you grant me the chance to meet and that you contact Tracy Turner at (555) 555-5567 or via *tturner@email.com*. I will call to confirm your receipt of this e-mail (original to follow in the mail) and to discuss your reactions to my request for consideration.

Sincerely,

Chris Smith

Chris Smith

Freelancer: Editor and Writer

Chris Smith
123 Any Street • City, ST 12345 • (555) 555-5555 • *csmith@email.com*

June 1, 200–

Pat Cummings
Publisher
Any Publishing Company
456 Any Street
City, ST 12345

Dear Ms. Cummings:

I am a freelance editor and writer of educational and reference materials targeting college students and adults. The books and articles I have written or edited to date have been in the areas of careers, self-help, and parenting. Recently, I identified titles by Any Publishing Company that reveal your interest in targeting similar topics and readers. Therefore, I would like to learn more about your freelance writing and editorial needs and acquisition process.

The attached resume documents projects to date, as well as my academic background, early experiences as an editorial assistant, and current status as a part-time English instructor. Others say I have a facility for synthesizing information and conveying it in a creative and well-organized way. They also share that my editorial style is focused and goal-directed and that it effectively inspires authors to use consistent tone and finish projects on time. Whether editing or writing textbook materials, teacher workbooks, or ancillary activities and worksheets, I can tailor the content, tone, and approach to a variety of purposes and audiences.

May I speak with you about working on some of your projects as either editor or author? Attached is a piece I wrote for an online newsletter as well as a brief note written by Kerry Williams, an editor at Textbook Company. I hope these documents reveal the potential I possess to contribute to Any Publishing Company's efforts. Of course, I can provide additional writing samples and references.

Let's talk by phone or communicate via e-mail soon. I am available whenever convenient. Thank you for your consideration.

Sincerely,

Chris Smith

Chris Smith

- Quickly reveals some accomplishments and goals in first paragraph, using industry-specific phrases.

- Supports candidacy in second paragraph, including identification of attached writing sample and reference note.

- Attaching note is a pro-active and assertive way to enhance impact of job-search advocate.

Gaps in Employment History: Assistant Curator

Chris Smith

123 Any Street • City, ST 12345 • (555) 555-5555 • *csmith@email.com*

- First paragraph is very focused, revealing targets and qualifications strongly, and diminishing concerns about so-called "gaps" that the reader may or may not be concerned about.

- Attaching reference list shows that any perceived gaps were not a result of negative experiences.

- Closing comment addresses in a positive way issues related to gaps of concern to candidate.

June 1, 200–

To: Pat Cummings, Curator of Any Museum
FAX: (555) 555-5557

I am seeking a position blending museum and gallery experience as well as a keen interest and academic background in fine art. Ideally that will be as your Assistant Curator. As detailed in the attached resume, I have completed two extensive internships for successful galleries in Alabama. In each position, I contributed to all aspects of operations, including artist relations, sales, show planning and implementation, and administrative duties. Responsibilities and accomplishments included assisting customers, setting up displays, and completing mailings for exhibitions. Both galleries included modern and classic pieces and artists working in eclectic media and genre.

I have a Bachelor of Arts degree in Art History, have participated in several related seminars, and I have had occasion to visit many of the world's great museums. I am a frequent visitor to the Any Museum and a member of Friends of Any Museum, so I am familiar with your mission, target patronage, educational, and outreach efforts.

In addition to a targeted resume, I have also provided a reference list of individuals familiar with my past experience who can share views regarding my future potential. I would very much like to discuss my qualifications for current or anticipated opportunities further. I will call to discuss your thoughts regarding a brief meeting.

I would like to discuss full-time or part-time options. As you are aware, those passionate about art must be creative when seeking ways to build a professional repertoire of skills and achievements. To date, whenever given the opportunity to work in an arts environment, I have succeeded. I hope I have that chance at Any Museum.

Sincerely,

Chris Smith

Chris Smith

Military Background: Transportation Operator

Chris Smith
123 Any Street • City, ST 12345 • (555) 555-5555 • *csmith@email.com*

June 1, 200–

Pat Cummings
Controller
Any Corporation
456 Any Street
City, ST 12345

Dear Mr. Cummings:

Seven of my past twelve years were spent with the United States Army in transportation-related roles and assignments. Since the completion of my military service, I have worked in sales positions. Now, I am very interested in resuming a civilian career in transportation operations or in the sale of products or equipment allied to the transportation field. All my pertinent experience is detailed on the attached resume. Key points on this document, and those I would like to discuss during an interview, include the following:

- Experience managing all phases of civilian and tactical transportation operations (vehicles from two-and-one-half-ton cargo trucks to ten-ton tractor trailers and petroleum tankers).
- Experience teaching courses and training troops about the total transportation cycle in the United States and abroad.
- Record of success contributing toward the efficient military operations and potential to do so at an in-house traffic, transportation, and distribution function or a commercial transportation depot.

Also, I am a trained professional, a graduate officer of the U.S. Army Transportation School, and a college graduate with my bachelor's degree. I would appreciate the opportunity to further describe my qualifications and the immediate and long-term contributions I could make to Any Corporation. I will call to discuss your thoughts regarding my candidacy and, if you judge appropriate, to arrange an interview. If you wish to contact me, please feel free to call me at the above number at any time.

Sincerely,

Chris Smith

Chris Smith

- First sentence and paragraph identify military background and, most important, goals.

- Closing paragraph clearly identifies desire to speak directly with potential employer.

No Clear Career Path: Accounting

Chris Smith

123 Any Street • City, ST 12345 • (555) 555-5555 • *csmith@email.com*

- First sentence and paragraph express desire for a career-oriented position and specific program goal.

- If candidate is not successful, a follow-up letter requesting referrals to clients or other accounting firms would be appropriate and effective.

June 1, 200–

Pat Cummings
Hiring Manager
Any Accounting Firm
456 Any Street
City, ST 12345
FAX (555) 555-5557

Dear Mr. Cummings:

I am now actively seeking a career-focused position in accounting that will utilize my experience in financial management and customer service, as well as my strong academic background. While researching area firms, I learned of Any Accounting's training and development program. This opportunity seems an ideal way to begin and build an accomplishment-filled career with your firm, and a long-term career is exactly what I seek. To this program and your firm, I would bring the following:

- A Bachelor of Science degree, cum laude, in Finance
- Four years of collections experience
- Successful collection of 90 percent of overdue accounts
- Experience in accounts payable and accounts receivable
- Knowledge of Excel, Lotus 1-2-3, Word, QuickBooks, and varied accounting applications
- The competence and commitment required to pass the CPA examination and adhere to strict professional and ethical standards

I hope you will give me the opportunity to speak to you about the training and development program at Any Accounting Firm. I will call to confirm your receipt of this fax (originals to follow via mail) and, if you judge my candidacy worthy, to arrange a telephone or in-person interview. Thank you for your consideration.

Sincerely,

Chris Smith

Chris Smith

Overseas Employment History: Marketing Assistant

Date: June 1, 200–
From: *csmith@email.com*
To: *pcummings@email.com*
Subject: Marketing Assistant Position

Chris Smith
123 rue Vert
Paris, France
011-123-45-55-55
csmith@email.com

June 1, 200–

Dear Ms. Cummings:

Anticipating relocation home to the United States, I am now actively seeking a marketing support position with Any Corporation. As you review the attached vita, I trust you will conclude that I can effectively contribute to an international service-oriented organization dedicated, as your mission states, "to expanding international commerce through effective state-of-the-art and traditional marketing strategies." I understand you currently have a number of international clients and anticipate landing new accounts with multinational firms. Summarizing some of the points I would like to share via phone discussions and in-person interviews, I offer Any Corporation:

- Experience as an interpreter and translator working on international market research with the Marketing Department at the University of Paris, Sorbonne.
- Knowledge of concepts and terminology associated with marketing and advertising.
- Confidence and history of success as administrative assistant to professors and business executives.
- Trilingual fluency in English, French, and Italian, and strong proficiency in Spanish.
- Skills and perspectives gained completing a Bachelor of Arts degree in French, summa cum laude, from University of Rochester, in Rochester, New York.
- Communication and presentation skills gained tutoring individuals in foreign languages and English as a Second Language.
- Familiarity working and interacting with multilingual, multicultural individuals and groups.

I will be in New York February 14–28 for a pre-relocation visit. Would it be possible to schedule an interview for that time? While I hope we will have had telephone and e-mail communications prior, it would be wonderful if we could meet during my upcoming visit. Of course, I am eligible to work in the United States and I anticipate paying all relocation expenses. Thank you for your attention.

Sincerely,

Chris Smith

Chris Smith

- First paragraph expresses immediate relocation status and goal, as well as some research done on the specific employer.

- Closing paragraph concisely presents desire for an interview, details how it can be arranged, and diminishes any concerns regarding international candidacy.

Part-Time Employment History: Store Manager

Chris Smith
123 Any Street • City, ST 12345 • (555) 555-5555 • *csmith@email.com*

- First paragraph identifies goal, summarizes background, and refers to Web-based efforts.

- Closing paragraph reveals knowledge of the field while focusing on part-time history as traditional and the foundation upon which success can be built.

June 1, 200–

Pat Cummings
District Manager
Any Retail Chain
456 Any Street
City, ST 12345
FAX (555) 555-5557

Dear Ms. Cummings:

I would very much like to join the Any Retail Chain's management team. A very strong and clear sense of career focus, previous retail experience, knowledge of your stores and target markets, and a desire for a full-time management position have prompted me to forward the attached resume. I have uploaded this document and provided additional information through your firm's website, but I also wanted to share my candidacy directly via this fax.

During the past seven years, as documented on my resume, I have held progressively responsible positions in retail sales, from salesperson to manager. In my most recent position as store manager for Raintree Designs, by motivating my colleagues and completing efficient buying, we accounted for an increase in branch sales from $.5 to $1.2 million in one year. I have hands-on experience in sales, inventory control, and product promotion. As assistant manager for Rips, Inc., in Brooklyn, I supervised a staff of twelve, oversaw the production of a promotional video, and assisted in selecting chain-wide promotion techniques.

As my resume indicates, and as is the history of many who build successful careers, some of my retail management experience has been part-time. I am now seeking a permanent position and the opportunity to build a career while I contribute to the growth of Any Retail Chain. Please allow me the opportunity to share in an interview how past experiences and accomplishments can predict future achievements. I will call to clarify all steps associated with the selection process and, if you judge appropriate, to arrange an interview. Thank you for your time and consideration.

Sincerely,

Chris Smith

Chris Smith

Recent Graduate: Assistant to Museum Director

Chris Smith
123 Any Street • City, ST 12345 • (555) 555-5555 • *csmith@email.com*

June 1, 200–

Pat Cummings
Museum Director
Any Museum
456 Any Street
City, ST 12345

Dear Ms. Cummings:

Throughout my undergraduate years I sought to learn both in the classroom and beyond. I did so via specific courses and, most important, through practical internships and training. Now, I seek an opportunity to put my newly developed skills and knowledge to use in a position at Any Museum. Perhaps I can do so as an assistant to the curator or in patron relations, education, or fundraising roles?

As my resume indicates, I recently participated in a program for art history majors at the Louvre. This involved studying European art and attending seminars on museum operations. Prior, I worked for two summers at the Metropolitan Museum of Art as a museum assistant at the information booth.

Coursework in African-American art, modern art, and museum science, all detailed in my resume, also prepared me for a position in a museum. As a recent graduate of the University of South Dakota, with an art history background and practical museum experience, I now seek an opportunity to continue my quest for knowledge and professional development with you and your Any Museum colleagues.

The eyes of a young visitor to your museum have grown into those of a diligent student, recent graduate, and hopeful candidate. While my heart still contains the enthusiasm and excitement I felt during early visits, my head is now full of knowledge and career focus. Please grant me the opportunity to interview and, someday, to become part of your staff. I will call to see if an in-person interview would be an appropriate next step.

Sincerely,

Chris Smith

Chris Smith

- First paragraph identifies desired goals via a well-crafted closing question.
- Second paragraph presents most significant experience as strongest qualification.
- Third paragraph focuses on academics and could include a brief listing of courses.
- Closing paragraph reveals motivations as well as qualifications hoping to inspire an interview.

Recent Graduate: English Teacher

Chris Smith

123 Any Street • City, ST 12345 • (555) 555-5555 • *csmith@email.com*

June 1, 200–

Pat Cummings
Human Resources Manager
Any School District
456 Any Street
City, ST 12345

Dear Mr. Cummings:

In response to last week's advertisement in the *New England Journal of Higher Education* for an English teacher, I enclose my resume, completed application, and supplemental materials for your consideration.

As is noted on my resume, I recently graduated from Boston College and I am certified to teach English and Special Education. As I trust you are aware, I fulfilled student teaching requirements at Newton High School and through your district's special education program. At Newton High, I developed and implemented lesson plans and an entire unit on college admissions essays, while observing my master teacher's instructional style. Through experience and observation, supplemented by courses in curriculum and instruction, I became a student-centered and reality-based instructor, motivator, and classroom manager.

Supporting special education offerings, I learned of IEPs and district approaches to inclusion. I was proud to assist students with learning disabilities, as well as those who needed assistance with physical disabilities. I used lesson planning, instructional, as well as tutorial talents gained in classrooms and other settings. Throughout my undergraduate years I participated in a volunteer literacy program, tutoring both youth and adults struggling with reading difficulties. The skills and perspectives gained as a student teacher and tutor will be foundations upon which I will build a successful teaching career.

Also attached are letters of recommendation and a favorite lesson plan. As you read these documents, I hope you gain a sense of the teacher I wish to be. I know I can instill knowledge, inspire continued learning, and refine students' writing talents. I will call to confirm that I have completed all required steps and to inquire regarding the interview and selection process.

Sincerely,

Chris Smith

Chris Smith

- First sentence focuses on position and where it was advertised.

- Second paragraph presents most significant student teaching experience as strongest qualification.

- Closing paragraph cites supplemental materials, focuses on sample lesson plan, introduces readers to teaching philosophy, and strongly requests an interview.

Recent Graduate: Gerontology Aide

Date: June 1, 200–
From: *csmith@email.com*
To: *pcummings@email.com*
Subject: Gerontologist Position

Dear Ms. Cummings:

Thank you for speaking with me today. As I mentioned on the phone, I am interested in beginning a career in gerontology. Ideally, that will be either as an Aide or a Residential Care Specialist. These are the two opportunities you identified as appropriate options. Summarizing my general qualifications as detailed on the attached resume, I offer the following:

- Academic knowledge and curiosities generated as a Sociology major at the College of the Holy Cross, and through courses including: Poverty and Crisis, the Political Economy of Health Care in the United States, Race Relations, and Women in Society.
- Commitment to community service and experience working with diverse constituents in programs offering services to elderly adults and at-risk youth.
- Patience and sensitivities needed to address individual and group needs of elderly in their homes and within residential or day facilities.

Most significant, and related to those requirements stated on your agency's website:

- As a member of Volunteers for a Better World, I helped organize and assisted with serving food to the homeless and co-directing a successful annual campus food drive.
- I served as a volunteer at Holy Cross Hospital, which required training and interaction with elderly patients and their families.
- I have a realistic understanding of daily care needed by agency clients, including those with early stages of Alzheimer's or those with physical disabilities.
- I have the ability to pass state licensing examinations and desire to complete specialized training, and I hold a valid drivers license.

Now, I most sincerely wish to assist clients of Any Agency as an Aide or as a Residential Care Specialist. I do hope that after you have reviewed my resume that I can meet with you for a formal employment interview. I look forward to your response.

Sincerely,

Chris Smith

- First paragraph of e-mail response to phone conversation focuses on specific positions.

- Closing paragraph reflects realistic rather than academic interest in field and desire to interview.

Recent Graduate: Legal Assistant

Chris Smith
123 Any Street • City, ST 12345 • (555) 555-5555 • *csmith@email.com*

- First paragraph imme-
diately identifies referral
source and the nature
of the position sought.

- Second paragraph
introduces academic
background.

- Third paragraph is the
most significant summary
of related experience and
again notes referral.

- Closing paragraph
reflects realistic under-
standing of functions,
using appropriate phras-
ing, and identifies can-
didate's next steps to
seek an interview.

June 1, 200–

Pat Cummings
Attorney-at-Law
Any Firm
456 Any Street
City, ST 12345
FAX (555) 555-5557

Dear Mr. Cummings:

Justice Ellen Malone of the Allentown Courthouse suggested that I contact you regarding an opening you may soon have for a legal assistant. Judge Malone is aware of
my desire to find a challenging paralegal, legal research, and administrative-focused
position, and she encouraged me to immediately seek consideration to join you and
your associates at Any Firm.

I will be graduating this May from Temple University with a Bachelor of Arts in African-American Studies. In addition to major courses, I have studied several areas,
including business administration and computer applications. While completing my
course of study, I have actively explored and gained knowledge of and skills associated with the field of law.

As is described in great detail on the attached resume, I have worked in a variety
of legal settings throughout college. Currently, I am a volunteer for Temple's Student
Legal Aid, supporting the efforts of law students helping undergraduates and community members with legal problems. I worked part-time over the past three years as a
peer probation mentor for the Allentown juvenile court. In addition to these experiences, last summer I served as a research assistant for the Chief County Clerk of Allentown, when I met Judge Malone.

All these positions have given me a strong sense of the law, the legal system, and most
important, the impact that effective research, document management, and citation
preparation can have on litigation and other activities. Before applying to law school
in a few years, I wish to fine-tune my knowledge of law and gain a greater sense of
career focus and special interests. Ideally, I can do so at Any Firm. I will contact you
within the week to further discuss the possibility of interviewing for this position.
Thank you for your consideration.

Sincerely,

Chris Smith

Chris Smith

Recent Graduate: Set Designer

Chris Smith
123 Any Street • City, ST 12345 • (555) 555-5555 • *csmith@email.com*

June 1, 200–

Pat Cummings
Stage Director
Any Production Company
456 Any Street
City, ST 12345

Dear Mr. Cummings:

Lynne Winchester recently indicated that you may have an opening for a set designer and suggested that I contact you. I am seeking a position involving stage design for television, theater, and video productions.

As noted on my resume, I graduated recently from Clemson University with a Bachelor of Arts degree in Theatre Arts and a concentration in Studio Art. Courses in modern drama, music and sound in theatre, set creation and design, intermediate painting, and woodworking all contributed to the skills I possess and focused my aspirations towards stage design. As a an undergraduate, I designed and helped create props for numerous campus productions, including *The Tempest* and *Marco Polo Sings a Solo,* and I developed many storyboards and set design presentations.

Design, carpentry, and related talents have been nurtured in settings outside of the theater. Recently, I co-designed and co-created props and decorations for several fundraisers, weddings, and events held at the Civic Center and Columbia Country Club. Also, I have gained valuable craft-specific skills working as an apprentice to a busy home-renovation specialist and painting murals with a freelance artist.

Enclosed is a resume as well as some photographs of my work. Of course, I would like to show you my entire portfolio and discuss with you how I might contribute to Any Production Company's current and future projects. I have some great ideas for the sets of *Trivia Tunes* and *Videos After Dark* and hope to have the opportunity to discuss them with you. I will call to confirm your receipt of all supporting materials, including a letter from Lynne, and to arrange either a formal employment interview or informal conversation regarding my candidacy. Thank you for your consideration.

Sincerely,

Chris Smith

Chris Smith

- First paragraph immediately identifies referral source and the nature of the position sought.

- Second paragraph presents most academic experiences, including a list of courses and projects.

- Third paragraph refers to important and "creatively connected" experience.

- Closing paragraph reveals desire to share portfolio (the most significant supporting document), again notes referral source, and requests formal or informal meeting.

Recent Graduate: Translator

Chris Smith
123 Any Street • City, ST 12345 • (555) 555-5555 • *csmith@email.com*

June 1, 200–

Pat Cummings
Director
Any Council
456 Any Street
City, ST 12345

Dear Ms. Cummings:

I would like to interview for the translator position advertised in the *Local News*. As detailed in my enclosed resume and most significant to this opportunity, I have been employed as an interpreter and translator for a Parisian film corporation. I interpreted for negotiations over film co-productions and have translated agreements, film scripts, and scenarios. In addition, I translated foreign correspondence. I also worked as the assistant to the Parisian representative for Desliases Associates, an import/export company. In addition to a strong academic background, I offer practical experience and, yes, accomplishments.

Academically, I graduated with a Bachelor of Arts in International Relations and French Language from Northwestern University. Throughout university studies I was recognized for scholarship, being consistently on the Dean's list, and graduating one year early, with honors. I was active in co-curricular events and organizations, including a residential honors program, in which I studied ethics and politics. By my junior and final year, I had become a Model United Nations Advisor, an alumni ambassador, and president of the International Affairs Society.

I would enjoy the opportunity to work for Any Council, and I am prepared to pay for any expenses associated with interviews and relocation. Please consider me a strong, enthusiastic, and immediately available candidate for the translator position. I have traveled great distances to gain the bilingual and translating skills I now offer. Please don't allow distance to negatively impact my candidacy. I will call to discuss your assessment of my potential, to schedule a formal telephone interview or, ideally, to arrange an in-person meeting.

Sincerely,

Chris Smith

Chris Smith

- First paragraph immediately identifies job and posting source and highlights the most significant experiences and qualifications.

- Closing paragraph reflects realistic understanding of issues related to long-distance job search and seeks to defuse them.

- Both resume and cover letter should be written and presented in French and English, front and back, revealing bilingual abilities.

Temporary Employment: Administrative Assistant

Chris Smith
123 Any Street • City, ST 12345 • (555) 555-5555 • *csmith@email.com*

June 1, 200–

Pat Cummings
Director
Any Temporary Agency
456 Any Street
City, ST 12345
FAX (555) 555-5557

SUBJECT: Temporary Administrative Positions

Attached is a targeted resume supporting my candidacy for temporary assignments. Ideally, Any Temporary Agency has immediate opportunities and, after those are completed, I can continue to serve the needs of your clients who seek temporary workers.

Five years of diverse temporary employment through agencies like yours, have provided me with skills and qualifications applicable to many different fields. Also, each has provided a reference that can support my candidacy for future opportunities.

In short, I offer a potential employer:

- Three years of accounting, financial, and administrative experience.
- Computer knowledge, including PC and Macintosh operating systems.
- Proficiency in a variety of word-processing, database, and spreadsheet programs, including Word, WordPerfect, Lotus 123, Excel, Access, and FileMaker.
- Outstanding communication, organizational skills, and project-management talents.

I would prefer to receive assignments in the Van Nuys area, and compensation requirements are negotiable. I look forward to speaking with you regarding steps I should follow to be considered for and, I hope, serve in temporary assignments for Any Temporary. I will call to discuss those steps and, should you judge appropriate, to conduct an interview and any testing. Thank you for your consideration.

Sincerely,

Chris Smith

Chris Smith

- Basic qualifications and experiences are presented as paragraph text and as bullets.
- Closing focuses on specific needs and reveals clear understanding of temporary placement process.

Chris Smith

123 Any Street • City, ST 12345 • (555) 555-5555 • *csmith@email.com*

- Brief note is appropriate for goals.

- Focus of letter is on experience, not education.

- Closing identifies knowledge of industry-specific issues and asks for an interview, as well as referral.

June 1, 200–

Pat Cummings
Manager of Operations
Any Airport
456 Any Street
City, ST 12345

Dear Ms. Cummings:

Described on my resume, I am currently the Parking Supervisor for the Parkinson Hotel and Conference Center. This position was a rapid promotion to management after only one year of service as a parking attendant. As supervisor of parking facilities, I oversee all financial collections, maintain customer service standards, resolve problems, and manage a large staff of hourly workers. I also administer work schedules, evaluate performance, coordinate payroll matters, assign duties, and interface with hotel management. While I am proud of my achievements to date in an area that requires practical knowledge and experience, I do wish to find expanded challenges and rewards.

With increased concerns about security has come increased focus on parking operations at facilities like Any Airport. I hope I have contacted you at a time when consideration can be given a candidate who has proven by past experience that "learning by doing" is the best education. I would like to speak with you about current or future opportunities. Of course, references are available upon request. If you now use an outside vendor for parking operations, referrals to the proper person in that organization would be appreciated. Thank you.

Sincerely,

Chris Smith

Chris Smith

Chapter 7

In Response to Employer-Identified Postings

Remember the three Ps of job search—Postings, Places, and People? This sample collection reveals the best way to respond to postings. Typically, job-seekers ask, "Which letter is best, why, and when?" This chapter will answer this query and inspire you to draft, finalize, and then transmit dynamic and effective cover letters.

Research and Respond

While you shouldn't forget about being proactive in your job search, a reactive job search also works when done effectively. Responding to job ads is an important part of the reactive job search.

When you find a posting you'd like to respond to, do some quick research before you sit down to write your cover letter. A brief review of the company's Web site is all you need to glean a few bits of information to include in your cover letter.

Remember, cover letters written in response to a posting must reveal knowledge of self, knowledge of the job, and knowledge of the employer. The samples that follow illustrate varied approaches, but they all are targeted with similar components. The initial paragraph clearly states the job being applied for, states the desire to interview, and may introduce key qualifications. Second and, when needed, third paragraphs clearly highlight qualifications, directly connecting accomplishments and talents requirements of the job. It's here that you should demonstrate that you've researched the company. The closing section reinforces a request for an interview and may highlight something worthy of special consideration.

Administrative Assistant

Chris Smith

123 Any Street • City, ST 12345 • (555) 555-5555 • *csmith@email.com*

June 1, 200–

Pat Cummings
Office Manager
Any Corporation
456 Any Street
City, ST 12345
FAX (555) 555-5557

Dear Mr. Cummings:

I would like to interview for, and should you judge my candidacy as worthy, someday soon become, your administrative assistant. Upon reading the advertisement in the *Jackson Review* I was inspired to contact you immediately and offer this cover letter and attached resume to formalize my interest.

As described on my resume, as an administrative assistant at Lambert Hospital, I was in charge of all receptionist, computer support, word processing, database, spreadsheet, and administrative functions. By prioritizing tasks, managing time efficiently, and communicating effectively with those whom I reported to, as well as those who reported to me, I maximized the output and customer service efforts of a very demanding office.

Summarizing, the duties I now perform effectively parallel those stated as required of your next administrative assistant. These include, but are not limited to, purchasing, equipment maintenance, daily office operations, supervising staff and volunteers, and coordinating various projects with staff and outside vendors. I would be so excited if I could support you and your colleagues' efforts at Any Corp. Being among those who manufacture, market, and distribute health-care products would be challenging and professionally rewarding.

I hope you will give me the opportunity to discuss the available position with you. Because you have requested no calls, I will eagerly await word regarding next steps. Also, I have requested that one of my references fax you a letter of recommendation that reflects his views regarding my potential to be a productive administrative assistant. Thank you for your consideration.

Sincerely,

Chris Smith

Chris Smith

Administrative Judge

Chris Smith
123 Any Street • City, ST 12345 • (555) 555-5555 • *csmith@email.com*

June 1, 200–

Pat Cummings
Chairperson
Any Municipal Court
456 Any Street
City, ST 12345

Dear Ms. Cummings:

Over 10 years of experience as a litigator, and my constant curiosity as a student of the judicial system has, I trust, prepared me to be a competent and appropriately confident candidate for the Administrative Judge position. The posting in the May 30th issue of *Lawyers Monthly* inspired me to formalize my candidacy via this letter, the attached resume, and additional supporting materials.

Upon review of the attached resume, you will find that I have held a number of positions since graduating from University of Chicago's School of Law. Also, since earning my JD, I have continued to learn via ABA-accredited professional training and Illinois State Association of District Attorneys seminars. An Administrative Judge must be well versed and familiar with the most up-to-date rulings, regulations, and procedural details. All professional development is cited on my resume.

During the past four years as Assistant Attorney General, I gained broad experience in the litigation of personal injury actions and workers' compensation claims. In this position, I utilized legal knowledge; skills in research, analysis, and writing skills; and trial and negotiation talents to yield my office's highest conviction rates. I am honored to have a number of judges among professional references, and I hope to someday model these men and women who personify all roles and responsibilities of an Administrative Judge.

I welcome the opportunity to discuss my qualifications with the selection committee. I will call to confirm your receipt of this letter and to determine if you require any additional documentation. Of course, feel free to contact me at the above address, phone, or e-mail.

Sincerely,

Chris Smith

Chris Smith

Enclosures: resume, reference list, performance review

Analyst

Date: June 1, 200–
From: *csmith@email.com*
To: *humanresources@email.com*
Subject: Analyst Position

I would like to offer my credentials for the Analyst position posted on Any Company's website. As detailed on my attached resume, my current position as an Analyst at Another Company requires a skill set similar to the one stated as required for your position. I have monitored and analyzed accounts receivable and accounts payable, and I have worked with internal accountants to complete monthly, quarterly, and annual reports. Having reviewed your announcement as well as additional information on Any Company's website, I am intrigued by the possibility of joining you and your colleagues.

Overseeing special projects and supervising other analysts would definitely be an appropriate next step on my career path, and one I would enthusiastically take. Through telephone or in-person interviews I can expand upon my qualifications and, yes, motivations. I am eager to learn more about the circuit-board manufacturing and marketing industry as I continue to offer my finance and strategic planning skills as an analyst.

Through academics and employment I have been involved with financial, strategic, and marketing analysis. My part-time MBA studies at the University of New Hampshire involve regular, detailed projects and case studies using the most sophisticated analytical techniques, including regression analysis. My undergraduate business studies also provide a foundation of accounting, finance, operations, and general business knowledge.

I would like to schedule an interview to discuss my ability to handle the responsibilities of the Analyst position. The above noted information is how you can contact me. If appropriate, I would like to call to confirm your receipt of this e-mail and the attached resume.

In the interim, I will look forward to your return response.

Yours sincerely,
Chris Smith
123 Any Street
City, ST 12345
(555) 555-5555

Assistant Curator

123 Any Street • City, ST 12345 • (555) 555-5555 • *csmith@email.com*

June 1, 200–

Pat Cummings
Curator
Any Music Library
456 Any Street
City, ST 12345
FAX (555) 555-5557

SUBJECT: ASSISTANT CURATOR POSITION

Please consider me a strong, enthusiastic and focused candidate for the Assistant Curator position recently advertised on *www.jobs.com*.

My experience acting as Assistant Editor of *Classics Quarterly*, writing classical music reviews for the *Complete Record Guide*, conducting interviews, and writing concert reviews for *Chicago Rock*, and rock and country album reviews for *Inside Edge*, have fine-tuned my writing talents and enhanced my knowledge of music genres. As the Classical Music Listings Coordinator for the *Complete Musical Almanac* summer and fall supplements, I updated a comprehensive database and oversaw creation of a system that stores and retrieves past editions, using key words, dates, composers and genre. Currently, I am copyediting part-time for *Art Illinois*. Clearly, my professional past, as detailed on the attached resume, reveals a commitment to music education, archiving, and dissemination.

The foundation upon which I built the above accomplishments is my academic training. I earned a Bachelor of Arts in Music and a Master of Arts in Musicology from DePaul University. A study of music and the arts at Cambridge University (England) preceded part-time doctoral studies at the University of Chicago. I am ready, eager and, I trust, qualified to serve full-time in roles associated with my exploration of all aspects of musicology.

I have often relied on the resources available at Any Music Library, and I would welcome the opportunity to join your curatorial staff. I would be happy to further discuss the position. Would your schedule allow for a brief discussion next week? I will call your office to schedule a convenient interview time. Thank you for your consideration.

Sincerely,

Chris Smith

Chris Smith

Assistant Editor

Date: June 1, 200–
From: *csmith@email.com*
To: *pcummings@email.com*
Subject: Assistant Editor Position

Dear Mr. Cummings:

I would like to take all appropriate steps to formalize my candidacy for the position of assistant editor. When I reviewed the posting advertised on the *Jobs.com* website, I wanted to immediately share the attached resume and writing samples.

As you review my resume entries, please envision the research, document development, drafting, and verbal communication skills developed in each setting and situation. Summarizing, through internships, cocurriculars, and practical experience, I now offer Any Corporation:

- Writing, editing, and layout skills gained as features editor, art editor, graphic artist, and reporter for various college publications.
- Specialized expertise demonstrated by Columbia Scholastic Press Association's First Place Gold Circle Award for graphic art.
- Knowledge and technical skills gained from courses and projects associated with advertising art and desktop publishing.
- Experience using PageMaker, Word, WordPerfect, Excel, PowerPoint, and varied graphics software to draft, edit, and finalize publications and presentations, and to create dynamic graphics.
- Capacity to use the Internet for detailed research and to disseminate newsletters, graphics, and text.

I understand the assistant editor will be involved in creation of all Any Corporation promotional materials, public relations documents, and internal communication pieces. This would be an ideal step on a clearly focused writing and editing career path. I hope you will give me the opportunity to discuss your expectations for this position and the above bullet items, point by point. Thank you for your consideration.

Sincerely,

Chris Smith
123 Any Street
City, ST 12345
(555) 555-5555
csmith@email.com

P.S. I will send original copies of this letter, my resume, and writing samples. Sometimes seeing certain written pieces and designed works in context gives a better sense of perspective.

Assistant Hospital Supervisor

Chris Smith

123 Any Street • City, ST 12345 • (555) 555-5555 • *csmith@email.com*

June 1, 200–

Pat Cummings
Administrator
Any Corporation
456 Any Street
City, ST 12345
FAX (555) 555-5557

RE: Assistant Hospital Supervisor Position

I am writing in response to your advertisement in the *Phoenix*. As you determine my worthiness for an interview, please focus on my comprehensive and related employment background detailed in the attached resume. For twelve years, I provided a range of administrative, financial, and research support to the Chief Executive Officer of the Deaconess Hospital, Ms. Kelly Employer. As evidenced by the attached letter of recommendation, Ms. Employer is a strong advocate of my candidacy, and she would be happy to discuss my capabilities with you.

Recently, I took a sabbatical and finished my Masters of Public Health at Emerson College, so I am now actively seeking opportunities to build upon academic and employment skill sets. Throughout my graduate studies, I learned about issues that will impact health care for decades to come, specifically those related to HMOs, PPOs, and the aging population. Most critically, I learned to use financial analyses to make intelligent managerial and procedural decisions. I am proud of my aptitude for numbers and extensive experience with the most pertinent software applications used in our industry. Please pay particular attention to the summary of qualifications section of my resume, where all competencies are clearly noted, indicating my potential to succeed as your Assistant Supervisor.

I would be interested in speaking with you further regarding this position. I am hopeful that you will consider my background in administrative support, as well as my word processing, database, and spreadsheet skills an asset to Any Corporation. Thank you in advance for your consideration.

Sincerely,

Chris Smith

Chris Smith

Associate Desktop Publisher

Date: June 1, 200–
From: *csmith@email.com*
To: *pcummings@email.com*
Subject: Qualified Associate Desktop Publisher Candidate

In support of my candidacy for the Associate Desktop Publisher position on your firm's website, attached is a copy of my resume. Also, please review my web portfolio at *www.csmith.com*. While a picture may be worth a thousand words, I do hope that we can share a few words together via an interview. I do want to share my motivations as well as qualifications.

My ten years of progressively responsible computer experience, all detailed on my resume, include researching, developing, and documenting the operational procedures of a software seller. I was responsible for all aspects of the design, creation, and dissemination of many user-friendly yet state-of-the-art manuals. I also coordinated and published the sales and marketing of a newsletter distributed monthly to key accounts and sales representatives.

Successful completion of such projects requires skills that match those stated as required of the Associate Desktop Publisher post. These qualifications include:

- Experience transforming data from research into factual, detailed, and accurate copy and graphics.
- Record of success planning, overseeing, and delivering projects on time and error-free.
- Comprehensive graphic and text-editing talents, with capacity to maximize the efforts of writers, graphic artists, designers, and freelancers.
- Proficiency using, supporting, and teaching others Word, PageMaker, PhotoShop, PhotoShow, Visual Studio, Picture It, QuarkXPress, Illustrator, Front Page, Print Shop, and Publisher.

I will be visiting Richmond next week, and I would be happy to meet with you at your convenience. I will call to confirm your receipt of this e-mail and to discuss the possibility of meeting. Of course, I will forward original samples from my portfolio as well as a copy of my resume. Thank you for your consideration.

Sincerely,
Chris Smith

Athletic Director

Chris Smith
123 Any Street • City, ST 12345 • (555) 555-5555 • *csmith@email.com*

June 1, 200–

Pat Cummings
Headmaster
Any School
456 Any Street
City, ST 12345

Dear Ms. Cummings:

Please accept this letter, my accompanying resume, and letters of recommendation as expressions of my desire to interview for and, someday, serve in the position of Any School's Athletic Director. When I reviewed the announcement on the National Association of Independent Schools' website, I wanted to express my desire to interview for this wonderful opportunity.

For the past nine years I have coached rowing at my undergraduate alma mater. The athletic director of Any School must be a strong administrator, educator, coach and, yes, role-model. Young men and women completing secondary studies must envision their futures as college students and competitors, as well as academic and athletic achievers. To do so, they must have the best opportunities to perform in the classroom and on playing fields, courts, and pools.

I will contribute to Any School's achievement-oriented environment and transform the words of your mission statement into student-focused outcomes. I certainly believe that "Minds, bodies and spirits of youth must be the foundations for present and future learning." During an interview, I would tell of events that inspired me to seek an administrative position and focus my efforts on private secondary schools.

Recently, I became responsible for running Yale's boathouse and two national secondary rowing competitions. Over the past two seasons, I addressed all ordering, budgeting, donation solicitation, parts inventory, and travel arrangements for crew teams. I now wish to continue my relationships with secondary coaches and educators within administrative roles. Experience has proven that I can influence student athletes as an athletic director, not just as a coach. I now seek to do so at Any School.

Sincerely,

Chris Smith

Chris Smith

Business Consultant

Chris Smith

123 Any Street • City, ST 12345 • (555) 555-5555 • *csmith@email.com*

June 1, 200–

Pat Cummings
Director of Recruiting
Any Corporation
456 Any Street
City, ST 12345

Dear Mr. Cummings:

Your advertisement in the *Herald-Leader* captured my attention! I am very interested in interviewing for and pursuing a successful and achievement-filled career as a software consultant with Any Corporation. My recent academic and professional achievements, all documented on the attached resume, demonstrate my potential to succeed in the Business Consultant position. Please allow me to highlight in this letter my qualifications as they relate to your stated requirements. The announcement cites that a candidate should possess:

- Experience consulting to and working in small-business environments
- Marketing experience related to services and intangible products
- Technical knowledge and computer competencies

My qualifications and capabilities include:

- Skills and perspectives gained via graduate business studies, including comprehensive and practical case-study methodology, acting as a consultant, and analyzing and solving business problems.
- Record of creative, managerial, and entrepreneurial success as the founder of Widgetsoft, a software development business.
- 4.5 years of progressive and profitable marketing experience.
- Expertise with Word, Excel, Access, PowerPoint, dBase, and Internet applications.
- Programming experience in C++, C+, Fortran, and COBOL.
- Bilingual Spanish-English abilities, knowledge of international business strategies, and capacity to expand marketing activities globally.

Although I lived in Spain while completing graduate studies at Spain's premiere business school, I am an American citizen with a bachelor's degree from the University of Kentucky. I have recently returned home to Lexington. I hope to someday soon discuss how the above qualifications will allow me to achieve as an Any Corporation Business Consultant. Thank you for your consideration.

Sincerely,

Chris Smith

Chris Smith

Campus Police Officer

Chris Smith
123 Any Street • City, ST 12345 • (555) 555-5555 • *csmith@email.com*

June 1, 200–

Pat Cummings
Director of Security
Any College
456 Any Street
City, ST 12345
pcummings@email.com

Dear Ms. Cummings:

I am interested in expanding my career in law enforcement and security management as a member of the Any College Campus Security Force. Your advertisement in *Careers in Law Enforcement* notes requirements that I possess and capabilities I would like to discuss during an interview.

As is described in detail on the attached resume, in my present position I maintain the highest possible site and operations security for a defense contractor. Prior, for almost a decade, I served in the United States Army, maintaining peak law enforcement/security alertness and the welfare of all personnel. In that capacity, I received numerous letters of commendation for superior job performance.

Also noted on my resume, I am a graduate of military police school, and I completed additional law enforcement seminars. Currently, I am enrolled in a criminal justice program and anticipate earning a Bachelor of Science in the spring. Upon completion of these studies, it would be ideal if I could provide security and related services to students of Any College. As a student, I have become sensitive to campus security issues and the need for security personnel to relate to all members of an academic community.

I would like to discuss my qualifications and outline the potential I have to be a strong member of your security force. I will call to confirm your receipt of this e-mail and accompanying resume (originals to follow by mail) and to arrange either phone or in-person discussions. Of course, travel to Whittier is easy to arrange. In advance, thank you for your consideration, and I look forward to your response.

Sincerely,

Chris Smith

Chris Smith

Chris Smith

123 Any Street • City, ST 12345 • (555) 555-5555 • *csmith@email.com*

June 1, 200–

Pat Cummings
Director of Social Services
Any Agency
456 Any Street
City, ST 12345
FAX (555) 555-5557

Dear Ms. Cummings:

Upon reading your announcement in the *Star Ledger*, I wanted to express my interest in interviewing for the Case Manager position. I am proud of my accomplishments to date, all documented on the attached resume, and I would welcome the opportunity to personify the mission of Any Agency. I will build upon my professional experience, which is focused on motivating and guiding at-risk youth and incarcerated clients, as well as helping them achieve academic and personal objectives.

As noted on my resume, I have guided at-risk youth as well inmates through individual counseling and structured programs. This involved extensive case documentation, referrals, and goal identification, as well as communication and interaction with boards of trustees, agency personnel, and others. All cases were clearly, concisely, and professionally tracked and documented, so appropriate groups, including psychologists, teachers, judges, and parole boards could review them. Regular interaction with and referrals to social workers and judicial agency professionals are a part of day-to-day efforts. Presentations, reports, and meetings were, of course, also required of past roles and responsibilities and, I hope, future ones as a Case Manager at Any Agency.

Academically, I earned undergraduate degrees in psychology and sociology as well as a graduate degree in social work at Rutgers University, where I completed a diverse number of courses, projects, and practica. I would welcome a meeting to discuss my academic as well as professional background and to learn more about the undertakings of Any Agency. I will call to confirm your receipt of this fax (originals to follow by mail) and to clarify appropriate next steps.

Yours sincerely,

Chris Smith

Chris Smith

Chief Financial Officer

Chris Smith
123 Any Street • City, ST 12345 • (555) 555-5555 • *csmith@email.com*

June 1, 200–

Pat Cummings
Controller
Any Corporation
456 Any Street
City, ST 12345

Dear Mr. Cummings:

As detailed on the attached resume, I have a record of success managing corporate financial operations for profitable and fast-growing manufacturing companies with multistate and international operations. My sixteen years of progressively responsible experience has included management of all financial and treasury functions. My professional duties have encompassed the fields of corporate real estate, human resources, and general operations. Titles and responsibilities have ranged from Chief Financial Officer, Vice-President of Finance, to Cost Accounting Manager. My achievements in directly increasing profits are many and are cited on the resume. Ideally, you will, upon review of my supporting documentation, determine that I am worthy to interview for the Chief Financial Officer Position of Any Corporation.

I have been a Certified Public Accountant for over two decades, completing continued professional studies required of updated certification. In addition, I have earned an MBA in Finance and a Bachelor of Arts in Accounting. Most important, I have always supported the educational and professional development of my staff and hired those committed to continued learning and professional excellence.

During initial telephone conversations and in personal discussions, I can learn more about the visions that you and other senior managers have for Any Corporations and about how I can transform visions into realities. Because my interest in joining you and your colleagues is sincere and strong, I can offer you references, but I must respectfully request that you only contact those listed.

I will call to discuss your thoughts regarding my candidacy and, I most sincerely hope, to arrange formal and detailed discussions. Please feel free to contact me in care of the above address, phone, or e-mail. In advance, thank you for your consideration.

Yours sincerely,

Chris Smith

Chris Smith

Child-Care Assistant Director

Date: June 1, 200–
From: *csmith@email.com*
To: *pcummings@email.com*
Subject: AnyCenter Assistant Director Position

As a licensed child-care provider in the state of Ohio, with three years' experience in a private center, I found the position described in your Assistant Center Director posting on Toledojobs.com to be exactly what I seek. By focusing all professional attention to caring for and facilitating the academic, behavioral, and social skills of children, and after observing some of the best administrative role models, I am ready for this important career move.

Most recently, I directly cared for and supervised others caring for over forty children. In this capacity, I have been solely responsible for the daily needs of ten or more children, ranging in age from six months to five years. For those in my care, I distribute meals and snacks, monitor playtime, create recreational and instructional plans, and motivate the educational and social growth of diverse students.

Through my experiences at ChildCare Center, I had the opportunity to observe the critical impact that parent education and outreach, scheduling, employee relations, and budgeting can have on the daily activities of a facility and, most important, on the children and their families. As AnyCenter's Assistant Director, I will continue my passionate commitment to children yet expand my efforts to include supporting the professional growth of my colleagues as well as effective marketing, parent relations, and management undertakings.

During an interview, I can elaborate upon qualifications cited in this letter and the summary of qualifications of my resume. Ideally, we might also discuss the inspiration I gained and sought to give as the author of a children's book, *Home We Go!* Clearly, I would appreciate the opportunity to speak to you further about this position.

Sincerely,
Chris Smith

Claims Adjuster

Chris Smith
123 Any Street • City, ST 12345 • (555) 555-5555 • *csmith@email.com*

June 1, 200–

Pat Cummings
Claims Supervisor
Any Insurance Company
456 Any Street
City, ST 12345

Dear Mr. Cummings:

I would like to apply and, if qualified, interview for the claims adjuster position advertised in the *Citizen Times*. For the past fifteen years I have been with a major insurance company, primarily focusing on workers' compensation claims. My accomplishments, all cited on the attached resume, required a sound background in claims management, cost containment, customer relations, employee training, and administrative support. I am proud that annually, for the past five years, I have cost-effectively negotiated well over two hundred claims. I would be as proud of my future achievements if you allow me to become a member of the Any Insurance team.

In summary, my qualifications, motivations, and achievements include:

- Over 15 years of progressively responsible claims experience, encompassing life, health, and auto, but specializing in worker's compensation.
- Knowledge of laws and regulations pertaining to claims and potential outcomes of litigation.
- Experience conducting extensive research, working with investigators, and appropriately interacting with policy-holders, physicians, health-care practitioners, and legal professionals.
- Record of success coordinating detailed data and negotiating effectively with claimants, professional peers, corporate management, and others to arrive at mutually favorable solutions.
- Experience training, establishing goals for, monitoring, and supervising claims professionals.

I hope I can share my qualifications for the adjuster position with Any Insurance. My salary requirements are appropriate for the position, so please, let's discuss my desire to become a strong contributor to your claims efforts. References are available upon request. I will call to confirm your receipt of this letter and to clarify appropriate next steps.

Sincerely,

Chris Smith

Chris Smith

Clinical Research Nurse

Chris Smith

123 Any Street • City, ST 12345 • (555) 555-5555 • *csmith@email.com*

June 1, 200–

Pat Cummings, R.N.
Head Nurse
Any Hospital
456 Any Street
City, ST 12345
FAX (555) 555-5557

Dear Ms. Cummings:

I would like to interview for the Clinical Research Nurse position recently advertised on the Any Hospital website. I am a dedicated professional with a record of successfully working with patients, physicians, and nursing peers, as well as research, laboratory, and professional specialty groups. As a result of patient care and research-related experiences, I have nurtured skills stated as required in the posting. These include:

- Past experience as a clinical research nurse.
- Capacity to develop and follow detailed protocols, procedures, and database collection efforts.
- Commitment to flawless patient recordkeeping and confidentiality.
- Knowledge of issues pertaining to AIDS and experience working with this patient population.
- Experience working in research contexts, supporting clinical trials and laboratory research efforts.
- Graduate and undergraduate studies in nursing, including anatomy and physiology.

I have a Bachelor of Science in Nursing and over fourteen years of comprehensive and diverse experience, ranging from staff nurse and charge nurse to clinical research nurse with a major teaching hospital. My graduate studies have focused on epidemiology and international health. Through courses as well as professional experience I have worked on studies involving psoriasis, cardiology, AIDS, sickle-cell anemia, amyloid, diabetes, and oncology. Also, I have sound knowledge of nursing quality-assurance programs and in-service education programs.

The opportunity to support research efforts related to AIDS treatment would be one I would act upon with great professional enthusiasm. I hope to speak with you soon. Thank you for your consideration.

Sincerely,

Chris Smith

Chris Smith, R.N., B.S.N.

Conference Director

Date: June 1, 200–
From: *csmith@email.com*
To: *pcummings@email.com*
Subject: Conference Director Position

Dear Mr. Cummings:

The position of Conference Director announced via the Deafcommunity.com user-group is of great interest of me. Please accept this e-mail and the attached resume as formal documentation of my request for consideration. Ideally, upon review of these materials, you will determine that an in-person or TTY interview would be an appropriate next step.

As a deaf person who has held a number of positions requiring strong leadership, planning, organizational, administrative, and communication skills, I believe I have the qualifications required to succeed as the Conference Director. Throughout a career focused on community outreach, event planning, and volunteer management, I have worked with individuals and groups in diverse settings within public, private, artistic, and government sectors. All professional experiences are detailed on my resume. When making determinations regarding interviews, please pay attention to the accomplishments associated with my roles as Director of Volunteer Services, specifically those related to planning and implementing annual educational, fundraising, and community awareness events.

Also, I am well versed in visual and performing arts, having served as a performer, coordinator, instructor, and facilitator. In academic as well as employment capacities, I planned events, provided services for, and instructed the deaf community and the general public. In summary, I have the event planning, media relations, promotions, and logistics management talents needed to transform your vision for an annual conference for Any Deaf Theatre into an effective and, yes, profitable undertaking.

Should you need additional information, or wish to arrange an interview, please contact me at (555) 555-5555 TTY or at *csmith@email.com*. I look forward to your response.

Sincerely,
Chris Smith

Cosmetologist

Chris Smith
123 Any Street • City, ST 12345 • (555) 555-5555 • *csmith@email.com*

June 1, 200–

Pat Cummings
Owner
Any Boutique
456 Any Street
City, ST 12345

Dear Mr. Cummings:

Attached, please find my resume and a list of references, as well as a letter of recommendation. While these documents do inform you of my professional experiences and capabilities, through an interview I can learn more about your vision for Any Boutique, what you expect of a cosmetologist, and the nature of your clientele. Clearly, I am very interested in interviewing for the position of Cosmetologist that was advertised in the *Post Intelligencer*.

Now, at the Other Boutique, I am proud to say that I have:

• Developed a strong and loyal clientele.
• Introduced an exciting new and profitable line of cosmetic products.
• Expanded bridal and wedding party business.
• Accounted for sales in excess of $4,000 for 14 months.

Thank you in advance for your consideration. I look forward to meeting with you to discuss this opportunity. I will stop by the boutique tomorrow to discuss your thoughts regarding my candidacy.

Sincerely,

Chris Smith

Chris Smith

Customer Service Manager

Chris Smith
123 Any Street • City, ST 12345 • (555) 555-5555 • *csmith@email.com*

June 1, 200–

Pat Cummings
Director of Public Relations
Any Corporation
456 Any Street
City, ST 12345
FAX (555) 555-5557

Dear Ms. Cummings:

During the past several years at Fortmiller, Inc., I have achieved much in customer service capacities and have motivated my colleagues to exceptional efforts as well. As detailed on the attached resume, my achievements have been in the areas of billing, credit, collection, training, and, most critically, customer service. I now wish to apply all the skills and perspectives nurtured in the past, to future successes as Any Company's Customer Service Representative. Upon review of the posting on your organization's website, I was immediately inspired to present my candidacy and request an interview.

In my current position as customer service supervisor, I maintain the efficiency, accuracy, and customer-friendly aspects of a complex billing system. To do so, I set policies and procedures, implement systems, and participate in staffing and training of personnel who answer customer inquiries every day regarding billing, delivery, and returns. During my tenure, 55 percent of the entry-level staff I trained advanced to managerial positions within Fortmiller. I instilled within these men and women that customer service excellence does sustain loyalty, enhance sales, and, ultimately, yield profitability.

It would be with enthusiasm and the appropriate confidence that I would interview for this exciting opportunity. I do hope that after you review my resume, as well as the attached training memos, that you will wish to discuss my customer service experience. I definitely want to learn more about Any Corporations goals for their next Customer Service Manager. Thank you for your consideration, and I look forward to speaking with you regarding the possibility of meeting.

Sincerely,

Chris Smith

Chris Smith

Dental Hygienist

Chris Smith
123 Any Street • City, ST 12345 • (555) 555-5555 • *csmith@email.com*

June 1, 200–

Pat Cummings, DDS
Dentist
456 Any Street
City, ST 12345

Dear Dr. Cummings:

I would like to interview for the Dental Hygienist position you advertised in the *Times-Union*. However, my concerns for current patients are such that I must ask that my candidacy remain confidential. While I am eager to interview, share motivations and qualifications, and provide references, please do keep our communications private. Summarizing all that appears on the attached resume, I offer:

- Current experience as a Hygienist, Surgical Assistant, and Assistant Office Manager.
- Record of success providing state-of-the art prophylaxis treatment to adults and adolescents.
- Capacity to perform pre-surgical, surgical and post operative care roles.
- Progressively responsible experience as a Hygienist, Assistant, and Office Administrator.
- Sound knowledge of medical terminology and clinical procedures.
- Certified in first aid, cardiopulmonary resuscitation, and electrocardiography

I am confident that my training and experience can be effectively applied to the requirements of your practice and patients. I can be the professional and pleasant Dental Hygienist you seek. In addition to the resume, attached you will also find a letter of recommendation. If you would like any additional information, please do not hesitate to contact me. I look forward to meeting with you and further discussing my desires to join your team. Thank you in advance for your consideration.

Sincerely,

Chris Smith

Chris Smith

Dentistry Department Manager

Chris Smith
123 Any Street • City, ST 12345 • (555) 555-5555 • *csmith@email.com*

June 1, 200–

Pat Cummings
Chief Administrator
Any Hospital
456 Any Street
City, ST 12345

Dear Ms. Cummings:

The position you advertised is of great interest to me, and I hope to convince you of my capability to cost-effectively execute the responsibilities of Dentistry Department Manager.

My managerial experiences with Johns Hopkins Medical School's Department of Ophthalmology, Maryland Eye & Ear Infirmary, and Blue Cross/Blue Shield, all detailed on the attached resume, have involved overseeing all matters pertaining to fiscal and business reporting. Most relevant to your stated requirements, I have firsthand experience designing, implementing, and utilizing sophisticated proprietary programs designed to accommodate and control costs and enhance the profitable growth of business.

Department management, staff training and supervision, and administrative experience are, I have found over the years, essential requirements for maintaining a highly complex business unit and inspiring professionals to maximum and efficient performance. I can provide cost-effective fiscal management to maintain and increase profitability, even during the challenging times we now have. Through efficient tracking and control systems, budget planning, and administration, I have and can continue to generate cost savings and greater profit margins.

Through a telephone or in-person interview, I can detail information regarding the above accomplishments and learn more about your visions for the Dentistry Department. I can be reached at (555) 555-5555 or via *csmith@email.com*. In the interim, I encourage you to contact those individuals on the reference list provided. I do look forward to meeting with you in the near future and, ideally, to someday joining your management team.

Sincerely,

Chris Smith

Chris Smith

Director of Public Works

Chris Smith

123 Any Street • City, ST 12345 • (555) 555-5555 • *csmith@email.com*

June 1, 200–

Pat Cummings
District Supervisor
Any Office
456 Any Street
City, ST 12345

Dear Mr. Cummings:

I understand you and your colleagues are reviewing Director of Public Works candidates. When I saw the announcement on *Governmentjobs.com*, I wanted to actively explore this opportunity. Attached is my resume and a list of references, as well as performance reviews from the previous two years. All reveal past achievements. Through an interview, I can best present my future ambitions and my sincerest desires to work for the people of Liberty.

During the past thirteen years, within public and private roles, I have been involved in the management of diverse projects, which have required the ability to work with engineering, architectural, and construction professionals on public and private rehabilitation, restoration, and construction programs. My experience ranges from concept to sign-off and includes the supervision of in-house and field crews on both privately and city/federally funded building and highway contracts.

As described on my resume, I am an effective manager and budget administrator, and I have the ability to work with individuals and groups in construction/public works environments where concentration is on community services, safety, the environment, and constituency concerns. As a longtime resident of the town of Liberty, I will call upon professional and personal knowledge to provide quality DPW services. Clearly, I am confident of my ability to direct an efficient, cost-effective, and productive department. But in order to translate this confidence into performance-focused outcomes, I must convince you and your selection-committee colleagues of my potential to serve as the next Director of Public Works. I will call your office next week to see if it would be appropriate to schedule a meeting. Thank you for your consideration.

Sincerely,

Chris Smith

Chris Smith

Editor

Date: June 1, 200–
From: *csmith@email.com*
To: *pcummings@email.com*
Subject: Editor Position

Dear Ms. Cummings:

I am very interested in the Editor position listed on Jobs.com. Attached are my resume and a writing sample, both offered to support my candidacy and request for an interview. Research has enhanced my familiarity with Any Corporation's printed and web-based publications. Through an interview, I can learn more about your visions for future efforts and your expectation for the next Editor.

As detailed on my resume, my general qualifications include:

- Research, writing, and editorial talents for interviewing, fact-checking, scriptwriting, and proofreading.
- Book, magazine, newspaper, and broadcast writing and editing experience.
- Confidence drafting, editing, and finalizing news, feature, and sports stories.
- Production experience in varied print and broadcast media.
- Capabilities gained through graduate studies and positions in magazine, newspaper, and television.
- Bilingual Spanish-English skills as well as Macintosh, Windows, and Internet capabilities.

My specific abilities and achievements that match your stated requirements include:

- Over two years of experience in book acquisition, editorial production, and marketing roles.
- Special knowledge of youth and adult markets, focusing on lifestyle, sports, and leisure.
- A commitment to blending creativity with profitability.

I hope to have the chance to expand upon these points and describe how much my efforts at Books R Cool have prepared me to succeed at Any Corp. Should you need additional information or writing samples, please feel free to contact me via phone or e-mail. I am so eager to join the editorial team at Any Corporation that I will call your office next week to discuss your assessment of my candidacy and, I hope, to arrange an interview. Thank you.

Chris Smith
123 Any Street
City, ST 12345
(555) 555-5555
csmith@email.com

Event Planner

Chris Smith

123 Any Street • City, ST 12345 • (555) 555-5555 • *csmith@email.com*

June 1, 200–

Pat Cummings
Vice President of Public Relations
Any Corporation
456 Any Street
City, ST 12345
FAX (555) 555-5557

Dear Mr. Cummings:

Please accept this letter, my accompanying resume, and supporting documentation to formalize my candidacy for the Event Planner position advertised in the *Providence Journal* and the *PRSA Newsletter.* Current circumstances require that my interest in this position remain confidential, but please be assured I am most definitely ready to interview and accept an offer if one would be given.

I am confident my six years of experience in public relations, specializing in event planning, have prepared me to succeed in the position described in the posting. Simply, I offer you and your Any Corporation colleagues:

- Experience planning annual marketing, promotional, fundraising, and volunteer recognition events.
- Proven abilities to negotiate and liaison with catering, hotel, and travel professionals.
- Capacity to generate corporate partners and individuals willing to share event costs.
- Record of success using events to mobilize and motivate others and, ultimately, have bottom-line impact on sales or donations.

I welcome the opportunity to meet with you to further discuss my qualifications and your expectations for the Any Corp's next Event Planner. Having reviewed your organization's website, I am eager to share my ideas regarding how special events can supplement the efforts of the nation's largest manufacturer and marketer of bathroom, kitchen, and plumbing fixtures. I hope, after you review the attached documents (including news releases, invitations, and event programs) that you will be inspired to meet with me regarding my potential to do so.

I will call to confirm your receipt of this fax (originals to follow by mail), and to discuss next steps. Again, thank you for understanding my need for confidential consideration.

Sincerely,

Chris Smith

Chris Smith

Features Reporter

Chris Smith
123 Any Street • City, ST 12345 • (555) 555-5555 • *csmith@email.com*

June 1, 200–

Pat Cummings
Senior Reporter
Any Newspaper
456 Any Street
City, ST 12345

Dear Ms. Cummings:

I would like to interview for the features reporter position advertised on Jobs.com. As noted in my attached resume, clippings, and letter of recommendation, I have an eclectic journalism background. Lessons learned through internships with regional and local publications, through a range of editorial and writing positions for academic publications, and as a committed journalism student have prepared me to become a member of Any Newspaper's reporting staff.

Most recently, as an intern at the weekly *Emmitsburg News,* I sharpened my researching, interviewing, and feature-writing skills. At that publication, I completed field reporting, copy-writing, and editing tasks associated with various articles. My photography talents enabled me to provide photos for my stories that appeared in the weekly, including the attached samples. I am proud that all who supervised me in the past have documented professional progress. Specifically, I am pleased that Kelly Jones felt strongly enough to share her views in the attached letter.

In addition, while earning dual degrees in Journalism and Fine Arts at Mount St. Mary's, I worked as editor-in-chief of the yearbook and as layout editor and reporter for the school's weekly newspaper, where I became proficient in desktop publishing. While we all know that the works of journalists should speak volumes, through an interview I can share how enthusiastic, driven, and ready I am to begin and build a career at Any Newspaper. An in-person meeting would be most welcome! I will call to discuss your thoughts regarding my candidacy and, if you deem appropriate, to schedule an interview.

Sincerely,

Chris Smith

Chris Smith

Field Finance Manager

Chris Smith

123 Any Street • City, ST 12345 • (555) 555-5555 • *csmith@email.com*

June 1, 200–

Pat Cummings
Chief Financial Officer
Any Corporation
456 Any Street
City, ST 12345

Dear Mr. Cummings:

I would most definitely like to interview for the Central Area Field Finance Manager position advertised in the *Times-Dispatch*. While my current position with Other Company, Inc., detailed on the attached resume, is most challenging and rewarding, the opportunity to serve within the capacities described in the announcement is professionally exciting. It would be with great focus and the appropriate confidence that I would:

- Develop new, and enhance existing, relationships with dealers who use Any Corporation financing.
- Monitor existing accounts and provide detailed weekly, monthly, quarterly, and annual reports to senior managers and field representatives.
- Hire, train, and motivate field representatives.
- Focus on profitability, risk management, and underwriting responsibilities.

Generally, the qualifications I possess to enhance the central area's performance include:

- Experience advising Fortune 100 and small-company senior management on strategy, planning, finance, and budgeting.
- Strong accounting and finance academic preparation, combined with significant experience in loan analysis, operations, and field marketing roles.
- Expertise using Excel, as well as proprietary financial software and loan documentation programs.

I will call to confirm your receipt of this letter and to discuss your initial thoughts regarding a telephone or in-person interview. Thank you for your consideration.

Sincerely yours,

Chris Smith

Chris Smith

Film Archivist

Date: June 1, 200–
From: *csmith@email.com*
To: *pc@anylibrary.com*
Subject: Qualified Film Archivist Candidate

Please accept this e-mail as a formal request for consideration for the Film Archivist position posted in *Moving Picture Pictorial.* My professional and academic experiences, all detailed on the attached resume, have required that I develop capabilities associated with this position.

Currently, I am a reporter for the *Vertov Film Journal,* a monthly magazine. Within this capacity I research and write features, often interviewing producers, directors, and actors. Contributions are written in varied styles, targeting eclectic readers. As a senior at Brandeis, I researched, wrote, and edited an honors thesis on the filmmaker Sergei Eisenstein. This capstone project required many of the skills described as required for the Archivist position. The courses, projects, and papers cited on my resume reflect an in-depth knowledge of film history, film studies, and related subjects. Clearly, I would enjoy researching, archiving, and retrieving film and film-related literature.

In addition, I am capable of shooting, printing, and developing 35mm film and using digital photography equipment and software. I also have web-page development, editing, and database software abilities. I am aware that your library's film archive is the largest in the South, and that you are currently planning to create a web-based catalog.

Also attached are writing samples for you to review. I will call soon to confirm your receipt of this e-mail and, I do hope, to arrange a telephone or in-person interview. Thank you for your consideration and, sincerely, for all that your Any Library staff does to educate and inspire those passionate about film.

Be assured that I am willing to pay for any expenses associated with an interview. Of course, I would relocate if offered the position. Please do not allow distance to negatively impact my candidacy.

Sincerely,

Chris Smith

Chris Smith

Fundraiser

Chris Smith

123 Any Street • City, ST 12345 • (555) 555-5555 • *csmith@email.com*

June 1, 200–

Pat Cummings
Development Director
Any Organization
456 Any Street
City, ST 12345
FAX (555) 555-5557

Dear Mr. Cummings:

I am writing in response to your advertisement for a fundraiser that appears in this month's *Not-for-Profit Now!* Any Organization seems particularly dynamic and constituent-focused, dedicated to providing services for youth and adults. I hope that someday my enthusiasm and professionalism can contribute to the success of your development campaigns and grant-application efforts.

As described in my attached resume, after graduating from the University of New Mexico, I have been working in the University's development office. UNM is in its second year of a $450 million capital campaign. My responsibilities have been as the Campaign Registration Coordinator. Working with and supporting the efforts of the University's expert fundraisers, I have learned a great deal about prospect strategy development, donor relations, proposal writing, solicitation, and pledge-documentation related activities. This job demands efficiency and precision, writing and communication talents, and the ability to prioritize and complete several different projects simultaneously.

As a result of past experiences, I am confident I can perform in the capacity of fundraiser, including:

- Planning and implementing annual fundraising campaigns.
- Identifying and soliciting corporate and individual donor contributions as an ongoing effort.
- Proven capacity to effectively work with the Development Directory and all board members.
- Drafting, editing, and finalizing all annual reports, donor documentation, and fundraising-related publications, materials, and correspondences.

I look forward to speaking with you about my qualifications and about your expectations for the fundraiser who would be joining you and your Any Organization colleagues. I will call to confirm your receipt of this fax (originals to follow by mail) and to assess your thoughts regarding my candidacy.

Sincerely,

Chris Smith

Chris Smith

Gemologist

Date: June 1, 200–
From: *csmith@email.com*
To: *pcummings@email.com*
Subject: Gemologist Position

TO: Pat Cummings, Vice-President
Any Stores

I was very excited to read about the opening for a Gemologist on your company's website. Please accept this e-mail as well as my attached resume and letter of recommendation as documentation supporting my application for this position.

This year I graduated with honors from one of the nation's best gemology schools, the Gemologist Institute of America, in Santa Monica, California. While earning the title of Graduate Gemologist, I completed numerous courses, learned to use state-of-the-art equipment, and completed numerous internship and externship experiences.

The summary of qualifications section of my resume highlights my retail and manufacturing gemology experiences as well as previous public relations, sales, promotions, and retail achievements. I am eager to join Any Stores, a reputable retail chain that supports its gemologists with national and regional marketing campaigns, and provides its customers with excellent service and guarantees. Being an effective gemologist requires that I use and expand upon my technical, sales, buying, and appraisal skills in order to maximize the profits of my store and service to my customers.

After you have reviewed my qualifications, I would appreciate interviewing with you for this position. Perhaps an initial telephone conversation could be followed by a lengthier in-person discussion. Please note that I plan to follow up with a call in a few days, but please feel free to contact me via e-mail or the above-cited information. In advance, thank you for your consideration. Of course, I would be happy to relocate in order to begin and build a successful career with Any Stores.

Sincerely,
Chris Smith
123 Any Street
City, ST 12345
(555) 555-5555
csmith@email.com

Home Economics Department Coordinator

Chris Smith

123 Any Street • City, ST 12345 • (555) 555-5555 • *csmith@email.com*

June 1, 200–

Pat Cummings, Ph.D.
Home Economics Program Director
Any University
456 Any Street
City, ST 12345
FAX (555) 555-5557

Director Cummings:

It is with great professional enthusiasm and the pride of an alum that I now formalize my candidacy for the Home Economics Department Coordinator position. When I received the e-mail announcement and, later, after reviewing the description on the department's website, I wanted to offer the attached resume and references for your consideration.

Academically, in addition to earning a B.S. in Home Economics and Nutrition Education, I have completed supplemental professional development with each of my employers since graduation. Additional training now includes specialized seminars in preventive nutrition, community outreach, and budget management, all taught by the faculty of a well-respected teaching hospital.

Professionally, I have served within nutritionist, program management, and community education roles. In these capacities, all detailed on my resume, I developed and monitored annual budgets and completed purchasing; effectively planned meals for patients and participants in day elder-care programs; trained service staff and patient-care technicians; and served as a liaison with vendors and suppliers. In all settings, I interacted with health-care professionals, educators, peers, patients, and others of diverse backgrounds. It would be a dream come true to return to my alma mater and assist you with your efforts to build the best program in the nation.

I will be in Seattle next week. Would it be possible to meet informally, or formally, to discuss my qualifications for this position? I will call to confirm your receipt of this fax and to discuss the possibility of our meeting. I will also ask those on my reference page to send you letters of recommendation. Thank for your consideration.

Sincerely,

Chris Smith

Chris Smith

Hospital Administrator

Chris Smith
123 Any Street • City, ST 12345 • (555) 555-5555 • *csmith@email.com*

June 1, 200–

Pat Cummings
District Vice President
Any Health Resource Corporation
456 Any Street
City, ST 12345

Dear Ms. Cummings:

After reading your advertisement in the *Flint Journal,* I would very much like to interview for the Hospital Administrator position. All my past experience, as described in the enclosed resume, reveals that I possess the strong administrative, patient-relations, practice-management, and financial expertise you seek in a qualified candidate.

In management and financial capacities of a prosthetics, orthotics, and occupational-therapy products business with branches in multiple states, I directed all phases of operations, from leasing office facilities to identifying suppliers, purchasing products, hiring and training, and selling and marketing custom and over-the-counter medical products. Also, I have a strong background in Medicare and health-benefits finance, preparation of business plans and strategies, financial and budget analysis, and forecasts and projections. All accomplishments to date, bulleted as first entries on the resume, have been associated with the health-care field.

In addition, I am a strong organizer, enthusiastic speaker, capable leader, and team player who can interface effectively with you, your Any Health Resource colleagues, medical professionals, as well as support staff and vendors. In the role of Administrator, I offer the qualifications and motivations to achieve results. Through a telephone or in-person interview, I can reiterate the qualifications presented in this letter and on the accompanying resume. Most important, during our meeting I can learn about your goals for Any Health Resource Corporation and your expectations for the next Administrator. I will contact your office next week to schedule a mutually convenient time to meet. Thank you for your time.

Sincerely,

Chris Smith

Chris Smith

Hotel Manager

Chris Smith

123 Any Street • City, ST 12345 • (555) 555-5555 • *csmith@email.com*

June 1, 200–

Pat Cummings
District Manager
Any Hotel Corporation
456 Any Street
City, ST 12345
FAX (555) 555-5557

Detailed on the attached resume is my broad-based hospitality industry experience. Each step on my current career path has allowed me to develop qualifications for the hotel manager position announced in the *Hospitality Association Newsletter*. In summary, these include:

- Experience managing a hotel and conference facility with annual sales in excess of $10 million.
- Progressively responsible management and human-resource experience with several properties.
- Expertise using varied proprietary budgeting, human resources, reservations, and finance packages.
- Undergraduate education in hotel and hospitality management, supplemented by ongoing professional development and training.

To date, my positions have ranged from intern and trainee to front-desk manager, director of sales and marketing, to my current role as assistant general manager of a prestigious three-thousand-room hotel and conference center. I now assist with all operation of conventions, special events, training, front office, housekeeping, maintenance, reservations, quality control, and communications. I am also a member of the executive committee that oversees all budgetary and policy decision-making.

As you will see as you review my resume, I have been involved in hospitality management for ten years. While my present position is challenging and rewarding, being a manager for Any Hotels, which operates gems like The Biltmore and The Renaissance, would be ideal. I would welcome the chance to speak by phone or in person regarding this position. I will be attending the Hospitality Association Conference next week. If you will be there, perhaps we could meet then. I will call to discuss your thoughts regarding a meeting. Thank you for your consideration.

Sincerely,

Chris Smith

Chris Smith

International Buyer

Date: June 1, 200–
From: *csmith@email.com*
To: *pcummings@email.com*
Subject: Qualified International Buyer Candidate

Dear Mr. Cummings:

I trust that upon review of my resume and supplemental documentation, including letters of recommendation, that you will determine my candidacy as worthy of an interview for the International Buyer position. As I read the job description on Any Corporation's website, I identified a number of specific qualifications I possess that match those you seek. These include:

- An undergraduate degree in marketing.
- Trilingual Italian-French-English talents.
- Experience in buying capacities.
- Overseas living and work experience.

Other assets I offer, all detailed on my resume, include:

- Completion of one of the nation's top retail-management training programs.
- Experience as an assistant buyer of housewares and electronics.
- Negotiation, pricing, and finance skills to enhance potential for profitability.

I hope that you will allow me the opportunity to expand upon the above via an interview. It is my goal to become a successful buyer and build an achievement-filled career with Any Corporation.

I will call to confirm your receipt of this e-mail and attached documents (original to follow in the mail) and to discuss your assessment of my candidacy. Thank you for your consideration.

Sincerely,
Chris Smith
123 Any Street
City, ST 12345
(555) 555-5555
csmith@email.com

Legal Assistant

Chris Smith
123 Any Street • City, ST 12345 • (555) 555-5555 • csmith@email.com

June 1, 200–

Pat Cummings, JD
Partner
Any Law Firm
456 Any Street
City, ST 12345

Dear Mr. Cummings:

I am writing in response to your recent posting on Jobs.com for a legal assistant. Having recently earned a certificate of paralegal studies, I intend to relocate to Chicago. Related work experience and scholastic endeavors have prepared me for employment in a firm that specializes in general practice. Ideally, that firm will be Any Law Firm, and I will be given the opportunity to be a strong member of your legal support team.

This fall and past summer, I interned for a small general-practice firm where I was entrusted with a great deal of responsibility. In a paralegal capacity I researched, wrote, and proofed appellate briefs; composed memoranda pertaining to corporate, contract, and criminal law; and drafted complaints and answers. I was an active participant in attorney-client conferences, interviewing clients and addressing how the law affects clients' suits, as well as raising potential consequences of varied legal outcomes.

Attached is a copy of my resume, which illustrates my specialized paralegal studies, undergraduate accounting studies, and all pertinent internship experiences. During an initial telephone interview and, subsequent to my relocation, via an in-person meeting, I would be happy to detail my qualifications and motivations to join Any Law Firm as a Legal Assistant.

In advance, thank you for your consideration. I look forward to someday soon discussing my background over the phone and to meeting you in person.

With best regards,

Chris Smith

Chris Smith

Chris Smith

123 Any Street • City, ST 12345 • (555) 555-5555 • csmith@email.com

June 1, 200–

Pat Cummings
Head Librarian
Any Library
456 Any Street
City, ST 12345

Dear Head Librarian Cummings:

I was very excited to discover the availability of the Librarian position at Any Library. The description as posted in the *Billings Gazette* identifies a number of requirements that match my qualifications. I am a library professional with community, secondary school, and university experience. To summarize the information detailed on my enclosed resume, my professional profile illustrates the following:

- Capacity to translate services, policies, and procedures into patron-focused and educational outcomes.
- Specialized focus on community outreach, patron education, program-planning, and public-speaking roles.
- Experience using and instructing peers and patrons to use NLM Classification System, ALA filing rules, as well as various indexes and Internet resources.

Professionally, my experience at the Kathryn Bell Library for the past eight years has focused on patron services and education, while circulation and reference desk roles have enhanced the above capabilities. Prior, working at a private secondary school, I addressed issues pertinent to faculty, students, and parents. In all capacities, and via academic training, including a graduate degree in library science and an undergraduate English major, I nurtured research and acquisition as well as book manuscript, journal, and dissertation archival and retrieval efforts.

During an interview, I can elaborate upon the above and all that appears on my resume. Because I am moving to Montana next month, I am available to begin immediately. Of course, I would be happy to meet with you earlier for a personal interview.

Sincerely,

Chris Smith

Chris Smith

Loan Officer

Chris Smith
123 Any Street • City, ST 12345 • (555) 555-5555 • csmith@email.com

June 1, 200–

Pat Cummings
VP of Credit Services
Any Bank
456 Any Street
City, ST 12345
FAX (555) 555-5557

Dear Mr. Cummings:

Attached is a copy of my resume supporting my candidacy for the Loan Officer position recently posted in the *Times Herald*. When you review this document, I trust that you will judge my qualifications as worthy of an interview. The requirements stated as required in the announcement include:

- Over five years of loan, customer service, personnel, and related experience.
- Extensive lending knowledge and ability to work within commercial or personal loan origination.
- Willingness to travel.

My qualifications, capabilities, and achievements, all detailed in my resume, include:

- Outstanding record of achieving sales goals as Branch Manager; successfully conducting residential and commercial mortgage acquisitions and personal and commercial loan transactions.
- Extensive experience developing commercial lending packages for private clientele, including financial restructuring, REFI, and equipment financing; coordinating activities with COMIDA, GCIDA, IBDC, and ESDC, and attorneys, appraisers, title companies, and governments.
- Capacity to train, supervise, and motivate others to achieve maximum performance.
- Expertise to develop marketing strategies and collateral, internal management programs, and professional business plans through use of Word, Excel, and PowerPoint.
- Successful record of developing and implementing marketing strategies and collateral material.

I hope to continue an accomplishment-filled career with Any Bank. I look forward to hearing from you regarding your assessment of my qualifications. Thank you for your consideration.

Sincerely,

Chris Smith

Meeting Planner

Date: June 1, 200–
From: *csmith@email.com*
To: *pcummings@email.com*
Subject: Exceptional Meeting Planner Candidate

TO: Pat Cummings, Vice President, Marketing

I would like to be Any Corporation's meeting planner. After reading your announcement in the *Chronicle,* I was eager to share my qualifications via the attached resume and letters of recommendation. After evaluating those documents, I hope you would allow me the opportunity to interview for this exciting opportunity.

As you review my resume entries and statements made by colleagues, envision the many times I have worked with marketing professionals to plan, implement, and evaluate the cost-benefit ratio of special events. Over the years I worked with colleagues, caterers, hospitality professionals, musicians, florists, and an amazing number of others to create memorable events. Whether small gatherings for board committees or annual dealership and sales meetings attended by hundreds, each event followed well-conceived plans and achieved clearly defined goals. In many cases, events were promotional, launching new products or marketing campaigns, achieving maximum publicity and attendance, as well as consumer attitudes and actions. Often they were community focused, associating the employer's name with meaningful undertakings. Do you remember last year's 10K run for breast cancer that raised over $3 million?

I have held positions that required communications, sales, marketing, and supervisory skills in retailing, media, and educational environments. While I have had the titles of marketing assistant, campaign organizer, and account supervisor, no matter what I was called, I was an achievement-focused, detail-oriented, enthusiastic meeting planner. I hope soon we can discuss whether my future includes a role as Any Corporation's Meeting Planner. I will call to discuss your thoughts regarding an interview and, ideally, to creatively share ideas about your next events.

Sincerely,
Chris Smith
123 Any Street
City, ST 12345
(555) 555-5555
csmith@email.com

Multimedia Specialist

Chris Smith

123 Any Street • City, ST 12345 • (555) 555-5555 • *csmith@email.com*

June 1, 200–

Pat Cummings
Director, Human Resources
Any Corporation
456 Any Street
City, ST 12345
FAX (555) 555-5557

Dear Ms. Cummings:

Please consider me a strong, enthusiastic, and qualified candidate for the Multimedia Specialist position recently posted on Any Corporation's website. To support my candidacy and assist with your deliberation, I offer the following, comparing my background and achievements with the qualifications stated as required for the position.

Your requirements:

- Experience in, working with, or consulting to small businesses.
- Talents associated with using computers for multimedia training, marketing, and Internet efforts.
- Abilities to liaison with business writers, editors, and programmers to help design software.

My qualifications, capabilities, and accomplishments:

- Conceived of and authored an OS/2 Tips and Techniques software training tool for IBM.
- Contributed to MS Office's entry into small-business market segment by assisting product development and launch of Your Office campaign and related multimedia training tools.
- Developed, over 5 years as consultant, dynamic multimedia presentations used for sales, marketing, promotions, and training activities.
- Generated over 50 percent of consulting income in the past year from entrepreneurial clients.
- Developed a website (*www.chrisconsults.com*) to illustrate creativity and graphics skills as well as client listings and sample presentations.

Please, let's review these points together. I am confident our conversation would be informative and enjoyable. I will call to discuss your thoughts regarding my candidacy.

Sincerely,

Chris Smith

Chris Smith

Newspaper Intern

Chris Smith
123 Any Street • City, ST 12345 • (555) 555-5555 • *csmith@email.com*

June 1, 200–

Pat Cummings
Managing Editor
Any Newspaper
456 Any Street
City, ST 12345

Dear Mr. Cummings:

When I saw your posting for an internship on the University of Virginia's career-services website, I wanted to enthusiastically request consideration for this amazing opportunity. As documented on the enclosed resume, I am currently an English major in my junior year, with a strong interest in a journalism career.

As an intern at Any Newspaper, I would use and enhance writing, editing, and research skills gained as a dedicated student and through co-curricular activities, including those associated with student publications. Studying literature, creative writing, composition, and grammar, and via related papers, projects, and essays, I have learned to complete assignments accurately, on time, with openness to critique and constructive editorial efforts. As a reporter for my high school newspaper and contributor to the yearbook, I was initiated to journalistic style, layout and design, and publishing software, including PageMaker and Quark Xpress. Samples of my work in these contexts are also enclosed.

I now possess the heart of a liberal arts student, ever curious, eager to share newly discovered information with others, and open to new experiences. Yet I seek to nurture the mind of a journalist who must perform interviews to draft and finalize features, news pieces, obituaries, special-event announcements, and other copy. Please allow me the opportunity to contribute to Any Newspaper and grow professionally and emotionally, gaining greater career focus, as your summer intern.

I will call your office next week to confirm your receipt of my resume and inquire about the possibility of an interview. In the interim, if you have any questions, please do not hesitate to contact me through the information above. Thank you for your consideration.

Sincerely yours,

Chris Smith

Chris Smith

Occupational Health Manager

Chris Smith
123 Any Street • City, ST 12345 • (555) 555-5555 • *csmith@email.com*

June 1, 200–

Pat Cummings
Vice President
Any Corporation
456 Any Street
City, ST 12345
FAX (555) 555-5557

Dear Mr. Cummings:

I would like to interview for the Occupational Health Manager position recently advertised in the *Star*. Attached is a copy of my resume. This document clearly presents those of my professional and academic achievements associated with your position. Through a telephone or in-person meeting, I can also share my motivation and desire to join Any Corporation within these critical capacities.

Upon a foundation of general nursing and health-care experience, all detailed on my resume, I have built a specialized career in occupational health. I am a certified occupational health nurse with twenty-one years of experience developing and implementing occupational health programs. Each related position has required a sound knowledge of OSHA and general occupational health issues in manufacturing, research, and health-care settings. I have served in diagnostic, patient care, physician support, education, training, and regulatory compliance roles.

Ideally, my next professional step would be to develop, implement, and support the strategically sound policies of Any Corporation to provide preventive, diagnostic, and treatment services for employees actively involved in pharmaceutical research, development, and manufacturing. I believe I am the right person to oversee the cost-effective, efficient, and effective delivery of occupational health services to your local and national workforce.

I look forward to hearing soon regarding your assessment of my candidacy and my request for an interview. Thank you for your consideration.

Sincerely,

Chris Smith

Chris Smith, R.N.

Office Receptionist

Date: June 1, 200–
From: *csmith@email.com*
To: *pcummings@email.com*
Subject: Office Receptionist Candidate

Dear Mr. Cummings:

Please consider me a strong and enthusiastic candidate for the receptionist position advertised in the *Herald Sun*. Attached to this e-mail is a copy of my resume, a letter of recommendation, and a list of references. I am very pleased that three of my past employers feel so positively about my performance that they agreed to comment on my future potential and that one wanted to detail my strengths as a receptionist and administrative assistant.

In each work setting, I greeted customers and clients in person, answered phones, managed multiple schedules, and assisted with a variety of administrative tasks, including mail and duplicating. I remained enthusiastic and positive when communicating with everyone. The feedback I received was, as my references and recommendation reveal, always positive. In summary, receptionist and administrative skills include:

- Experience using multiple phone lines and serving as a telephone and in-person receptionist.
- Typing speed of 70 wpm and proficiency using word-processing programs and spreadsheet applications.
- Strong work ethic and record of success within corporate, medical, and retail settings.

I am available to interview at your convenience, and I can start immediately on a full-time or part-time schedule. I will call to discuss your thoughts regarding next steps.

Sincerely,

Chris Smith
123 Any Street
City, ST 12345
(555) 555-5555
csmith@email.com

Park Maintenance Supervisor

Chris Smith
123 Any Street • City, ST 12345 • (555) 555-5555 • *csmith@email.com*

June 1, 200–

Pat Cummings
Chairperson
Any Parks Department
456 Any Street
City, ST 12345
FAX (555) 555-5557

SUBJECT: PARK MAINTENANCE SUPERVISOR

Please accept this letter and the enclosed resume as documents supporting my candidacy for the park maintenance supervisor position advertised in the City of Youngstown Employee Online Newsletter. As a current town employee, it would be a wonderful and logical next step to serve in a role that would ask me to manage, motivate, hire, and train others to perform efficiently and professionally.

For the past twelve years, I have held positions within the Youngstown Fire Department. Although my current position is secure and rewarding, it is strictly administrative and does not allow me to physically participate, as I have in the past, in actual firefighting or other hands-on activities that provide the outdoor work environment I most enjoy. The maintenance supervisor position described in your advertisement matches motivations and qualifications presented on my resume and in this letter.

I have worked on a family farm, attended a degree program in agriculture, and by choice I have always worked full-time or part-time with tree and excavation services. I am thoroughly familiar with the operation, maintenance, and repair of equipment, including safety practices. I also have the background and communication skills to train and supervise work crews using this equipment. I feel confident that I can provide Any Parks Department with reliability, dedication, and quality performance.

Since the fire department is not aware of my interest in making a change, your confidence is appreciated. But please feel comfortable consulting with the references provided regarding my background. I look forward to your response. Thank you for your consideration.

Yours,

Chris Smith

Chris Smith

Pharmacist

Date: June 1, 200–
From: *csmith@email.com*
To: *pcummings@email.com*
Subject: Pharmacist Position

TO: Pat Cummings, Vice President
Any Pharmacy Corporation

Since my graduation from the University of the Pacific School of Pharmacy, I have successfully completed all my professional roles and responsibilities while working within a hospital setting. While my experiences at the David Grant Medical Center were challenging and rewarding, I now seek a position that will allow me to continue my career development in a retail pharmacy setting. All that I have learned from colleagues about Any Pharmacy is very positive. Therefore, it is with great focus that I now seek to interview for the Pharmacist position recently announced via the Professional Pharmacist Association's e-mail system.

My past professional training did include a Community Management Rotation at Longs Drugs Corporate Office, so I am quite realistic and enthusiastic regarding what would be required to serve the health-care needs of customers, support the educational and patient-care roles of physicians, and to maintain an efficient and, of course, profit-focused operation. My professional competency and specialized knowledge have been developed and demonstrated in all past work settings detailed on the enclosed resume. During an interview, I hope to convince you of my sincere desire to build an achievement-filled career with Any Pharmacy Corporation. I am available to interview whenever mutually convenient. I am also willing to relocate, and I am confident that the salary associated with the position matches my goals.

I will call to confirm receipt of this email and to arrange either an in-person or telephone interview. Thank you for your consideration!

Sincerely,
Chris Smith
123 Any Street
City, ST 12345
(555) 555-5555
csmith@email.com

Photographer/Writer

Chris Smith
123 Any Street • City, ST 12345 • (555) 555-5555 • csmith@email.com

July 22, 200-

Pat Cummings
Human Resources Director
Any Newspaper
456 Any Street
City, ST 12345

Dear Mr. Cummings:

As is detailed on the enclosed resume and illustrated via samples of my work, I am an accomplished photographer with over ten years of experience in commercial and industrial photography, portraiture, and wedding photography. My publications include *A Shutterbug's Notes* and *Picture Your Pet*. I also have broad experience creating all the copy and graphics for print and online newsletters. While my past experiences have all been rewarding, I now seek to bring my talents and determination to Any Newspaper. I believe strongly that I possess the qualifications and motivations required to succeed in the Photographer and Writer position appearing on your website.

Academically, I hold a Bachelor of Arts in English from Reed College, where relevant coursework included feature writing, photojournalism, and news reporting. I have attended seminars and workshops with the Fred Jones Workshop and the Winona School of Professional Photography. My photos have appeared in the Winona course catalog, BBI Printing Company's catalog, and numerous Smithco publications (including annual reports and newsletters). In addition, I wrote all copy for the above-cited books.

The prospect of visiting local and regional sites, interviewing and photographing residents, and documenting human interest stories via text and photos would be a professional dream come true. Please allow me the opportunity to share my vision of this position and see if it matches yours. We can do so via an in-person meeting and conversation. I will call to determine if that would be an appropriate next step. I do hope it will be. Thank you for your consideration.

Sincerely,

Chris Smith

Chris Smith

Political Staffer

Chris Smith

123 Any Street • City, ST 12345 • (555) 555-5555 • *csmith@email.com*

June 1, 200–

Pat Cummings
Director
Any Organization
456 Any Street
City, ST 12345
FAX (555) 555-5557

Dear Ms. Cummings:

I would very much like to interview for the Political Staffer position advertised in a recent edition of the *Evening Bulletin*. Upon review of the attached resume, letter of recommendation, and reference list, I trust you will conclude that I have the experience, education, dedication, and potential to excel in this post.

Currently, I am an Administrative Assistant at the State House in Providence. In this role, my primary responsibilities include writing press releases, researching and drafting legislation, and providing consistent constituent contact. I have also worked with various committees and legislators regarding an array of legislative issues. Prior, I worked as an intern at the Lieutenant Governor's office during the elections, and I actively worked for several political and social causes on campus and in the Boston area.

Academically, I hold a Bachelor of Arts from Boston University in Political Science with a concentration in Public Policy. As a student, I completed numerous courses, papers, and projects cited on my resume, yet I have always supplemented academics with practical experience and internships.

Therefore, I consider myself a competent staffer, capable of serving in all capacities described in your announcement. I am eager to continue building a successful career in legislative support, campaign, and related areas as an Any Organization Staffer. I have the commitment, energy, and drive necessary to contribute successfully to your cause, yielding election and legislative successes. I will call to discuss your thoughts regarding my candidacy and, if you believe appropriate, to arrange an interview. Thank you for your consideration.

Sincerely,

Chris Smith

Chris Smith

Preschool Director

Chris Smith
123 Any Street • City, ST 12345 • (555) 555-5555 • *csmith@email.com*

June 1, 200–

Pat Cummings
Director
Any Preschool
456 Any Street
City, ST 12345

Director Cummings:

As a child-care and education professional with a record of progressively responsible experiences, I feel qualified for the preschool director position advertised in the *Star Tribune*. The enclosed resume begins with an overview of my greatest assets and those most relevant for this post. They include:

- Over 9 years of experience within home and school settings, teaching and caring for children aged 2 months to 7 years.
- Commitment to needs of infants, preschoolers, and kindergarteners and a record reflecting learning and loving.
- Background including courses in Childhood Development, Early Childhood Education, and Educational Psychology.

I have contributed to the educational and care efforts of several recognized preschools. In these settings I observed and supported a number of creative, focused, and effective administrators. Each role model has taught me much, and I now wish to implement their lessons as the Director of the Any Preschool. I wish to be a child- and parent-focused, staff-sensitive, and, yes, mission- and budget-directed leader of inspired teachers, aides, and others. During an interview, I can learn your vision for an exceptional preschool program and share how I can transform it into a day-to-day reality for some time to come.

I look forward to speaking with you regarding how my qualifications meet your expectations of the next Any Pre School Director. To assist with your deliberation, I have asked a person on the attached reference page to contact you regarding my abilities. If you wish additional supporting materials, including lesson plans or student progress reports, please do not hesitate to ask. Thank you.

Yours sincerely,

Chris Smith

Chris Smith

Product Developer

Date: June 1, 200–
From: *csmith@email.com*
To: *pcummings@email.com*
Subject: Product Development Candidate

TO: Pat Cummings, Chief Executive Officer
Any Technology Corporation

I read with much excitement on your company website about your search for candidates interested in joining your new products development department. Please accept this e-mail and the attached resume as formalized documentation of my sincere, enthusiastic, and, I trust, strong candidacy.

When you review my resume, you will see that I have more than ten years of experience in manufacturing, research and development, management of new product development, and existing product redevelopment and upgrade. I am especially experienced with complex composite materials, precision metal castings, and PC board industries. In addition, I have extensive experience both as a teacher and lecturer at several well-known universities. A Ph.D. in Materials Science Engineering, as well as undergraduate studies in Mechanical Engineering support all my practical experiences.

I am eager to interview for and, should you and your colleagues assess my background as appropriate, to join the Any Technology team. While documentation can reveal much, only through an interview can I best present my past achievements and future potential. If you wish to arrange an interview, please do not hesitate to respond to this e-mail or call me at the number below. Thank you for your consideration.

Chris Smith
123 Any Street
City, ST 12345
(555) 555-5555
csmith@email.com

Production Quality-Control Manager

Chris Smith

123 Any Street • City, ST 12345 • (555) 555-5555 • csmith@email.com

June 1, 200–

Pat Cummings
Hiring Manager
Any Corporation
456 Any Street
City, ST 12345
FAX (555) 555-5557

RE: Production Quality-Control Manager

After seven years of progressively responsible experience in production, electro-mechanical assembly, soldering, testing, and total quality management with a precision manufacturing operation, I feel I have all the qualifications you require for the Quality-Control Manager position. When I read the announcement on Techiejobs.com, I wanted to share my background and request consideration.

As detailed on the attached resume, and as I will share during an interview, over the past several years my responsibilities as Group Leader required me to establish and maintain an efficient and harmonious work atmosphere. While accomplishing this objective, I developed training procedures that ultimately created a highly motivated collection of cross-trained and productive production personnel working at ten assembly stations. This assured that all stations could be covered despite employee absences. In addition, I implemented TQM efforts, which resulted in a 40-percent increase in productivity, a 20-percent decrease in production costs, and a flurry of letters from satisfied clients.

I am aware of Any Corporation's innovative approach to TQM and its reputation for profitability and product excellence. I most definitely wish to apply my manufacturing know-how to your production operations as your next Production Quality-Control Manager.

I will call to confirm receipt of this fax (originals to follow in the mail) and to discuss your assessment of my background. I do hope that you will invite me to interview for this amazing opportunity. Thank you for reviewing my credentials.

Yours sincerely,

Chris Smith

Chris Smith

Program Coordinator

Chris Smith
123 Any Street • City, ST 12345 • (555) 555-5555 • *csmith@email.com*

June 1, 200–

Pat Cummings
Language Coordinator
Any Institute
456 Any Street
City, ST 12345

Dear Mr. Cummings:

Please consider me a strong and enthusiastic candidate for the ESL program coordinator position advertised in the *Free Press*. I am particularly qualified for this opportunity as a result of my double language major, my current enrollment in two language-proficiency certificate programs, and my past experience in tutorial and teaching roles.

My dual degrees in Spanish and Italian were recently earned from the University of Michigan, an institution known for its challenging language programs. Through these studies I became aware of the demands and technical challenges involved in translation and transcription. Most relevant, I became motivated to enhance my instructional skills while building bilingual talents. As an undergraduate, and now, well after commencement, I tutor peers and younger students in the fundamentals of written and spoken Spanish and Italian.

Having grown up in a bilingual (Spanish/English) environment and having studied abroad in both Spain and Mexico, I am quite sensitive to the challenges of those for whom English is a second language. As your program coordinator, I will transform sincere motivations, knowledge of language lesson planning and implementation, and creative communication talents into well-conceived programs and resources of the Any Institute. I am confident of my abilities to teach ESL classes targeting adults, teens, and youth and to recruit, train, and motivate others to do the same. Please grant me the opportunity to share a sample lesson with you sometime soon and, through an interview, to support all the information contained in the enclosed resume.

Thank you for your consideration. *Gracias por su consideración.*

Sincerely,

Chris Smith

Chris Smith

Project Manager

Date: June 1, 200–
From: *csmith@email.com*
To: *pcummings@email.com*
Subject: Project Manager Position

Dear Ms. Cummings:

In response to your ad for Project Manager on Any Corporation's website, I have attached my resume for your review and consideration. When you review this document, I trust you will conclude that I possess the qualifications worthy of an interview for this position. Summarizing what is detailed on my resume, I offer:

- Over twenty years of construction experience in supervisory and labor capacities.
- Knowledge of the roles of project manager and of owner's representative, as well as those of general and sub contractors.
- Record of success managing commercial and residential projects regionally and nationally.
- Oversight, supervisory, and varied experiences with multimillion-dollar projects.

I look forward to discussing my credentials and the requirements of the position with you, focusing on the above bullet items and information appearing on the resume. I will call to confirm receipt of this e-mail (original to be faxed as well) and to discuss the possibility of an interview. Thank you for your consideration.

Chris Smith
123 Any Street
City, ST 12345
(555) 555-5555
csmith@email.com

Public Relations Associate

Chris Smith
123 Any Street • City, ST 12345 • (555) 555-5555 • *csmith@email.com*

June 1, 200–

Pat Cummings
Vice President
Any Firm
456 Any Street
City, ST 12345

Dear Mr. Cummings:

My past achievements instill within me a confidence that my future accomplishments as an Associate at Any Firm would be many. Please review the attached resume and supplemental documents to determine if you believe the same. To preview the information detailed on my resume, I offer:

- Ability to plan and direct successful fundraising, public relations, and promotions programs.
- Campaign development and implementation experience with major health agency.
- Extensive volunteer recruitment experience and success motivating diverse teams.
- Supervisory experience with both professional and nonprofessional staffs.
- Capacity to use Word, WordPerfect, Lotus 123, PageMaker, and FileMaker Pro for drafting and editing features and promotional materials, for budgeting tasks, and for graphic projects.

During an enjoyable and productive session, we could discuss how my qualifications match those cited as required in your advertisement in the *New York Times*. I would like to touch on particular aspects of my background that should be of interest to you. These include:

- Over five years of progressively responsible campaign-development experience.
- Undergraduate Public Relations degree from one of the nation's top communication programs.
- Capacity to successfully address needs and achieve goals of corporate and not-for-profit clients.

I will call to confirm receipt of this letter and, if you judge it appropriate, to arrange an interview at a mutually convenient time and date. In advance, thank you for your time and consideration.

Yours sincerely,

Chris Smith

Chris Smith

Publicist

Chris Smith

123 Any Street • City, ST 12345 • (555) 555-5555 • *csmith@email.com*

June 1, 200–

Pat Cummings
Publicity Director
Any Firm
456 Any Street
City, ST 12345
FAX (555) 555-5557

Dear Ms. Cummings:

Would you like your next publicist's professional profile to include the following?

- Experience as publicist, media consultant, publicity professional, and television booker.
- Extensive contacts within broadcast and print media, yielding successful placements of stories as well as interviews.
- Talent to establish and implement strategic media and promotional campaigns to generate multimedia coverage.
- Capacity to work with clients to attain marketing, attendance, and general publicity goals.

As you review the attached resume, letters of recommendation, and sample releases, I trust you conclude that I can be an enthusiastic, confident, and performance-driven associate. I very much want to discuss my qualifications for the posting that appeared in the *Constitution*. I will, with great pride, share how much I have learned as a personal publicist and consultant at Coverage Concepts Consulting, as a production assistant at CNBS Television, and as a publicity assistant at Barstow Publishing. Common to these positions is my dedication to achieving goals through creative yet strategically sound press relations, promotions, and placement efforts.

I wish to continue an accomplishment-filled career by serving the needs of Any Firm's existing clients, including Coca Cola, Eminem, Tony Hawk, and others. Of course, I want to help generate new accounts as well. Please, let's meet soon. I'll call to discuss whether you wish to do so. Thank you for your consideration.

Yours sincerely,

Chris Smith

Chris Smith

Publisher's Assistant

Date: June 1, 200–
From: *csmith@email.com*
To: *pcummings@email.com*
Subject: Qualified Assistant Candidate

TO: Pat Cummings, Vice President of Editorial
Any Corporation
RE: Publisher's Assistant Position

I am e-mailing to request consideration for the Assistant position posted on your firm's website. As you review the attached resume, I believe you will find that my training and related experience are well suited for this position. If so, please grant me the opportunity to learn about your expectations for your next Assistant and to share my qualifications via a telephone or in-person interview.

My achievements as an administrative assistant, magazine production assistant, and teacher demonstrate my capacity to prioritize, focus on details, and effectively address all challenges of providing superior executive support for you and your Any Corp's colleagues. As a current temporary assignment worker with Alltemps in Topeka, I have become highly computer literate in both Macintosh and Windows operating systems and software programs. In accomplishing all that is cited on my resume, I was organized and accurate, mastered new information rapidly, and communicated effectively with supervisors, peers, and subordinates. I also work well with diverse individuals.

Thank you for reviewing my credentials. I will call in a week to schedule a convenient time to discuss my qualifications and your expectations.

Sincerely,
Chris Smith
123 Any Street
City, ST 12345
(555) 555-5555

Purchasing Agent

Chris Smith
123 Any Street • City, ST 12345 • (555) 555-5555 • *csmith@email.com*

DATE   June 1, 200–

Pat Cummings
Employment Manager
Any Corporation
456 Any Street
City, ST 12345
FAX (555) 555-5557

Dear Mr. Cummings:

Please accept this letter and resume as documentation formalizing my application for the purchasing agent position advertised in the *Macon Telegraph*.

As detailed on my resume, I have six years of progressively responsible experience in purchasing for a growing organization that now purchases in excess of $3.5 million of raw materials, supplies, and equipment. Throughout my career, first as purchasing clerk and now as a senior buyer who wishes to become your next Purchasing Agent, I have learned to:

- Clarify the needs of end users.
- Source and communicate effectively with vendors and suppliers via phone and Internet.
- Create detailed spreadsheet cost-benefit analyses of potential purchases.
- Communicate with end users and negotiate with suppliers and vendors with great focus.
- Track, store, and retrieve all purchase documentation, delivery dates, warrantees, and installation agreements.
- Use purchasing, budgetary, and related software systems.

I am quite proud that recently I was a key contributor to the successful setup and startup of new branch locations, from bare walls to a fully stocked and efficiently operating facility. This involved working with managers, contractors, architects, and assorted on-site professions, with total purchases of over $500,000. During an interview, I can discuss how much I have learned completing this project and over the years in varied purchasing roles.

I appreciate your consideration of my candidacy and look forward to your reply.

Sincerely,

Chris Smith

Chris Smith

Real Estate Sales Associate

Chris Smith
123 Any Street • City, ST 12345 • (555) 555-5555 • *csmith@email.com*

June 1, 200–

Pat Cummings
Vice-President
Any Properties
456 Any Street
City, ST 12345
FAX (555) 555-5557

RE: Advertisement in *Real Estate Weekly*

Dear Mr. Cummings:

I am writing to apply for your Sales Associate position. As cited on the attached resume, I possess the following:

- Record of productivity and profitability as a real estate sales professional.
- Proven accountability, dependability, and decisiveness, servicing needs of buyers and sellers.
- Sales and marketing talent gained via experience, achievements, and customer relationships.
- Competencies from Century 21 Sales Curriculum, Dale Carnegie's Face-to-Face Selling Skills, Xerox Selling Skills, Creating Customer Focus, and other varied seminars and training courses.

The experience detailed in my resume involved the most sophisticated aspects of commercial and residential real estate sales and leasing, as well as associated areas of real estate development, property management, and rehabilitation. In addition to a current brokers' license, I have an excellent grounding in real estate and business law. At Century 21 I am a highly organized team player, with excellent verbal and written communications skills, an eye for detail, and the necessary persistence to conceive, package, and bring the big deals home. I am confident I will do the same at Any Properties.

Please give me an opportunity to talk about how I can add value to your team. I will call to confirm receipt of this fax and, I do hope, to arrange an interview. Thank you for your consideration.

Sincerely,

Chris Smith

Chris Smith

Regional Manager

Date: June 1, 200–
From: *csmith@email.com*
To: *pcummings@email.com*
Subject: Regional Manager Position

TO: Pat Cummings, Management Supervisor, Any Corporation

It is with great enthusiasm and the appropriate confidence that I seek to interview for the Regional Manager position advertised on Any Corporation's website.

As noted on the attached resume, I have over the years progressed quickly through sales associate, senior associate, and district manager roles. It would be a logical next step for me to continue my accomplishment-filled Any Corporation career as a Regional Manager. You are, of course, familiar with my performance, and we have discussed my commitment to our company's mission, sales goals, and continued profitable operations. My track record as a professional, along with my knowledge of the automotive supply industry and my ability to hire, train, and motivate sales professionals are clearly documented on my resume and in past annual reviews. Naturally, my insightful understanding of our retail partners would be an asset when seeking to exceed all objectives for the Eastern Region.

While I am proud of all the recognition I have earned, including the President's Award and Chairman Club membership, I am proudest of what I have learned completing Any Corporation's training seminars and when called upon to offer these opportunities to my peers. A great Regional Manager must transform a vision into the day-to-day performance of sales-persons on the front lines, of distribution professionals, and of those within our manufacturing and marketing capacities. As someone who has taught persons in each of these areas, I am confident the Eastern Region team will achieve.

Although my present position continues to provide challenges and rewards, I am ready to contribute to Any Corporation in new ways. Let's meet to discuss my qualifications and capabilities and your goals for the next Regional Manager. Thank you for your consideration.

Sincerely,
Chris Smith
csmith@email.com

Researcher

Chris Smith
123 Any Street • City, ST 12345 • (555) 555-5555 • *csmith@email.com*

June 1, 200–

Pat Cummings
Human Resources Director
Any Newspaper
456 Any Street
City, ST 12345

Dear Mr. Cummings:

I would most definitely like to be Any Newspaper's next researcher! Upon review of the position announcement in the *Post*, I wanted to formalize my candidacy via this letter, the accompanying resume, and a writing sample. To summarize what I trust these documents reveal, in the capacity of researcher, I will utilize and expand upon the following strengths:

- Research, fact-checking, and investigative skills gained as a reporter, copywriter, and editor for magazines, newspapers, and book publishers.
- Specialized knowledge and research skills developed as author and coauthor of books on sports and communications and articles on topics ranging from crime and sports to medicine and humor.
- Capacity to contribute to the process associated with conceiving of story ideas and conducting research at all stages.
- Expertise using the Internet, databases, printed references, and interview techniques.

During an interview, I can first learn more about your expectations for the researcher and then elaborate upon how each of the above-listed skills would contribute to my success as a critically important member of the Any Newspaper team. I will call to confirm receipt of this letter and to discuss your thoughts regarding whether a phone or in-person interview would be appropriate. Thank you for your consideration.

Sincerely,

Chris Smith

Chris Smith

Restaurant Manager Trainee

Chris Smith

123 Any Street • City, ST 12345 • (555) 555-5555 • *csmith@email.com*

June 1, 200–

Pat Cummings
Manager
Any Restaurant
456 Any Street
City, ST 12345
FAX (555) 555-5557

Dear Ms. Cummings:

Please accept the attached resume as a formal expression of my desire to interview for and ideally serve in the restaurant-manager trainee position. The posting in the *Post* revealed that the qualities you seek match those I possess.

During the past seven years, I have held positions of responsibility in banquet and special-event catering, function management, and restaurant food service operations. I have additional experience in front-desk operation of a conference facility. In each position, I nurtured ever-improving organizational, leadership, training, and supervisory skills in settings dedicated to providing quality service and performance in high-volume operations.

Looking ahead to what I believe can be an achievement-filled career with Any Restaurant, I feel confident that I can successfully perform all the duties of a trainee and, soon after completing training, be an effective profit- and performance-driven manager of an Any Restaurant location.

If past performance does predict future success, I will be very successful, if given the opportunity to do so. Please allow me the chance to share my past achievements and future ambitions during an interview. I will call to confirm your receipt of this fax (originals to follow in the mail) and to arrange a mutually convenient time and date for an interview. Thank you.

Sincerely,

Chris Smith

Chris Smith

Sales Representative, Medical Products

Date: June 1, 200–
From: *csmith@email.com*
To: *pcummings@email.com*
Subject: Qualified Sales Rep Candidate

I would like to apply for the position of sales representative advertised on Anyjobs.com. Honestly, medical product sales is my career goal! As the attached resume reveals, I possess qualifications and capabilities matching those stated as required for this position. In summary, these include:

- Knowledge of health-care, business, and economic-related topics gained from courses including Accounting, Microeconomics, Business Administration, Changing Concepts of Disease, Medical Sociology, Domestic Social Policy, Organizational Psychology, and Statistics.
- Confidence and experience communicating with physicians, health-care practitioners, patients, and others associated with medical devices.
- Research, project management, time management, writing, and oral communication skills gained from employment education and activities.
- Capacity to conduct topic-specific research to identify trends or key issues and to document findings in reports as well as presentations.
- Persuasive communication style, necessary for clarifying medical product and treatment protocols and studies.
- Word, Excel, PowerPoint, Access, and Internet capabilities.

I have built these skills on a strong academic foundation of health and society, business, economics, and policy studies completed at the University of Rochester. Now, please allow me to build an achievement-focused career with Any Corporation. Through initial telephone conversations and in-person discussions, I can present my sales competencies to you and your sales colleagues. I would be happy to pay to travel to any regional facilities or to corporate headquarters for an interview. Thank you for your consideration.

Sincerely,

Chris Smith

Chris Smith

Senior HVAC Technician

Chris Smith

123 Any Street • City, ST 12345 • (555) 555-5555 • *csmith@email.com*

June 1, 200–

Pat Cummings
Human Resources Director
Any Corporation
456 Any Street
City, ST 12345

Dear Ms. Cummings:

At the suggestion of Donald Lee of your HVAC department, I am requesting an interview for the Senior HVAC Technician position recently posted on Any Corporation's website and announced to employees via e-mail. Donald is well aware of my background, so he encouraged me to share my resume and request consideration for this opportunity.

When you review my resume, you will see I possess nine years of experience in after-warranty maintenance, preventive maintenance programs, and complete overhaul of major heating, air conditioning, and ventilation systems. I have successfully installed and repaired systems within various buildings and work settings, often in facilities that are challenging and require creativity as well as technical know-how. I have also completed extensive and continuous education and training on the latest and most cost-efficient energy and control systems.

The opportunity to apply my technical as well as supervisory skills to the needs of Any Corporation is one I now seek to actively explore. If you judge it appropriate, allow me the chance to discuss your requirements and my ability to handle the responsibilities of this position. I will call to confirm receipt of this letter and accompanying resume and to arrange an interview. Of course, feel free to discuss my candidacy with Donald. Thank you.

Sincerely,

Chris Smith

Chris Smith

Site Location Supervisor

Chris Smith
123 Any Street • City, ST 12345 • (555) 555-5555 • *csmith@email.com*

June 1, 200–

Pat Cummings
General Manager, Properties
Any Corporation
456 Any Street
City, ST 12345
FAX: (555) 555-5557

RE: Executive Position, Site Location, and Store Build-Outs

During the past fifteen years, my experience as a developer, general contractor, owner, and property manager of residential, commercial, and industrial projects has been extensive. In conjunction with these projects, I was actively involved in investment analysis, whole loans and structured transactions, and financial control to assure quality completion within schedules and budgets.

As a result of all my past achievements documented on the enclosed resume, I am confident that I am the person you seek for the position posted in the most recent edition of the *Evening Bulletin*. Ideally, after an interview, you will judge me as qualified to join Any Corporation as a Site Location Supervisor, capable of working effectively with clients in real estate development, property management, and finance roles. Because of a broad and diverse background, I can provide consulting and management services to clients with problems involving planning, financing, budgeting, scheduling, or monitoring any phase of site development, renovation, and expansion-related efforts. It would be with professionalism and profit-focus that I would fulfill management responsibilities while expediting project completions from inception to final inspection.

Although my resume does detail all pertinent information, I would be able to provide you with additional insights regarding my capabilities and ambitions during a personal interview. I am free to relocate and/or travel, and the compensation package I seek is negotiable. In advance, thank you for your consideration.

Sincerely,

Chris Smith

Chris Smith

Social Worker

Date: June 1, 200–
From: *csmith@email.com*
To: *pcummings@email.com*
Subject: Social Worker Candidate

RE: Social Work Position

In response to your advertisement on Socialjustice.com, I would like to present my candidacy for the Social Worker position at Any Agency. I am confident you will find my experience and abilities worthy of an interview for this opportunity. As detailed on the enclosed resume, I possess the academic and practical experience required to be a competent, caring, and effective professional, serving diverse needs of Any Agency clients. Previewing and reviewing what appears on my resume, I offer the following:

• Capability to serve in comprehensive social-work capacities in school or health-care settings.
• Experience creating and implementing treatment plans for clients with psychosocial, behavioral, and health-related disorders.
• Capacity to manage cases, maintain accurate case records, and create detailed reports.

My most recent experiences at Baltimore Central School District, Johns Hopkins Children and Teen Clinic, Baltimore County Juvenile Court Clinic, and Johns Hopkins University Hospital have all contributed to my development of professional competencies. Academically, I earned a master's degree in social work from Johns Hopkins and undergraduate degrees in psychology and sociology from Colby College. While a graduate student, I volunteered as a literacy tutor for children residing in a housing project and as a geriatric aide at a day facility for Alzheimer's patients.

Clearly, I have worked with diverse clients in varied settings, so I am ready to successfully address the needs of those who use Any Agency services. I look forward to speaking personally with you about my motivations and qualifications. Feel free to respond to this e-mail, or call me at the number above.

Sincerely,
Chris Smith

State Administrator

Chris Smith
123 Any Street • City, ST 12345 • (555) 555-5555 • *csmith@email.com*

June 1, 200–

Pat Cummings
President, New England Offices
Any Organization
456 Any Street
City, ST 12345

Dear Mr. Cummings:

In response to your advertisement in the *Herald*, enclosed is a copy of my resume as well as a letter of recommendation and reference list for your review. When you have evaluated these documents, I trust you will determine my candidacy is worthy of an interview for the position of State Administrator available at Any Organization.

During the past twelve years, I have held diverse and progressively responsible fundraising, development, and special-event planning positions for nonprofit service organizations, universities, and educational institutions. In these capacities, I have been directly involved in development strategies, million-dollar annual fund campaigns, marketing and mailing programs, and media and public relations efforts. While these positions have been challenging, rewarding, and broad in scope, I now wish my expertise to be utilized by Any Organization. Your mission to provide lobbying and financial support for those individuals and groups committed to the education of deserving students is one I seek to transform into record-breaking fundraising, dynamic public relations, and effective policy papers.

I hope that, after reviewing my credentials, you and members of the selection committee will speak with me regarding my qualifications to be the State Administrator. Clearly, I am confident in my abilities and committed to the efforts of Any Organization, and I would like to schedule an interview to reinforce my qualifications and motivations.

I appreciate your time and look forward to speaking with you.

Sincerely,

Chris Smith

Chris Smith

Chris Smith

123 Any Street • City, ST 12345 • (555) 555-5555 • *csmith@email.com*

June 1, 200–

Pat Cummings
District Supervisor
Any Stores
456 Any Street
City, ST 12345

Dear Ms. Cummings:

A profitable and accomplishment-filled retail career and a true enthusiasm to join Any Stores now motivate me to seek a store management position with your chain. As detailed below, my background matches the qualifications cited in your advertisement in the *Herald-Tribune.*

You require managerial experience, superior training and motivational skills, and budget management abilities. As detailed on the attached resume, I offer the following:

- Skills and perspectives gained as a manager and assistant manager within record, clothing, and toy-store settings.
- Success in merchandising, inventory control, ordering, cash control, and maintenance roles.
- Experience hiring, training, and nurturing strong sales performance in store personnel.
- Recognitions earned for exceeding sales and profit goals as well as display competitions.
- Academic background in retail management supplemented by extensive training.

May we discuss how I may contribute to Any Stores? Because I work typical retail hours, it would be best if I called to determine a mutually convenient time and date to meet. Of course, I would be happy to relocate, and I am confident the compensation offered a manager would meet my objectives. Thank you for reviewing my credentials. I look forward to speaking with you.

Sincerely,

Chris Smith

Chris Smith

Systems Engineer

Date: June 1, 200–
From: *csmith@email.com*
To: *pcummings@email.com*
Subject: Systems Engineer Position

TO: Pat Cummings

In response to your advertisement on Compjobs.com, I would like to apply for the position of systems engineer. The professional profile that begins the attached resume summarizes the qualifications I offer you and your Any Corporation colleagues. These include:

- Extensive and diversified hardware and software knowledge.
- Expertise in prototype computer testing.
- Comprehensive investigative and research skills.
- Knowledge of programming languages, operating systems, as well as word processing, database, and spreadsheet software applications including DOS, Windows, Macintosh, Word, WordPerfect, Excel, Lotus 1-2-3, Access, Oracle, and RoboHELP.

Professionally, I have served within Systems Engineering roles for Maximillian Data and Computer Systems and, prior, as a Systems Programmer at the University of Georgia. I am proud to offer Any Corporation the skills I now possess, the drive to enhance those skills, and the expertise needed to design and test prototypical hardware that is defined by end-users as state of the art. It would be an honor to interview for and, if you judge my background as worthy, to join the Any Corporation team. Academically, I earned an undergraduate degree in computer science and a comprehensive set of courses that involved learning a number of programming languages and use of varied testing techniques for eclectic projects. Please review the detailed list on my resume as you assess my candidacy. I look forward to speaking with you by phone in advance of an in-person interview. Please confirm receipt of this e-mail and, if you judge appropriate, communicate regarding interviews. In advance, thank you for your time and consideration.

Sincerely,
Chris Smith
123 Any Street
City, ST 12345
(555) 555-5555

Technical Writer

Chris Smith

123 Any Street • City, ST 12345 • (555) 555-5555 • *csmith@email.com*

June 1, 200–

Pat Cummings
Communication Director
Any Tech
456 Any Street
City, ST 12345
FAX: (555) 555-5557

I would like to apply for the technical writer position advertised on Any Tech's website. As detailed on my attached resume, I am currently a Technical Writer and Senior Project Administrator at Rizzo Associates. Within these capacities, I complete all research, drafting, editing, and finalizing of documentation for a defense contractor. Prior, as a technical writer for a technical publishing consulting firm, and as an editor and writer for an engineering firm, I developed the foundation for skills I have built into a successful technical writing career. Now, it is these skills that I offer.

Summarizing what appears on the attached resume, the capabilities and abilities I will use to succeed at Any Tech include:

- Proven abilities to structure technical writing projects and motivate others to complete components accurately and on time.
- Capacity to transform technical information into detailed illustrations and documentation.
- Sensitivity related to creation of classified training and support materials for military hardware.
- Security Clearance Level IA.
- Project- and team-management skills nurtured via observation and experience.
- Capacity to identify specific task components, set realistic deadlines, and monitor and motivate others.
- Expertise with the Word, WordPerfect, PowerPoint, Lotus 1-2-3, Excel, and CAD.

I hope to be able to discuss the available position with you further. I will call to confirm your receipt of this letter and to determine if an interview will be an appropriate next step. Thank you for your consideration.

Sincerely,

Chris Smith

Chris Smith

Telemarketer

Date: June 1, 200–
From: *csmith@email.com*
To: *pcummings@email.com*
Subject: Qualified Telemarketer

TO: Pat Cummings, Director of Marketing and Sales

I am responding to your advertisement for a telemarketer appearing on Jobs.com. The attached resume provides details of my accomplishment-filled and goal-directed career in marketing and sales. Achievements to date include:

- Induction into performance clubs and earning of multiple recognitions over the past three years.
- Personal responsibility for over $500,000 FY annual sales.
- Record of consistently reaching or exceeding established goals for over four years.

My qualifications, gained with ESP Telecom and the Test Review Education Group, include:

- Outstanding selling and closing capabilities illustrated by a proven track record of exceeding goals.
- Well versed in active listening techniques, nurturing conversations through appropriate questioning.
- Drive and focus required to meet contact and sales quotas, meeting personal and other established deadlines.
- Confidence in cold-calling and direct-sales roles, marketing services and products to businesses and clients.
- Pride associated with using earnings as telemarketer to pay for college tuition and expenses.
- Business Administration, Public Speaking, Persuasive Writing, and marketing courses.

My past accomplishments are many, but I am driven to achieve more. Please allow me the opportunity to share my ambitions and learn more about your goals for those who succeed in telemarketing roles at Any Corporation. Of course, I will call you to discuss my candidacy. Thank you for your consideration.

Chris Smith
123 Any Street
City, ST 12345
(555) 555-5555
csmith@email.com

Television Camera Operator

Chris Smith
123 Any Street • City, ST 12345 • (555) 555-5555 • *csmith@email.com*

June 1, 200–

Pat Cummings
Production Manager
Any Television Station
456 Any Street
City, ST 12345

Dear Mr. Cummings:

When I read your job description for a Television Camera Operator in the *Sunday Times,* I wanted to share my background via this letter, accompanying resume, and sample tapes. As you review each, I hope you will see that I have the potential to be a successful member of the Any Television Station team.

During the past three years, I have worked as a Production Assistant and Technical Operator in a television studio. At LA Productions, I was involved in all aspects of video production, supporting writing, direction, production, and editing efforts associated with three short 8mm films and several music videos that were shot and edited using digital equipment. All projects completed to date have allowed me to fine-tune my filming and editing talents. In addition, I gained additional experience in and training associated with video and camera operation from Ellis Technical Training School.

Once given the opportunity to share some of my work and demonstrate my talents, I am sure that I can prove worthy of an offer to join your station. I look forward to sharing my tapes with you and interviewing for this position. I look forward to hearing from you regarding a mutually convenient time and date. Thank you for your consideration.

Sincerely,

Chris Smith

Chris Smith

Translator

Chris Smith
123 Any Street • City, ST 12345 • (555) 555-5555 • csmith@email.com

June 1, 200–

Pat Cummings
Head Translator
Any Organization
456 Any Street
City, ST 12345

Dear Mr. Cummings:

I am writing to seek consideration for the Translator position. Upon review of the posting in the *Constitution*, I was immediately intrigued by this opportunity and inspired to share my background via this letter and enclosed resume.

As you review each document, front and back, you will see my trilingual English-Spanish-Russian talents. Also, examination of supporting documents will reveal that I possess the professional and academic accomplishments to be an effective translator. While completing my Bachelor of Science degree in Russian at Emory University, I worked as a Translating Assistant on campus. In this capacity, I transcribed business and creative writings from Spanish and Russian into English and vice versa. I also regularly served as a translator. It was with great enthusiasm and attention to detail that I assisted many international businesspersons, academicians, students, and those traveling to Atlanta for pleasure.

Also, while at Emory, I spent a semester studying abroad in St. Petersburg, Russia, where I served as a personal tutor for students taking Russian and Spanish and as a teacher of English as a Second Language. In summary, my previous experience as a translator, my trilingual writing and conversational abilities, and the competency I have gained via extensive travel throughout Latin America, Europe, and the United States qualify me for this unique experience. I hope to someday soon discuss these in detail via an interview. Also find enclosed letters of recommendation written by several clients. Thank you for your consideration, and I look forward to meeting with you. I will call to discuss your reactions to my candidacy and, ideally, to arrange a mutually convenient interview.

Sincerely,

Chris Smith

Chris Smith

Travel Agent

Date: June 1, 200–
From: *csmith@email.com*
To: *pcummings@email.com*
Subject: Experienced Agent Candidate

TO: Pat Cummings, Any Travel Agency

I would like to apply for the position of travel agent advertised on the Travel Professional Association's website. As the attached resume indicates, I have about a decade of progressively responsible experience in the travel and tourism field.

My relocation to Connecticut motivates me to respond enthusiastically to your posting. During initial phone conversations, followed by in-person meetings, you can assess my potential to be a very positive and profitable addition to your professional team. During these discussions I will highlight how much I learned at Surge and Siege Travel, Quick Trip Travel, and Gotta Fly Tours, in the roles of Air and Sea Coordinator, Travel Consultant, and Computer Operator/Intern.

My recent efforts at coordinating all travel and accommodations for attendees of a major conference held at the Mohegan Sun have enhanced my relationship with the Greater Connecticut Convention and Visitor's Bureau and the Connecticut Chamber of Commerce, as well as heightening my awareness of this region. I now strongly believe in the potential to market services to those traveling to and from Connecticut, for business as well as personal reasons.

I look forward to speaking with you regarding my qualifications and motivations. To this end I will call soon. Thank you for your consideration.

Sincerely,
Chris Smith

Writing Instructor

Chris Smith
123 Any Street • City, ST 12345 • (555) 555-5555 • *csmith@email.com*

June 1, 200–

Pat Cummings, Ed.D.
Writing Center Director
Any College
456 Any Street
City, ST 12345
FAX (555) 555-5557

Dear Director Cummings:

Please consider this letter and the attached resume as a formal application for the position of Writing Instructor. As detailed on these two documents and, I trust, illustrated in the additional materials attached, I have been a college-level writing teacher and tutor for the past eleven years. In varied capacities, I have consistently offered strong writing, editing, and proofreading skills, traits I have also inspired in students, faculty, and others.

As teacher, tutor, and writing advocate at community colleges, research universities, and liberal arts colleges, I learned much and taught much. Any College, with its commitment to a liberal arts mission, focus on a new curriculum with introductory and capstone writing course requirements, and proactive faculty is where I wish to continue my accomplishment-focused career. I am confident that my qualifications are clearly illustrated through the entries on my resume and the information provided via documents promoting writing center services and syllabi for various classes. But it would be through an interview that I would best be able to share my motivations as well as qualifications. Please give me the chance to do so.

I would be delighted to discuss further how my abilities match your requirements and learn of your vision regarding how the Any College's next Writing Instructor should contribute to the educational goals of the institution. Most important, I want to share how very much I wish to inspire students to superior writing talents.

Sincerely,

Chris Smith

Chris Smith

P.S. I faxed this letter to expedite consideration, but original documents will soon follow by mail.

Chapter 8

In Response to Confidential Postings

When reviewing job postings, you will find announcements that do not reveal the name of the employer. These are confidential postings or, as they have been called in the past, "blind ads." They are either posted by search firms or by organizations that do not want their recruiting efforts to be public knowledge. These are sometimes frustrating for job-seekers, but they shouldn't be. Don't be concerned with the company name. Focus on the job title and function. Follow-up can be done for confidential postings as well as employer-identified postings.

Applications Programmer

Chris Smith
123 Any Street • City, ST 12345 • (555) 555-5555 • *csmith@email.com*

June 1, 200–

SUBJECT: Applications Programmer

After reviewing your posting on Jobs.com, I wanted to contact you to let you know that I am seeking consideration for the Applications Programmer position. I offer the following qualifications (detailed on my resume, attached):

- Knowledge of C, COBOL, COBOL II, Pascal, FORTRAN, Visual Basic, Assembly, CC+, Cajon, Pascal, LISP< IBM< PL/I, Prolog, AION Databases: SQL/DS, Oracle.
- Effective design, resource allocation, and status-evaluation skills associated with large projects that shaped production-testing and data-collection processes.
- Proficient design and implementation of program enhancements, including an online message system, database repair/troubleshooting utilities, and release system to update clients.

As you review descriptions of my experiences with Bentley Life Insurance, Medware Corporation, and Shadow Associates, I trust you will conclude that I am a programmer analyst with expertise in application development and maintenance, as well as enhancement of programs in purchasing, inventory control, contracts management, and related logistics applications. Most of these roles have required interaction with various departments and users.

I hope to have the opportunity to speak to you further about an available position. I look forward to hearing from you.

Yours,

Chris Smith

Chris Smith

Assistant Personnel Officer

Chris Smith

123 Any Street • City, ST 12345 • (555) 555-5555 • *csmith@email.com*

DATE: June 1, 200–
TO: Human Resources Director
SUBJECT: Assistant Personnel Officer Position

I would most definitely like to interview for the assistant personnel officer position recently advertised in the *Post*. As the attached resume indicates, I have extensive experience in personnel, including my most recent position as assistant staff manager at Virginia General Hospital. To succeed in this capacity, I recruited and trained administrative and clerical staff members, ancillary and works department staff, and professional and technical employees. I also evaluated personnel, conducted disciplinary and grievance interviews, signed employees to contracts, and advised staff on conditions of employment, entitlements, and maternity leave. It is with great professional pride and the appropriate ambition that I now seek the challenges and rewards associated with the position described in your announcement.

I look forward to hearing from you if my qualifications meet your needs and, most important, to presenting my capabilities to you and all others involved in the search. I do want to become a strong and contributing member of your human resources team, providing strategic and objective-focused hiring, training, benefits administration, and employee relations resources for senior management and employees at every level.

Sincerely,

Chris Smith

Chris Smith

Biomedical Engineer

Date: June 1, 200–
From: *csmith@email.com*
To: *jobs@email.com*
Subject: Biomedical Engineer Candidate

As I recently earned my undergraduate biomedical engineering degree, it is with great enthusiasm that I now seek to interview for the engineering trainee position recently posted on Jobs.com. Summarizing what appears on the attached resume, I offer:

- Capacity to investigate and solve engineering problems dealing with biological systems or chemical properties.
- Skills and perspectives gained within comprehensive research roles.
- Strong verbal and leadership skills, including the ability to conduct research and solve complex problems in large groups.
- General knowledge of computer programs, including Scion Image, Origin, Math Cad Professional, Word, and Excel.
- General knowledge of slide preparation, sterile technique, fluorescence microscopy, confocal imaging, protocol design, spectroscopy, NMR, gas chromatography, cell cultivation, and preparation protocols for experimental procedures.

During an interview, I can expand upon all of the above bullet items, learn more about this position and your organization, and detail how much I learned in the classroom, and beyond, as well as describe how much I want to learn as I begin my biomedical engineering career. I would like to detail for you the benefits of my Research for Undergraduates in Biomechanics and Imaging Program Laboratory Internship, when I completed a project titled Endothelial Coated Beads for Cell Adhesion Studies. I have also greatly matured professionally as a Laboratory Technician over the past two-plus years. I appreciate your reviewing the attached documents and look forward to hearing from you soon. Of course, I will e-mail a copy of my transcript and a letter of recommendation soon, to further support my candidacy.

Sincerely,
Chris Smith
123 Any Street
City, ST 12345
(555) 555-5555

Business Consultant

Memo from Chris Smith
123 Any Street
City, ST 12345
(555) 555-5555
csmith@email.com

June 1, 200–

TO: Human Resources Director
RE: Business Consultant Candidacy

I am responding to your advertisement for a business consultant in the *Financial News*. It is likely that my consulting experience with large and small businesses matches the requirements for this position. My qualifications, detailed on the attached resume, include:

- Ability to manage cases from evaluation and data collection to analysis, presentation, and implementation.
- Significant knowledge of government systems, structures, funding, and organizational oversights.
- Ability to use Excel and Access to create financial models and related databases and Word, PowerPoint Project, WordPerfect, Visio, and LexisNexis for research, presentation development, and report writing.

Over five years of progressively responsible experiences with American Management Systems have required me to develop the above skills while completing numerous client-focused cases and projects. I am eager to discuss how past accomplishments qualify me for future performance as a member of your consulting practice. I hope you judge my candidacy as worthy of an interview. During that discussion, I will share how I wish to apply the professional capabilities gained as a Senior Consultant, Consultant, and Research Analyst to your position. Please feel free to contact me in care of the e-mail or phone appearing above. In advance, thank you for your consideration.

Yours professionally,

Chris Smith

Chris Smith

Legal Associate

Chris Smith
123 Any Street • City, ST 12345 • (555) 555-5555 • *csmith@email.com*

June 1, 200–

SUBJECT: Legal Associate Position

Please consider me a strong candidate for the legal associate position advertised in *Lawyers Weekly*. Upon reading this announcement, I wanted to provide you the enclosed resume, recommendations, and transcripts. As you will note from my resume, I hold a Juris Doctor degree and recently received a Master of Tax and Accounting, with a concentration in estates and trust. As described on each of my supporting documents, my career started as a general practitioner, and, with time, became more involved in estate-planning activities. Thus, it is from a comprehensive foundation of knowledge and professional experience that I now seek to interview for and, I hope, serve in the capacity of Legal Associate.

During our conversations, I will detail the complexity of my work to date and the litigation I have done over the years. As I learn more about your practice's needs and your expectations for the Associate you hire, I will in more specific ways connect my qualifications to the requirements of this position.

I do hope you judge my candidacy as worthy of telephone and, ultimately, in-person meetings. I eagerly await your response to this letter. Thank you for your consideration.

Sincerely,

Chris Smith

Chris Smith

Marketing Analyst

Memo from Chris Smith
123 Any Street
City, ST 12345
(555) 555-5555
csmith@email.com

June 1, 200–

TO: Department of Human Resources
RE: Marketing Analyst Candidacy

I would like to apply for the marketing analyst position advertised in the *Daily News*. As detailed in my attached resume, I have most recently served as a Market Research Consultant and, before that, in diverse roles related to marketing and strategic management research. As you review this document, I trust you will conclude that my candidacy is worthy of an interview. To serve as a review and preview, I offer the following:

- Expertise conducting the research required to develop strategically sound business plans used to generate capital.
- Confidence addressing consumer product, health-care, government agency, and non-profit issues.
- Capacity to develop state-of-the-art, statistically viable projects and cite findings in comprehensive reports.

During an interview, I can share how my previous experience building consumer behavior models using multivariate techniques, including regression and other analyses, have allowed clients, senior management, and others to make informed decisions and create sound campaigns. I have analyzed national survey data, as well as information gained from specialized assessments, offering interpretations of trends in easy-to-review and dynamically illustrated reports and presentations. Please allow me the opportunity to present my greatest assets to you and to learn more about what you expect of your next Marketing Analyst. Thank you for your consideration.

Sincerely,

Chris Smith

Chris Smith

Medical Assistant

Chris Smith
123 Any Street • City, ST 12345 • (555) 555-5555 • *csmith@email.com*

June 1, 200–

SUBJECT: Medical Assistant Candidate

After reviewing your posting on Healthsupport.com, I seek to become an active candidate for this position by submitting the attached resume. As detailed on my resume, I offer the following qualifications:

• Skills and perspectives gained via experience as a home health aide, inpatient claim representative, and, most recently, medical assistant with Smith Rehabilitation Hospital.
• Knowledge of medical terminology, procedure codes, and medical office systems, including related computerized applications.
• Completion of medical assistant studies and current status as a candidate for an associate's degree in Nursing.

The resume provided through your electronic posting system details all of my current diagnostic support, patient care, and preventive health-care education, as well as scheduling, file maintenance, and billing roles. I hope to hear from you if my qualifications meet your needs and, ideally, to arrange an interview. Thank you.

Sincerely,

Chris Smith

Chris Smith

Operations Manager

Chris Smith
123 Any Street • City, ST 12345 • (555) 555-5555 • *csmith@email.com*

June 1, 200–

TO: Personnel Director
RE: Operations Manager Position

I would definitely like to interview for the operations manager position recently posted in the *Democrat-Gazette*. The enclosed resume documents all my professional and academic experiences. While the announcement does reveal some of what you are seeking, during an interview I can learn more about what you would expect of the next operations manager, and I can target my own specific capabilities.

As you review my resume to determine if an interview is appropriate, please pay particular attention to my employment and educational histories. During the past seven years, I have held progressively more responsible positions in sales and marketing, market development, product management, new product introduction, warehousing, and distribution. My titles have included sales and marketing representative and product manager. In these roles, I have been responsible for startup, marketing, and promoting new technology for a manufacturer of architectural and industrial coatings and finishes. Clearly, my overall operations experience would enable me to succeed in similar capacities for your organization.

Academically, I earned a Bachelor of Arts in Economics, and I have completed advanced professional and technical study associated with manufacturing and marketing. Those courses and projects taught me to apply research findings as well as analytical, communication, and decision-making skills to challenging operations, marketing, finance, and personnel-related issues. Now, I wish to apply all the lessons I have learned in the past to future accomplishments as your Operations Manager.

In addition, I will soon be forwarding a reference list and letters of recommendation to support my candidacy. I trust all documentation assists you with your deliberations. Thank you.

Sincerely,

Chris Smith

Chris Smith

Pharmaceutical Sales

Date: June 1, 200–
From: *csmith@email.com*
To: *jobs@email.com*
Subject: Enthusiastic and Qualified Sales Candidate

After success selling tangible products and software services, it is with great focus and the appropriate confidence that I now seek to interview for the pharmaceutical sales position recently posted on *Pharmjobs.com*. Highlighting what appears under the "Objective" heading on my attached resume, I offer:

- Record of success within direct marketing and information-driven sales roles.
- Confidence nurturing relationships via direct calls using information dissemination strategies.
- Capacity to understand and share knowledge of pharmaceutical products and protocols.
- Abilities to set goals, document efforts and outcomes, and maximize achievements.
- Bilingual English-Mandarin abilities and cross-cultural sensitivities.

I do hope that upon review of my credentials, you will agree with the above analysis and allow me the opportunity to expand upon these bullet items in an interview. During direct phone or in-person discussions, I can learn more about this position and your organization and detail how confident I am that I can be a profit-driven and successful sales representative, enhancing prescription rates and sales figures.

I appreciate your reviewing the attached documents, and I look forward to hearing from you soon.

Sincerely,
Chris Smith

Chapter 9

"Cold" Contact Letters to Employers

Communications with potential employers are often self-initiated, or "cold." When making cold contact, you are neither responding to a posting nor contacting someone at the advice of others. You're being proactive in your job search and contacting companies to see if they have a position available that would fit your candidacy. With these letters, it is particularly important to reveal your knowledge of the company you're writing to and the kind of job you're looking for.

Administrative Assistant

Date: June 1, 200–
From: *csmith@email.com*
To: *pcummings@email.com*
Subject: Administrative Assistant Candidate

TO: Pat Cummings, Director of Human Resources
RE: Administrative Assistant Opportunities

Having reviewed Any Corporation's website, I am motivated to share my availability for an administrative assistant position. While no specific opportunities were posted, I want to express my strong desire to meet with you to share motivations and qualifications and to seek consideration for current or anticipated openings.

As detailed in the attached resume, which is targeted to my goal of serving in administrative support roles, I am particularly strong in computer knowledge and user-support experience, with related practical and academic experience. As you will see, I graduated recently with an associate degree in Computer Information Systems from the University of Anywhere. At the University, I worked at the main computer lab for two years and developed knowledge of various PC and Macintosh software used to complete database management, spreadsheet, scheduling, and word-processing tasks. Most recently, I worked as a receptionist with Other Consulting, where I gained exposure to all facets of administrative support, specifically for a firm, like Any Corporation, that markets and provides state-of-the art information technology services. I am well aware of Any Corp's commitment to "excellence in specialized customer service," as stated in your mission statement. I now seek to be among those who transform these words into day-to-day actions and achievements.

I will call to confirm receipt of this inquiry and to discuss whether you believe an in-person meeting would be an appropriate next step. Thank you for your consideration.

Sincerely,
Chris Smith
123 Any Street
City, ST 12345
(555) 555-5555

Admissions Counselor

June 1, 200–

Pat Cummings
Director of Admissions
Any University
pcummings@email.edu

Dear Ms. Cummings:

I'm sure you've heard many say, "I want to work in admissions." Rather than restate the obvious, I would like you to review the attached resume and reference list and think about whether you believe past experience can predict future performance. I am proud of my undergraduate experience, which included working within an admissions office and serving in a number of student life and orientation roles. Now, through this letter, I seek consideration for a position within your office.

Summarizing all that appears on the resume, I offer:

- Specialized admissions experience gained as undergraduate.
- Diverse experiences in student activities, residential life, and orientation areas.
- Confidence in outreach capacities, specifically answering admissions and student life questions, and promoting academic, co-curricular, and developmental strengths of an institution.
- Capacity to educate prospective students and parents, to evaluate admissions documentation, and to effectively contribute to efforts associated with yielding the best students possible.

In an interview, I can describe all of these statements. I do want to become associated with Any University and educate potential applicants, parents, and guidance counselors regarding:

- A curriculum that allows students to learn what they love and love what they learn.
- The challenges and rewards of undergraduate research and Quest courses.
- Specialized offerings like the Early Medical Scholars, Take 5, Study Abroad, Internships, the Senior Scholar Program, 3-2 Programs, and Certificate programs.

I will call your office to confirm your receipt of this e-mail (originals to follow in the mail) and, I do hope, to arrange either a formal employment interview or informal discussion regarding anticipated opportunities. In advance, thank you for your consideration.

Sincerely,

Chris Smith

Chris Smith

Advertising Sales Associate

Chris Smith
123 Any Street • City, ST 12345 • (555) 555-5555 • *csmith@email.com*

June 1, 200–

Pat Cummings
Director of Sales
Any Station
456 Any Street
City, ST 12345

Dear Mr. Cummings:

Given past sales achievements and a desire for a future career in advertising, I would like to explore opportunities at Any Station. While the attached resume details all my accomplishments, I hope to learn about your goals for the station, share how sincere my goals are, and use my persuasive talents when presenting qualifications for a sales position in a phone or in-person meeting.

I have been successful in sales and customer service at a major U.S. freight and parcel carrier. Through my specialized training and experience, I learned the art of creating a strong rapport with clients, assessing their needs, presenting quantitative and qualitative analyses, and demonstrating outstanding customer service to achieve and exceed goals. I am confident that I can contribute to annual sales and profits of Any Station. I will actively support all efforts to raise the station's revenues well above third in the market! I believe the ratings and demographics of the station could be effectively marketed to large and small local, regional, and national businesses, all focused on youth and male target audiences. The newly acquired WWE programming should be an advertising salesperson's greatest asset.

I want to discuss your reactions to this letter and accompanying resume and assess your thoughts regarding adding a new sales professional to your team. Of course, we can address compensation potential as well, for a good salesperson is motivated by outcomes as well as performance-based incentives. I will call you next week to inquire about an interview. Thank you.

Sincerely,

Chris Smith

Chris Smith

Associate Editor

Memo from Chris Smith
123 Any Street
City, ST 12345
(555) 555-5555
csmith@email.com

June 1, 200–

Pat Cummings
Human Resources Director
Any Publishing Company
456 Any Street
City, ST 12345

Dear Ms. Cummings:

As detailed on my attached resume, I have publishing experience associated with scholarly journals and social science, physical science, and engineering publications. Ideally, you will find my background strong enough to warrant consideration for an editorial post at Any Publishing. Specifically, I am seeking a position as an associate editor, project editor, or the equivalent in new book or journal development. The nature of my responsibilities is more important than the titles I have held. On the other hand, book titles like *Medical Miracles, Scientific Breakthroughs of the 90s,* and *The Search for Life,* among those you published last year, would be most important!

The accomplishments we can discuss during an interview include the following:

- Development of a new book series in sociology through all phases of publication, from author contract negation to the creation of a series-marketing plan.
- Acquisition of *Earth Day Every Day,* which was nominated for the Fortmiller Foundation's Prize and is already an academic bestseller.
- Participation in a dynamic engineering program that included the launch of three new journals: *Physical Science, Micro Journal,* and the *Journal of Alternative Energy.*

My academic history includes undergraduate degrees in English literature and social sciences as well as courses relevant to medical publishing: anatomy, physiology, and biology. I hope the depth and breadth of my potential will motivate you to discuss existing or future opportunities. I will be relocating to the New York area later this summer, so I will be available to begin employment anytime thereafter. I will be in New York next week. Could we meet then?

Sincerely,

Chris Smith

Chris Smith

Audiovisual Specialist

Date: June 1, 200–
From: *csmith@email.com*
To: *pcummings@email.com*
Subject: Audiovisual Specialist Candidate

RE: Audiovisual Position

To initiate consideration for audiovisual opportunities with your company, attached is a resume for your review. As you will note, I have fifteen years of educational and media experience. To date, I possess proficiency operating a wide variety of photographic, video, and audio equipment, and I have done so in conference and educational settings. Within each, I was responsible for processing, duplicating, and setting up multimedia presentations, including synchronized slide and audio, laptop, and video-based presentations. Also, as an instructor at Any Community College, I taught a course in multimedia presentation development, focusing on software used in PC and Macintosh environments. My software expertise includes PowerPoint, Firefly, PhotoShop, and MusicMix. Therefore, it would be with great focus and confidence that I would like to assist Any Corporation with:

- Creating and maintaining multimedia and web-based presentations.
- Purchasing, scheduling, and setting up equipment as needed.
- Providing user support for all who develop presentations and use related equipment.

I will be relocating to the area, so it would be ideal if I could interview during my next pre-relocation visit and begin employment soon after. The nature of your manufacturing and marketing of consumer products, specifically all promotions, sales, and marketing efforts, requires a variety of audiovisual needs. I look forward to speaking with you about how I can creatively and enthusiastically address those needs. Thank you for your consideration.

Sincerely,
Chris Smith
123 Any Street
City, ST 12345
(555) 555-5555
csmith@email.com

Chef

Chris Smith
123 Any Street • City, ST 12345 • (555) 555-5555 • csmith@email.com

June 1, 200–

Pat Cummings
Manager
Any Hotel
456 Any Street
City, ST 12345

Dear Ms. Cummings:

I would like to inquire about culinary opportunities at Any Hotel. During the past decade, my titles have ranged from pastry chef and bakery manager to pastry cook. Most recently, in my role at the Bevenshire, I plan and prepare desserts for the restaurant and catering operations, and I have created and manage an extremely popular retail bakery outlet. My first position after graduating from the American Pastry Arts Center and the Gourmet Institute of America was at the Willard Hotel, in Boston, so I do have a strong hotel and catering background. Now, as you at Any Hotel complete your renovations and prepare to expand your wedding planning efforts, I seek to join your team and, as your mission statement cites, "to blend customer service and culinary excellence with profitability."

Because of my ability to organize, train, and work effectively with personnel in quality, high-volume operations, I am able to maintain a conscientious, highly productive work force and profit-focused outcomes. I can oversee training of chefs and other kitchen staff to ensure efficient and profitable operations.

During an interview, I can share how proud I am of the awards I have received for my creative culinary skills and how truly proud I will be to become affiliated with Any Hotel, the recent recipient of the AAA Diamond Award. Perhaps we could meet at the end of the month when I will be in Kentucky for a conference? Alternately, we could begin discussions of potential opportunities by phone. I will call to confirm your receipt of this letter and to discuss next steps. Thank you for your consideration.

Yours sincerely,

Chris Smith

Chris Smith

Computer Software Designer

Date: June 1, 200–
From: *csmith@email.com*
To: *pcummings@email.com*
Subject: Software Design Candidate

TO: Pat Cummings
RE: Software Design Opportunities

As a candidate who will soon earn an MS in Computer Science, I am actively seeking a position in application or system-oriented software design. I hope Any Corporation is now recruiting or will do so in the near future. The opportunity to apply all the skills and talents I have gained in academia and in business settings to the benefit of a major software developer would be challenging and rewarding.

I understand you and your colleagues are now working on major government contracts for specialized applications, on next generations of your popular and profitable AnySoftware programs, and on numerous research and development projects. During an interview, we can discuss my attached resume, and you can determine how and where my background best fits.

Two years as a database designer and six months as an intern at Puttnee Bowles ensured my transition from academic and theoretical thinking to the accurate, on-time development of practical, user-friendly, robust, and secure software projects. As a result of these experiences, and the breadth of my studies, I am confident I can be a successful software designer at Any Corporation. I have considerable experience with DBMS packages, like Oracle, Ingres, DB2, FoxPro, and OS/2 Data Manager.

My competencies include Unix, C, SAS, Pascal, and a variety of other programming languages, including, but not limited to, SUNOS, DOS, and VAX operating systems. I have used, taught, and provided user support for graphics, spreadsheet, database, desktop publishing, word processing, and telecommunication applications.

I hope to get an opportunity to talk with you soon about current or future opportunities at Any Corporation. I look forward to hearing from you.

Sincerely,
Chris Smith
123 Any Street
City, ST 12345
(555) 555-5555
csmith@email.com

Consulting/Management Information Specialist

Date: June 1, 200–
From: *csmith@email.com*
To: *pcummings@email.com*
Subject: MIS Consulting Position

TO: Pat Cummings, Any Consulting
RE: MIS Consultant Candidacy

I trust Any Consulting is in need of a hardworking and intelligent consultant/management information specialist with over ten years of experience. If that is the case, please consider my following qualifications:

- Extensive and diverse computer hardware and software knowledge related to personal computer usage within business and educational settings.
- Expertise assessing hardware and software needs, estimating costs, purchasing, and installing.
- Capacity to hire, train, and monitor performance of Information Systems professionals.
- Experience working with outside consultants, service and product vendors, and third-party temporary and permanent placement agencies.
- Ability to use, teach, and support programming languages, operating systems, and network configurations, as well as word-processing, Internet, database, and spreadsheet applications.

As noted on the attached resume, for the past eight years I have been a performance-driven Information Systems Manager at Maximum Data Systems. Within these capacities I have worked with several IT consulting firms, including Any Consulting. Therefore, I am well aware of the nature of your work, the competencies of your professionals, and the "consultative model" you follow. Also, before that, I served as a consultant for one of your small competitors. It is with focus and reality-based commitment that I seek to re-enter consulting and apply all of my talents to the client-focused efforts of Any Consulting.

I hope to talk to you about current or future opportunities at Any Consulting. I will call to confirm your receipt of this e-mail and, I hope, to arrange either a phone or in-person interview. Of course, I have completed all necessary forms through your online recruiting system. Thank you for your consideration.

Chris Smith
123 Any Street
City, ST 12345
(555) 555-5555
csmith@email.com

Editorial Assistant

Chris Smith
123 Any Street • City, ST 12345 • (555) 555-5555 • csmith@email.com

June 1, 200–

Pat Cummings
Personnel Director
Any Magazine
456 Any Street
City, ST 12345
FAX (555) 555-5557

Dear Ms. Cummings:

I would like to interview for an assistant position or an internship in the editorial department at Any Magazine. Relevant courses and co-curricular experiences have allowed me to develop strong writing, editing, and research skills. My experience associated with music, culinary arts, and contemporary city living should also be of interest to you and your Any Magazine colleagues. It would be wonderful if I could utilize my existing skills and knowledge in the context of my goal to work for a music and lifestyle-related publication. In general, my qualifications presented on the attached resume include:

- Academic and practical strengths in research, editing, writing, and project management gained through undergraduate journalism studies at NYU and experience with student publications.
- Skills and perspectives gained as a research intern for Tradewinds Publishing.
- Writing experience related to contemporary music, culinary arts, and lifestyle issues.
- Ability to interact with authors and editorial colleagues, sharing drafts, revisions, information, and analyses through written and oral communications.

I would welcome the chance to discuss the above qualifications and my attached writing samples in detail. Most important, I look forward to learning more about what would be expected of an assistant or intern and how I could meet and exceed all expectations. I will call to confirm your receipt of my resume and, at your convenience, to arrange an initial phone interview and an in-person meeting. Chicago is home, so I am actively exploring opportunities in the area, and I will be visiting for interviews regularly. Thank you for your consideration.

Sincerely,

Chris Smith

Chris Smith

Elementary School Teacher

Chris Smith
123 Any Street • City, ST 12345 • (555) 555-5555 • csmith@email.com

June 1, 200–

Pat Cummings, Ph.D.
Headmaster
Any Private School
456 Any Street
City, ST 12345

Dear Dr. Cummings:

It is with great enthusiasm for and commitment to elementary education that I inquire about teaching positions at Any Private School. My qualifications and related accomplishments, as noted on the enclosed resume, include:

- Certification in Elementary Education, Music, and Secondary English.
- Experience teaching elementary, junior high, and high school students.
- Competencies teaching choral and instrumental classes and directed choirs and bands.
- Success developing youth music programs by creating musicals tailored to student abilities.
- Experience producing musicals involving students in composing, acting, choreographing, playing instruments, and singing.
- Experience using audio-visual and electric piano computer systems in the classroom.
- Creation of Music & More, a civic musical theatre company composed of multicultural youth.
- Accomplishments as pianist, singer, accompanist, conductor, composer, and writer.

As you prepare to dedicate the new Blake Entertainment Center, I am confident that you and your Any School colleagues, parents, and students anticipate expanding music instruction, choral, and performance offerings. Of course, I would like to discuss how my background could address these special goals, as well as those associated with traditional classroom instruction.

Academically, I earned a Master of Music and Bachelor of Music, as well as teaching certification at the College of Music. Professionally, I have held varied instructional positions. Please, let's meet to discuss your assessment of my potential to be a strong member of Any School's instructional team. Also find enclosed for your review letters of recommendation, sample lessons, and documentation of student performances. Thank you for your consideration.

Sincerely,

Chris Smith

Chris Smith

Financial Analyst

Chris Smith

123 Any Street • City, ST 12345 • (555) 555-5555 • *csmith@email.com*

June 1, 200–

Pat Cummings
Comptroller
Any Corporation
456 Any Street
City, ST 12345
FAX (555) 555-5557

Dear Ms. Cummings:

As a financial analyst with diverse experience, including credit and collections, I have been instrumental in substantially improving cash-flow control and reduction of bad debt risk for a rapidly growing and profitable bank and trust. Now, as I seek to relocate to the St. Louis area, it is with great excitement that I wish to discuss my potential to contribute to the finance area of Any Corporation.

As described on the attached resume, my performance in past years as an analyst, internal audit trainee, and intern has been strong and marked by enhanced responsibilities. When Cartel was acquired by Bridell, I was retained and continued to contribute bottom-line results. However, my desire to move home to St. Louis motivates me to identify new opportunities with companies that can benefit from my expertise. Any Corporation's growth over the past years, including expansion to Canadian and Mexican markets and the aggressive acquisition of smaller competitors, requires strong financial oversight and flow of information to key decision-makers, like you.

I am confident of my ability to set up and manage audit, financial analysis, credit leveraging systems, procedures and controls, and employee training programs that will address Any Corporation's expanding needs.

I would appreciate the opportunity to discuss your visions for the finance area of Any Corporation and how I might contribute as an analyst. I will call to discuss your reactions to this fax (originals to follow by mail) and, I hope, to arrange a meeting when I am next in St. Louis. Thank you.

Sincerely,

Chris Smith

Chris Smith

Fundraiser

Date: June 1, 200–
From: *csmith@email.com*
To: *pcummings@email.com*
Subject: Qualified Fundraising Candidate

TO: Pat Cummings, Any Organization
RE: Fundraising Position

I would like to inquire about fundraising opportunities at Any Organization. I trust the attached resume reveals my commitment to a career in nonprofit development, public relations, and especially fundraising. I have spent the past three years nurturing public relations and fundraising skills as a student, intern, and within varied cocurricular roles. My fundraising, outreach, and related qualifications and achievements are noted on the resume. In summary, these include:

- Experience as fundraiser and program recruiter for campus organization.
- Confidence in event planning, marketing, strategy development, and outreach.
- Capacity to draft and finalize correspondence, promotional materials, and brochures.
- Skill in research, analysis, and presentation associated with lobbying and topical reports.
- Business knowledge gained from courses including Accounting, Finance, and Marketing.

The prospect of someday soon serving in any number of fundraising roles is most exciting—preparing grant proposals, developing and disseminating documentation for fundraising events, writing correspondence and campaign proposals, contributing web-based or printed newsletters, generating donation acknowledgments, and planning special events. Transforming Any Organization's mission "to enhance the potential for young men and women to maximize educational and career opportunity" would be a personal and professional passion. I welcome the chance to speak with you by phone and, ultimately, in person. In fact, I would be happy to pay for my travel if invited to meet with you. In addition to my resume, attached are several writing samples. Thank you for your consideration. I look forward to hearing from you.

Sincerely,
Chris Smith
(555) 555-5555
csmith@email.com

Investment Banking Analyst

Chris Smith

123 Any Street • City, ST 12345 • (555) 555-5555 • *csmith@email.com*

June 1, 200–

Pat Cummings
Managing Director
Any Bank
456 Any Street
City, ST 12345

Dear Ms. Cummings:

I would like to interview for an analyst position at Any Bank. As detailed on my attached resume, which I have uploaded to your firm's online application system, academic and internship experiences inspire me to seek a position like this one. As an Economics major at the University of Rochester, I completed quantitative, modeling, and analytically oriented courses including Macroeconomics, Microeconomics, Money, Credit, Banking, Econometrics, and Statistics. Also, to earn a Management Studies Certificate, I completed Financial Accounting, Corporate Finance, and Marketing Projects and Cases.

My knowledge of cash-flow analysis, asset management, financial markets, and economic variables, and my related research, report-writing, and presentation skills have been fine-tuned in multiple internship settings. Most significant, I worked at UBS Paine Webber in Philadelphia, where I utilized financial data programs to research municipalities to identify risk criteria and investment potential of bond issues.

The qualifications I possess to become a successful analyst include:

- Capacities to succeed within an global investment bank, using research and analytical skills nurtured by a comprehensive Investment Banking Internship as well as economics and business courses.
- Experience conducting research as part of a team, analyzing case studies, completing projects, and making presentations.
- Time-management skills and motivation, enhanced and exemplified through experience as a scholar-athlete.
- Ability to apply knowledge of Word, Excel, Power Point, HTML, Bloomberg, SDC, and Internet applications to research, modeling, spreadsheet, and related projects.

I would welcome the chance to discuss my qualifications for an analyst position when you visit campus. If it would be more convenient for me to visit your office, I would be happy to do so.

Sincerely,

Chris Smith

Chris Smith

Legal Assistant

Chris Smith

123 Any Street • City, ST 12345 • (555) 555-5555 • csmith@email.com

June 1, 200–

Pat Cummings
Director of Human Resources
Any Law Firm
456 Any Street
City, ST 12345
FAX (555) 555-5557

Dear Mr. Cummings:

I would like to inquire about a possible opening for a legal assistant at Any Law Firm. As detailed on my attached resume, I have recently earned a Comprehensive Certificate in Paralegal Studies and a Bachelor of Science in Business Administration. My specialized studies have developed my paralegal skills and perspectives. In addition, my general academic knowledge of accounting, tax, and finance issues provide a strong foundation upon which I can build an accomplishment-filled legal research, litigation support, project management, and paralegal career at Any Firm.

As I completed the above-cited studies, I served as a mediation intern with the Attorney General's office during school and in the summers. In these capacities I fine-tuned my research, mediation, writing, editing, document management, and file preparation talents. Also, I have experience in all aspects of administrative support, so I am proud that those considered "support professionals" are critical team members. Please allow me the privilege to join the 30 or so members of the Any Firm team, working on labor, contractual, and corporate issues, for esteemed clients including ABC Management, Inc., and Any Corporation. In academic and employment settings, I have completed many projects requiring time management, writing, editing, and presentation talents. I certainly wish to do so as a legal assistant at your firm.

I hope that I have the chance to discuss my qualifications with you in person or, if more convenient, by phone. I will call to confirm your receipt of this fax (originals to follow by mail) and to discuss your reactions to my request for consideration and an interview.

Yours sincerely,

Chris Smith

Chris Smith

Librarian

Date: June 1, 200–
From: *csmith@email.com*
To: *pcummings@email.com*
Subject: Librarian Position

Pat Cummings
Director, Personnel
Any Library
456 Any Street
City, ST 12345

As detailed on the attached resume, I am an experienced researcher who has worked extensively with archival records and secondary sources. Currently, I am seeking an opportunity to apply my research skills in a full-time position as a librarian.

By training and experience, I have long sought to transform the importance of precise organization and the thoughtful use of evidence to make clear historical arguments. My work in the Library of Congress, the Boston Public Library, and the Hauptstaatarchiv Stuttgart, all involving the support of library professionals, has revealed to me the power of those who hold positions like the one I now seek at Any Library. To be among those who support the research efforts of our nation's finest scholars, students, and faculty would be a professional dream come true.

Most recently, as a librarian and as a consultant at Boston University, I have gained valuable experience supervising staff members, working directly with students and professors, and instructing departments on new reference procedures. I also have experience with automated library reference networks and web-based archival and retrieval systems. Please, let's do speak regarding how I may best contribute to the staff of Any Library. I will call to confirm your receipt of this e-mail and, I hope, to arrange a meeting when we can discuss any current or anticipated openings for a librarian. Thank you for your consideration.

Sincerely,
Chris Smith
(555) 555-5555

Management Consulting Analyst

Chris Smith
123 Any Street • City, ST 12345 • (555) 555-5555 • *csmith@email.com*

June 1, 200–

Pat Cummings
Undergraduate Recruiting Coordinator
Consulting Firm
456 Any Street
City, ST 12345

Dear Ms. Cummings:

I am an Economics and Statistics major at the University of Rochester. In addition, I will also earn a Certificate in Management Studies, with a Finance and Accounting track, for completion of business, finance, and accounting courses. I would like to interview for a position as an Analyst at Consulting Firm.

Ideally, I will contribute to the following practice areas: financial analysis, management strategies, and business development. Detailed in the attached resume, I offer fine-tuned research, analysis, and writing capabilities. My courses to date include Finance, Statistics, and Econometrics. In academia I have learned to utilize fact-gathering, regression and trend analysis, valuation, and writing techniques, all directly applicable to the efforts of consulting case teams. I seek to transform "value added through analysis and implementation," from words into mission-driven activities.

My knowledge of economic research, statistical analyses, report-writing, and presentation skills have been developed in academic contexts. They are reflected in academic achievements, and, I trust, are applicable to being an Analyst at Consulting Firm. I welcome the chance to meet with you to discuss my qualifications. During that conversation, I can elaborate upon my internship with the Organization for Economic Cooperation and Development, upon statistics classes including Linear Regression Models and Sampling Techniques, and upon the numerous data-driven papers I have written. Of course, samples of my writing are available upon request.

Ideally, you will judge my candidacy as worthy of an initial telephone or in-person interview. I would be happy to travel home to the Washington, D.C., area at any mutually convenient interview date and time. Thank you.

Sincerely,

Chris Smith

Chris Smith

Chris Smith

123 Any Street • City, ST 12345 • (555) 555-5555 • *csmith@email.com*

June 1, 200–

Pat Cummings
Director of Human Resources
Any Corporation
456 Any Street
City, ST 12345

Dear Mr. Cummings:

I would like to inquire about any openings for a departmental manager at Any Corporation. In my six years at Kimco, as detailed on my enclosed resume, I was responsible for directing and coordinating the activities of accounting and support personnel in a $10 million manufacturing operation. I concurrently managed the cutting room and handled the purchase of approximately $5 million in raw materials, supplies, and capital equipment.

To succeed in these broad managerial roles required problem-solving skills, goal identification, entrepreneurial perspectives, and the ability to manage varied responsibilities in a small yet active manufacturing operation, very similar to the activities of Any Corporation. While I was departmental manager, the company increased profits and was able to expand its staff by 15 percent. I understand that Any Corporation is about to expand its manufacturing operations and hire additional staff. I hope to be among those who join your organization and one who positively influences continued profitable growth.

I would appreciate the opportunity to further discuss my qualifications for a management position. I will call your office to confirm your receipt of this letter and, if you judge my candidacy as worthy, to arrange a meeting. If you prefer, we can conduct telephone interviews prior to an in-person meeting. Of course, references are available upon request. Thank you for your consideration.

Sincerely,

Chris Smith

Chris Smith

Marketing Director

Chris Smith

123 Any Street • City, ST 12345 • (555) 555-5555 • *csmith@email.com*

June 1, 200–

Pat Cummings
Vice President of Marketing
Any Corporation
456 Any Street
City, ST 12345
FAX (555) 555-5557

Dear Ms. Cummings:

It takes a seasoned marketing professional to provide leadership, motivation, and strategies to introduce new products, oversee manufacturing and distribution, establish and implement advertising and promotion campaigns, develop profitable territories, and direct a productive and profitable marketing team. I am proud of all the marketing-related accomplishments appearing on my attached resume. It would be with continued professional pride, ambition, and goal-direction that I would serve as a marketing director, brand manager, or related title at Any Corporation. Please grant me the opportunity to discuss my hopes for the future, as well as your goals for your organization during an interview.

I offer extensive marketing experience, including over a decade as director of marketing operations and brand manager for a multimillion-dollar imaging and scanning systems manufacturer. This position required marketing decision-making and management abilities at the broadest levels and successfully establishing new markets and major contacts regionally and nationally.

During my time in this marketing-director position, I have achieved much. My qualifications for a related position with Any Corporation, a manufacturer and marketer of optical scanning and mapping devices, are all cited on my resume, along with details of all my achievements. But a resume can reveal only so much. If you feel that my abilities would benefit you and your marketing colleagues, I hope you will give me the opportunity to discuss them with you further. My travel to the Bay Area is frequent. Please, let's meet soon. Thank you for your consideration.

Yours sincerely,

Chris Smith

Chris Smith

Mutual Funds Broker

Chris Smith

123 Any Street • City, ST 12345 • (555) 555-5555 • *csmith@email.com*

June 1, 200–

Pat Cummings
Vice President, Asset Management
Any Brokers, Inc.
456 Any Street
City, ST 12345
FAX (555) 555-5557

Dear Mr. Cummings:

As is described with pride and in detail on my enclosed resume, I have over a decade of experience in the financial services arena. Now, as I look ahead to future challenges and, of course, rewards, I seek to focus on a specialized area of expertise—mutual funds. Therefore, it is with great focus, confidence gained from a history of success, and the enthusiasm of seeking new circumstances that I seek consideration for a brokerage position at Any Brokers.

Highlighting all I wish to discuss during telephone and, ultimately, in-person interviews, my qualifications include:

- Over a decade of progressively significant roles and achievements in planning portfolio management and client services.
- Personal responsibilities for more than $210 million in client assets.
- Recognition for outstanding asset-based performance and customer services.
- After completion of the ABC Financial Consultant Sales Training and Advanced Training, served as trainer and curriculum developer.
- Licensed Series 6, 7, 63 and health and life insurance.

Much of the advice given to clients deals with purchasing of mutual funds and managing portfolios with these funds, so I am well aware of the intricacies of this field, of the distinctions between products, and the clientele most likely to invest in particular funds. The attached newsletters reveal my views. Please, let's talk about my potential to succeed at Any Brokers, about my desires to either expand your business on the island, and, if more appropriate, about my willingness to relocate to Southern California. I will call to confirm receipt of this fax and to discuss next steps.

Sincerely,

Chris Smith

Chris Smith

Public Relations Assistant

Chris Smith

123 Any Street • City, ST 12345 • (555) 555-5555 • *csmith@email.com*

June 1, 200–

Pat Cummings
Vice President, Human Resources
Zepf, Costigan, and Nardizzi
456 Any Street
City, ST 12345

Dear Ms. Cummings:

I would like to inquire about the possibility of a position as a public relations assistant with Zepf, Costigan, and Nardizzi. Since earning degrees in Journalism and Public Relations, I have gained experience as an assistant with a modeling and talent agency and a modeling school. As an active supporter of and participant in model recruitment and placement efforts, I have worked with key accounts driven to achieve enhanced image-building and high visibility for client services or products. I have served as a liaison with public relations professionals who were planning and implementing special events and seeking to maximize publicity for these efforts. In fact, I worked on the Dodge, NBA, and Clinique campaigns with members of the Zepf, Costigan, and Nardizzi team. Please feel free to discuss my potential to serve as an assistant with Francis Justin, Kelly Burton, or Jordan Blake.

Media relationships were developed as I selected and placed models for television commercials. I have the skills to coordinate creative programs and innovative functions involving clients and the general public, and, clearly, I feel confident I could successfully apply my experience to a position in your firm.

Please allow me the opportunity to directly share my motivations as well as qualifications via an interview. I will be in Los Angeles at the end of the month and wonder if it would be possible to arrange for an interview. Of course, I would be happy to travel at my own expense to meet at any time convenient for you. Thank you for your consideration.

Sincerely,

Chris Smith

Chris Smith

School and Community Counselor

Chris Smith
123 Any Street
City, ST 12345
(555) 555-5555
csmith@email.com

June 1, 200–

Pat Cummings, Ph.D.
Director
Any Center
456 Any Street
City, ST 12345

Dear Ms. Cummings:

My involvement with a number of counseling centers has given me the opportunity to become familiar with counseling models used to address the needs of many special populations. In anticipation of a relocation to Dallas, I have researched a number of facilities and am particularly intrigued by Any Center's offerings. Therefore, I would welcome consideration for a full-time or part-time counseling position.

Professionally, I have developed my counseling, advising, referral, and case management skills as a mental health intern, graduate assistant, and school counselor. Client issues ranged from adolescent development and alcoholism to substance abuse, as well as learning and emotional disabilities. I have successfully followed all protocols and documentation required of schools, state facilities, and private residential and day treatment programs. I have counseled clients ranging in ages from 4 to 24, and specifically addressed ADHD, ODD, and learning disabilities within a team context, including teachers, parents, outside professionals, and the student in planning and implementation. It would be an ideal next professional step to work at Any Center, with adolescents dealing with many of the issues cited, and using a rational emotive and behavioral approach to treatment.

Academically, I earned a Ph.D. in Counseling and Human Development, and my doctoral dissertation reveals a strong interest in ethnic identity issues. These interests are reinforced within my attached statement of professional philosophy. Please, let's discuss anticipated openings and how my background might match Any Center's needs. I will be in Dallas permanently as of next month. Perhaps we could meet then. Thank you for your consideration.

Sincerely,

Chris Smith

Chris Smith

Television Production Assistant

Date: June 1, 200–
From: *csmith@email.com*
To: *pcummings@email.com*
Subject: PA Position

TO: Pat Cummings, Production Director

I would like to inquire about a Production Assistant or intern position at Any Television Station. This May, I graduated from the University of Hawaii-Hilo, with a Bachelor of Arts in Communications. Throughout my education, I have completed relevant broadcast communication courses dealing with production, writing, and research. In development of my copywriting and editing skills, I was also actively involved in the university newspaper. For a number of course projects, all detailed on the attached resume, I wrote copy for, taped, and edited two- and five-minute feature and news stories and critiqued the efforts of my peers. In addition, I researched local events and entertainment talent, conducted interviews, and wrote articles for the entertainment section of the paper.

Last summer, and most relevant to my request to interview for a PA position, I worked as an intern for KBZT-TV's *Island Beat*. In these capacities, I had the opportunity to co-produce a local talk show, which required that I pre-interview and schedule guests, handle financial and transportation details, and research show topics. I also networked resource organizations to locate potential guests and panel members. I wish to bring all the talents, ambition, and commitment I developed as an intern and a student to Any Station. While I am most interested in PA opportunities, I would welcome consideration for an internship as well.

I will be in Honolulu next week. Would it be possible to schedule an interview? If not, I would be happy to meet with you whenever convenient. I will call to confirm receipt of this e-mail and to discuss your thoughts regarding next steps. Thank you for your consideration.

Sincerely,
Chris Smith
123 Any Street
City, ST 12345
(555) 555-5555

Chapter 10

Broadcast Letters to Employers

Broadcast letters are, by definition, distributed to many employers. Thus, they are less focused. Format may appear similar to other letters, and it is most important to have the company name appear prominently early. While less company-specific information is contained, you must still show readers that you know the organization's name and the nature of their business. Be aware that quantity of letters is not as crucial as the quality of content. Broadcast letters can be good first efforts and momentum builders, if you maintain appropriate expectations and follow up effectively.

Administrative Assistant

June 1, 200–

TO: Pat Cummings, Any Medical Office
SUBJECT: Administrative Assistant Position

Are you currently in need of an administrative assistant with over a decade of experience and a commitment to supporting the needs of patients and supervisors and to working effectively with peers? If yes, please review the attached resume and consider my candidacy for a position with Any Company.

Summarizing, the qualifications I offer include:

- Skills and perspectives gained through progressively responsible administrative roles.
- Abilities to prioritize tasks and complete tasks accurately and on time in deadline-sensitive settings.
- Professionalism required to address concerns of patients and clients while maintaining office efficiency.
- Flexibility required to transform instructions and feedback of diverse supervisors into projects completed independently and thoroughly.
- Capacities to use, support, and train others to use Word, WordPerfect, Excel, Access, and FileMaker Pro.

As detailed on my attached resume, I have worked in a hospital setting, where I learned all critical terminology, how to address specialized billing and support issues, and what is required to support the needs of physicians, nurses, and health-care practitioners. I now am actively seeking the opportunity to return to a challenging and rewarding medical setting. I do hope that it is with Any Medical Office. I will call to confirm receipt of this letter, to determine if you have current or anticipated openings, and, if you wish, to arrange an interview. Thank you for your consideration.

Sincerely,

Chris Smith

Chris Smith

Admissions and Enrollment Manager

Chris Smith
123 Any Street • City, ST 12345 • (555) 555-5555 • csmith@email.com

June 1, 200–

Pat Cummings
Vice President of Enrollment Management
Any School
456 Any Street
City, ST 12345

Dear Ms. Cummings:

I trust the enclosed resume, specifically the Admissions Achievements section, highlights my qualifications for an admissions and enrollment management position. Within my professional capacities, I have held titles of Senior Assistant Director and Director of International Recruitment, as well as Assistant Director and Counselor. I have successfully worked in recruitment, candidate assessment, yield, and retention. Now, I seek enhanced roles and responsibilities and challenges at Any School.

With the assistance of colleagues, I doubled the number of international candidates completing applications and interviews and those receiving offers to enroll at Seton Hall University. The key to successful recruitment has been promoting the educational, cocurricular, and employment assets of undergraduate programs, while providing candidates exceptional and personal customer service and advising. Well-informed applicants, generated through extensive outreach, are the cornerstone of any successful admissions undertaking. Admissions and enrollment management success is a function of sharing knowledge of and passion for undergraduate education with local, regional, national, and international applicants.

My in-depth knowledge of admissions, enrollment strategies, and processes, along with my appreciation for how academic, athletic, cocurricular, and residential communities can be marketed, make me an enthusiastic and, I trust, qualified candidate for a position at Any School. I hope to build upon my experiences at Seton Hall and Rutgers at your school. I would be pleased if I could elaborate on my past experience and future ambitions through an interview; perhaps next week's AAAP convention would be a good time for us to talk. I will inquire soon to confirm your receipt of this letter, to learn if you are currently expanding your operation, and to identify appropriate next steps. Thank you for your consideration.

Sincerely,

Chris Smith

Chris Smith

Advertising Intern

Fax from Chris Smith
123 Any Street
City, ST 12345
(555) 555-5555
csmith@email.com

Recruitment Coordinator
Any Advertising
456 Any Street
City, ST 12345
FAX (555) 555-5557

I would very much like to interview for an internship at Any Agency. While a typical cover letter might list qualities and refer you to an enclosed resume (as this one will do), I trust that upon review of my resume and this letter, and after we meet, you will conclude that I am not a "typical candidate."

Honestly, prior to the completion of my active career exploration, I thought all jobs in the field required individuals to be "creative in an artistic way." Having done my homework, I now know that account management interns and professionals must be "imaginative in a business and project-focused manner" and able to inspire creativity in others. As a founding father of advertising once said, "The consumer isn't a moron; she is your wife. You insult her intelligence if you assume that a mere slogan and a few vapid adjectives will persuade her to buy anything. She wants all the information you can give her." I do not wish to insult your intelligence, but I do seek the opportunity to give you all the information I can through an interview.

At first, I can present my qualifications and motivations via this letter and attached resume. After, through telephone interviews, I can answer any questions you have and support my candidacy for an internship at Any Agency. I plan to be in New York during spring break, in mid-March. If an in-person interview is required, we could meet then. Should you wish to communicate with me, please do so via the e-mail or phone above. Thank you for your consideration.

Sincerely,

Chris Smith

Chris Smith

Chiropractor

Chris Smith
123 Any Street • City, ST 12345 • (555) 555-5555 • *csmith@email.com*

June 1, 200–

Pat Cummings
Managing Partner
Any Practice
456 Any Street
City, ST 12345
FAX (555) 555-5557

Dear Mr. Cummings:

I am a certified chiropractor currently exploring affiliations with established practices. As cited on my attached resume, I have worked in the Chicago area for over twenty years and, as a result, my reputation for quality care is well known. While I am confident your practice can offer me much, I do offer much in return.

Currently, I work as a chiropractic therapist with the Chicago Chiropractic Center, a position I have held for the past fifteen years. In this capacity, I provide spinal manipulation and handle necessary musculoskeletal needs of sports-injury patients, alleviate pain in elderly and work-related patients, and assist the industrial-accident–injured in regaining strength and stamina.

Like you and your Any Practice colleagues, I am an active member of the American Chiropractic Association, Illinois Chiropractic Society, Chicago Chiropractic Society, and the Sports Injury Council of the American Chiropractic Association. Perhaps we could discuss my desire to join your practice during the upcoming Illinois State ACA conference here in Chicago?

I look forward to hearing from you if my qualifications are of interest to you. Please feel free to e-mail or call via the information above and on my resume.

Sincerely,

Chris Smith

Chris Smith

Credit Manager

Chris Smith
123 Any Street • City, ST 12345 • (555) 555-5555 • csmith@email.com

June 1, 200–

Pat Cummings
Director
Any Company
456 Any Street
City, ST 12345

Dear Mr. Cummings:

I am seeking a position as credit manager, to which I bring many years of successful credit-management experience. Ideally, you and your colleagues are in need of someone to over-see credit operations, motivate credit professionals, and train those involved in this crucial area.

During the past ten years, as credit manager with a $20 million manufacturing and distribution firm, I have successfully set up and enforced credit controls, resulting in reducing DSO from 60 days to 33. I am continually involved in training personnel in credit and collection policies and procedures, troubleshooting and resolving sales and customer disputes, and making credit and collection decisions to reduce bad-debt risk and increase cash flow. Now, as I prepare to relocate to your area, I remain enthusiastic that I can find an exciting and challenging new employer and continue an accomplishment-filled career.

Based on my past contributions to the credit profession, I received recognition through NACM New England as Credit Executive of the Year in 2000 and was elected the president of the same professional credit association for the 2002–2003 term.

I look forward to hearing from you if you have a suitable position available or if you have any referrals. While I would welcome consideration for employment with Any Company, I would appreciate your suggestions regarding others I should contact in the area. Thank you for your consideration.

Sincerely,

Chris Smith

Chris Smith

Freight Supervisor

Chris Smith

123 Any Street • City, ST 12345 • (555) 555-5555 • *csmith@email.com*

June 1, 200–

Human Resources
Any Corporation
456 Any Street
City, ST 12345
FAX (555) 555-5557

During the past thirteen years, I have been actively involved in positions as field manager of container operations and night operations supervisor of freight stations and service centers, dealing with domestic and international freight deliveries. Now I seek to continue my career as a freight supervisor, ideally with Any Corporation.

In addition to supervising day-to-day operations, my experience encompasses hiring, training, and supervising drivers, office, and support personnel, as well as providing cost-effective, quality service within a multiple service network. All my previously held positions and references are listed on the attached resume. You will also find enclosed a letter of recommendation written by one of my freight and transportation colleagues. After you review these supporting documents, you will see that I have sound knowledge of computer systems for freight movement management. I am also clearly skilled in both troubleshooting and resolving problems related to the movement of materials and to the personnel who make these activities possible.

I would welcome the opportunity to discuss whether Any Corporation has a need for someone with my background and whether you would be willing to consider me for immediate or future employment. Please feel free to contact me through the information above. I will, of course, call the human resource office to confirm your receipt of this fax (originals to follow by mail) and to confirm the appropriate person to contact directly. Thank you for your consideration.

Sincerely,

Chris Smith

Chris Smith

Marketing/Sales Executive

Date: June 1, 200–
From: *csmith@email.com*
To: *pcummings@email.com*
Subject: Marketing/Sales Candidate

TO: Pat Cummings, Chief Account Executive
RE: Marketing and Sales Position

As you will see when you review the attached resume, I am a seasoned marketing and sales professional seeking to join an aggressive young firm like Any Corporation. Through telephone or in-person interviews, I can share my extensive experience and achievements in marketing, business development, and product management at national and international levels.

During an interview, I will describe how my past successes, described below, required skills that will lead to future achievements with Any Corporation. My sales and marketing accomplishments to date include:

- Developing sales programs and new businesses to increase penetration, market share, and revenue using advanced, technically sophisticated systems-management services.
- Participating in development and marketing teams for new service products for a service business generating $3.7 billion worldwide.
- Assuming profit-and-loss responsibility for an added-value services business generating $90 million.
- Establishing a record for producing positive bottom-line results in a high-tech, service-oriented business with worldwide markets.

I am well qualified to direct areas that are key to achieving your sales and profit objectives. If you have such a position open, I look forward to hearing from you. Please contact me in care of the information below. I will, as any good salesperson should, follow up this e-mail with a phone call and assess your interest in arranging an interview. Thank you for your consideration.

Sincerely,
Chris Smith
123 Any Street
City, ST 12345
(555) 555-5555
csmith@email.com

Optics Researcher

Chris Smith
123 Any Street • City, ST 12345 • (555) 555-5555 • *csmith@email.com*

June 1, 200–

Pat Cummings
Any Corporation
456 Any Street
City, ST 12345

Dear Mr. Cummings:

My postgraduate objective is to begin a career in optical engineering research at Any Corporation. Relevant courses in optics, mathematics, and physics, as well as my co-op and related experience, have enabled me to develop related practical skills and perspectives. These include:

- Knowledge of optical engineering theory and its application.
- Skills gained through optics, chemistry, imaging systems, and physics courses and laboratories.
- Product management skills, including the ability to identify a client's problems, implement solutions, and produce a desired end product.
- Quality-control experience including ISO and scratch/dig standards attained through work experience, technical courses, customers, and suppliers.
- Experience representing a company by interfacing with potential customers at a national trade show.
- Proficiency in applications including Matlab, Photoshop, MathCAD, Mathematica, MS Office Suite Applications, Explorer, and Netscape.

As noted on the attached resume, I will be graduating in December from the University of Rochester. I have experience working as a researcher and as an optical engineer. Specifically through my experience at Sine Patterns, I developed qualifications applicable to Any Company, including:

- Ability to operate microlithography and photographic equipment.
- Capacity to transform stated needs of customers into completed products including optical masks, resolution charts, reticles, and custom film.
- Knowledge of product management and quality-control issues.
- Specialized skills associated with team and independent tasks and projects.

Because I will be available to start immediately after receipt of my degree, around January 1, I would certainly appreciate the opportunity to speak with you soon regarding your anticipated hiring needs. Thank you for your consideration.

Sincerely,

Chris Smith

Chris Smith

Project Manager

Date: June 1, 200–
From: *csmith@email.com*
To: *pcummings@email.com*
Subject: Project Manager Position

As a program manager interested in establishing connections with a new, up-and-coming firm, I submit the attached resume for your review. The qualifications presented on my resume include over twelve years' managing experience with Ricochet Data. In this capacity, I developed and coordinated short- and long-range plans for designing and introducing four new microcomputers. I also created master charts to track major milestones and critical-path activities, directed a management task force to develop a set of work instructions for introducing outsourced products, and reduced product time to market by 25 percent. Thus, my project management achievements are well documented. Through an interview, I can share my potential to contribute to Any Company's manufacturing, marketing, operations, and distribution efforts.

My experience in retail management might also be of interest. While employed at Lorenz Company, I generated gross annual sales in excess of $2 million for four consecutive years, managed a sales and service team of twenty people, and provided superior customer service and support. Academically, I earned my bachelor's degree while employed, without negatively impacting my performance in any way. I also completed numerous project-management training seminars, all noted on my resume, and related cases and projects. I welcome the chance to discuss these with an appropriate Any Company representative by phone or in person. Should my qualifications match your current or anticipated needs, I hope to hear from you. Please use the information below if you wish additional information or if you want to schedule a formal interview or informal conversation.

Sincerely,
Chris Smith
123 Any Street
City, ST 12345
(555) 555-5555
csmith@email.com

Senior Vice President, Banking

Chris Smith

123 Any Street • City, ST 12345 • (555) 555-5555 • *csmith@email.com*

June 1, 200–

Pat Cummings
President
Any Bank
456 Any Street
City, ST 12345
FAX (555) 555-5557

Dear Ms. Cummings:

As you know through our regular interactions as members of the Missouri Bankers Association, I am currently a senior vice president at Central St. Louis Bank. The recent acquisition of CSB necessitates my communicating with other financial institutions, actively seeking consideration for a Senior Vice President position. Highlighting what is detailed on the attached resume, my qualifications and capabilities include:

- Fifteen years of diverse experience, ranging from acting branch manager and district manager to senior vice president.
- Supervision of all internal departments, including sales and account development, human resources, customer relations and customer service, and product and sales support.
- Responsibility for an increase in new business by 25 percent in one year through extensive interface with clients, decision-makers, and support personnel.

Although my present position is challenging, and I have a record of success within these capacities, my future is with another organization, like Any Bank. Ideally, my next position will address both national and international banking markets and will call upon me to continue an accomplishment-filled career as a leader, motivator, and achiever. Let's discuss your reaction to my request for consideration.

I look forward to hearing from you if an appropriate opportunity is currently available or if you anticipate one becoming available in the near future. Thank you for your consideration.

Sincerely,

Chris Smith

Chris Smith

Chapter 11

Contacting Employment Agencies

Employment agencies and those who work there most often deal with temporary, temp-to-perm, or experienced opportunities. In truth, they don't find jobs for people—they find candidates for the jobs posted with them. Depending on your job-search circumstances, temporary assignments with the possibility to lead to permanent offers are great transition positions. As a qualified and driven candidate, you should be attractive to employment agencies. Be aware of what they can and cannot do. Keep your expectations of any agency realistic, but do consider these organizations as additional resources.

Accounting Manager

Chris Smith
123 Any Street • City, ST 12345 • (555) 555-5555 • *csmith@email.com*

June 1, 200–

Pat Cummings
Director
Any Employment, Inc.
456 Any Street
City, ST 12345

Dear Ms. Cummings:

The enclosed resume outlines my diverse and in-depth experience in accounting and finance management. I am in search of an appropriate opportunity in the greater Missouri area. As detailed on my resume, the following are some of the strengths and capabilities I bring to a position:

• Solid understanding of financial statement preparation and review.
• Proficiency at budget preparation and written analysis.
• Expertise using Excel to complete spreadsheet analysis and proprietary software programs to track data and generate reports.
• Proven ability to organize department goals to meet overall corporate goals.
• Competence in resource management, both people and systems.
• Strong leadership qualities, including motivating staff.

I would welcome the opportunity to meet with you to discuss my background and credentials. Ideally, you currently have a client firm in need of a candidate with my abilities and capabilities. I do hope that you judge me qualified for one or more searches being conducted by Any Employment. After we speak, I trust you will refer my candidacy to employers who have posted those opportunities with you. I will call to confirm receipt of this letter and accompanying resume and to arrange either a telephone or in-person interview.

Thank you for your consideration.

Sincerely,

Chris Smith

Chris Smith

Chris Smith
123 Any Street • City, ST 12345 • (555) 555-5555 • *csmith@email.com*

June 1, 200–

Pat Cummings
Partner
Any Employment Agency
456 Any Street
City, ST 12345
FAX (555) 555-5557

Dear Mr. Cummings:

If one of your clients is in need of a highly motivated bookkeeper with the experience and enthusiasm needed to handle the day-to-day details necessary to ensure smooth operation, I would appreciate your consideration of my candidacy on behalf of that client. The attached resume illustrates my bookkeeping experience and the diverse nature of the settings where I have succeeded to date.

During the past nine years, I have been employed in a variety of industries, including manufacturing, distribution, property management, retail, and automotive services. In progressively responsible positions, I have gained in-depth experience in accounting, bookkeeping, administration, office maintenance, and customer service. I have sound knowledge of credit policies and collection procedures to control accounts receivable and loss reduction while retaining good customer relations and business. My accounts payable efforts have always balanced with cash flow and management responsibilities.

Although my preference is to stay in Hawaii, I would consider relocation to California, so referral to one of your California offices would be welcomed. Of course, factors including salary, benefits, and future opportunity for growth will influence my enthusiasm for particular opportunities that may now be available via Any Employment Agency. My present salary is $38,000, so I am motivated to maximize my earnings and increase this amount by at least 10 percent.

I will follow this fax with a call to determine if a telephone interview or in-person meeting would be appropriate next steps. In addition, I would welcome the opportunity to communicate directly with any of your client employers.

Sincerely,

Chris Smith

Chris Smith

Chef

Chris Smith

123 Any Street • City, ST 12345 • (555) 555-5555 • *csmith@email.com*

June 1, 200–

Pat Cummings
Director
Any Employment Agency
456 Any Street
City, ST 12345
FAX (555) 555-5557

SUBJECT: CHEF POSITION AND RELOCATION

I will be moving to the Dayton area, and I would like the assistance of Any Employment Agency as I search for exciting new positions. The advertisement in *Today's Cook* is most appealing. I would like consideration for this particular position, and your announcement also inspires confidence that you will have other client postings that match my qualifications.

As detailed on the attached resume, I have experience in a wide variety of settings, including restaurants, catering, and banquet facilities. My areas of expertise include all aspects of food preparation and presentation as well as kitchen management, including ordering, hiring, and training. I now work at the McGuiness Inn. I will leave this establishment with positive references and a history of planning seasonal menus, overseeing all preparation of traditional American cuisine. In addition to cooking to order, I perform in scheduling, inventory control, and customer-relations roles. Also, together with the owners, I expanded a fledgling wedding business to a strong revenue generator. My previous sous chef and apprentice positions are all described on the resume, and I have taken the liberty of providing some sample menus as well.

I will soon visit Dayton to secure housing. Perhaps we could meet to discuss my ambitions and qualifications? Ideally, you now have employers in search of candidates, and I could also interview with them during my upcoming visit. Also, please be aware that I would welcome consideration for positions within an hour's commute from Dayton. I will call to discuss your thoughts regarding my candidacy and to clarify next steps. Thank you for your consideration.

Sincerely,

Chris Smith

Chris Smith

Claims Processor

Date: June 1, 200–
From: *csmith@email.com*
To: *pcummings@email.com*
Subject: Claims Processing Position

TO: Pat Cummings, Employment Specialist

I would like to interview for the Claims Processor position recently posted on Jobs.com. My interest in this specific position, along with my desire to secure a position of claims processor with any of your client companies, has inspired me to forward my resume for your review. As a qualified and motivated candidate with a record of past achievements, I now seek opportunities to continue an accomplishment-focused career in claims with a firm that has now posted an opportunity with Any Employment Agency.

My directly related experience as an inpatient claim representative and as a medical assistant with Marifield Rehabilitation Hospital has required that I develop a knowledge of medical terminology, procedure codes, and medical office systems, including related computerized applications. Also, serving as a home health aide will enhance my abilities to conduct thorough, policy-holder–sensitive inquiries regarding claims. All my past experience is detailed on the attached resume.

I trust you recall that a number of years ago, I communicated with you and your colleague, Francis Williams, regarding my interest in claims. As a result, you placed me at Marifield Rehab. Now I seek your professional assistance again. Ideally, a new position would allow me to stay on Long Island, but I would be happy to interview for positions in Manhattan or those that would require relocation to New Jersey. I would very much like to discuss all of my professional and personal goals, including salary, with you or one of your Any Employment Agency partners. I will call to confirm your receipt of this email (originals to follow by mail), and I would be available to speak with any of your client employers whenever mutually convenient. Thank you for your consideration.

Sincerely,

Chris Smith

Chris Smith

Dental Assistant

Date: June 1, 200–
From: *csmith@email.com*
To: *pcummings@email.com*
Subject: Dental Assistant

Pat Cummings
Associate
Any Employment Agency
456 Any Street
City, ST 12345

Dear Ms. Cummings:

As described on my attached resume, I am a trained dental assistant with several years of clinical and administrative experience. I am conducting a search for a full-time or part-time position in the Indianapolis area. I have heard about your agency's placement record through several colleagues, so I am very enthusiastic about current or future client postings that match my professional abilities. Any assistance that Any Employment Agency could provide me in securing such a position would be much appreciated.

To highlight the details of my resume and the attached letter of recommendation, my qualifications are as follows:

- Over six years of experience as a dental assistant, contributing to direct patient care and patient relations.
- Honor graduate as a dental assistant from National Education Center.
- Sound knowledge of medical terminology and clinical procedures.
- Certified in first aid, cardiopulmonary resuscitation, and electrocardiography.
- Additional experience as a receptionist/secretary with an executive search/management consulting firm, a financial management company, and realty firms.

My compensation requirement is in the mid-twenties. I am available to start as soon as needed, and relocation is easy to arrange. Please, let's talk by phone regarding appropriate next steps, and, should you judge appropriate, to arrange an in-person meeting. I would be happy to travel to Indianapolis to meet with you or one of your clients whenever necessary. I look forward to speaking with you soon. In advance, thank you for your time and consideration.

Sincerely,

Chris Smith

Chris Smith

Executive Assistant

Chris Smith
123 Any Street • City, ST 12345 • (555) 555-5555 • *csmith@email.com*

June 1, 200–

Pat Cummings
Associate
Any Employment Agency
456 Any Street
City, ST 12345
FAX (555) 555-5557

Dear Ms. Cummings:

Please consider me an enthusiastic and qualified candidate for the Executive Assistant position recently posted in the *Mobile News*. As revealed in my attached resume, reference list, and letter of recommendation, I am an experienced executive/administrative assistant. Currently, I am seeking appropriate career opportunities in the corporate arena. This particular posting seems ideal, but I would also welcome your consideration for any other client postings you believe match my background.

In addition to five years of staff experience at Bradstreet and Associates, I have worked for three years as executive assistant to the president and to the executive vice-president of a software development company. In these capacities, my responsibilities have included a variety of assignments, both independent and team projects. I am skilled in writing and typing executive correspondence and other administrative activities. My Microsoft Office expertise includes Word, Access, PowerPoint, and Excel, and my technical background enables me to quickly develop expertise in other such applications.

Clearly, I have a strong background. I hope you identify my candidacy as worthy of referral to those who posted the Executive Assistant position and to other clients. I do believe Any Employment Agency can help me with my overall job search. Please, let's talk about all opportunities initially by phone and, after, in person. Please contact any of those references appearing on my resume, but keep my candidacy confidential. My current employer is unaware of my search.

Thank you for your consideration. I look forward to hearing from you.

Sincerely,

Chris Smith

Chris Smith

Legal Administrator

Chris Smith
123 Any Street • City, ST 12345 • (555) 555-5555 • *csmith@email.com*

June 1, 200–

Pat Cummings
Partner
Any Employment Agency
456 Any Street
City, ST 12345

Dear Mr. Cummings:

I have recently relocated to Florida, and I would like the assistance of Any Employment Agency to locate a court or paralegal-related administrative position with one of your clients. The Legal Administrator posting appearing on your website seems ideal!

As described in the enclosed resume, in Washington, D.C., I was a legal assistant for a well-respected law firm. There, my responsibilities included completion of legal research, drafting and proofing documents, interviewing witnesses and clients, and preparing documentation needed to support litigation activities of attorneys.

As a result, I have highly refined technical and organizational skills, including comprehensive computer expertise. I have extensive experience working on multiple projects and meeting deadlines in a team-oriented legal environment. Now, I seek to continue my legal support career here in Florida. I hope you will find me a qualified candidate for the position posted and refer me to the client seeking to hire a Legal Administrator. I also hope you have additional clients who have engaged you to find candidates for immediate full-time or part-time opportunities. I will call to discuss your reactions to this letter and to determine if a meeting would be mutually beneficial.

I look forward to speaking with you, with one of your Any Agency colleagues, or with one of your client firms whenever appropriate. Thank you for your time and consideration.

Sincerely,

Chris Smith

Chris Smith

Office Manager

Chris Smith
123 Any Street • City, ST 12345 • (555) 555-5555 • *csmith@email.com*

June 1, 200–

Pat Cummings
Associate
Any Employment Agency
456 Any Street
City, ST 12345
FAX (555) 555-5557

Dear Mr. Cummings:

If one of your clients is in need of a reliable, competent, well-organized individual to join their office management staff, I have the qualifications and motivation to fill the position.

As cited on the enclosed resume and reinforced by the accompanying letter of recommendation, during the past ten years, I have held progressively responsible positions in office management and administrative support with manufacturing, distribution, export, and service companies. I have broad experience with manual and automated accounting and administrative systems, customer service, personnel supervision, event and meeting planning, credit and collection, and executive support.

The accomplishments detailed on my resume and recommendation should reveal to you and any client employers now seeking candidates that I function best in a diverse, busy environment. I have established a reputation for being organized and capable of coordinating and handling multiple assignments efficiently, cost-effectively, and under the pressure of deadlines.

Should you know of any suitable opportunities, I would appreciate your forwarding all pertinent documentation along with your support. I would be happy to meet with you prior to interviewing with any clients. In that way, you can first assess my capabilities and share all appropriate information. If you wish to communicate with me, please do so via the contact information appearing on this fax. I will, of course, follow up soon with a phone call. I do look forward to using Any Agency as a resource in my job search.

Sincerely,

Chris Smith

Chris Smith

Property Manager

Chris Smith

123 Any Street • City, ST 12345 • (555) 555-5555 • *csmith@email.com*

June 1, 200–

Pat Cummings
Director
Any Employment Firm
456 Any Street
City, ST 12345
FAX (555) 555-5557

Dear Mr. Cummings:

I will soon relocate to the Chicago area. Ideally, during my next pre-relocation trip, we could meet to discuss how Any Employment could assist me. Attached you will find a copy of my resume, detailing my accomplishments as a property manager. I understand from colleagues that you are a specialist in real estate, so I believe our relationship can be mutually beneficial and rewarding.

Currently, I serve as property manager for 275 residential and four commercial units in three buildings. In this role I am actively involved in all sales, maintenance, and tenant relations activities. This includes advertising, promotion, and leasing or sales of vacant apartments and offices. Although our overall occupancy rate remains high, whenever necessary, we have always quickly found new tenants or owners and, frankly, increased our profit margin when we did. I completed all monthly, quarterly, and annual sales, lease, and market reports, including competitive analysis of rate structures. My reports and presentations are easy to review. They contain comprehensive, yet clear illustrations, and use state-of-the-art software to facilitate information retrieval, dissemination, and updating.

My experience also includes negotiations with contractors, liaison with banks as well as local and regional governments, relationships with service agencies, relations governing personnel, management of finances, and performance of all functions basic to effective management of complex properties. Prior, I worked for the Other Bank of New York focusing on commercial and real estate lending.

I will call to determine a convenient meeting time and date. Of course, I hope you have current postings that match my background and that soon you will refer me to interviews with potential employers.

Sincerely,

Chris Smith

Chris Smith

Research and Development

Date: June 1, 200–
From: *csmith@email.com*
To: *pcummings@email.com*
Subject: Research and Development Position

TO: Pat Cummings, Director

I will be relocating to your area next month, and I would be interested in a position requiring my chemical, electromechanical, and mechanical research skills. I believe I would be a good match for a progressive, technically oriented company seeking support in research, manufacturing, or production. But your professional perspective and assistance with my job search would be most welcomed.

As is described in great detail on my attached resume, during the past fifteen years, I have held progressively responsible and sophisticated positions with RHG Corporation, including automated manufacturing machine operator, research and development assistant, and senior laboratory technician. Some colleagues identify my greatest strengths as related to building and maintenance of testing equipment, prototypes, and maintenance of manufacturing equipment.

I consider myself a "jack of all trades," with past experience managing and supervising fleet maintenance for cars and trucks. I have an academic background in and additional training related to chemistry, biomedical engineering, mechanical engineering, accounting, and management. Please, let's soon discuss by phone your thoughts regarding my candidacy and whether Any Employment Agency might help. Do you know of any openings that match my qualifications? Would you refer me to an employer interview? What are appropriate next steps?

I look forward to speaking with you regarding your answers to these and other questions. I will call to speak with you soon, but feel free to e-mail or call me at the address and number listed below.

Sincerely,
Chris Smith
123 Any Street
City, ST 12345
(555) 555-5555
csmith@email.com

Sales/Customer Service Representative

Chris Smith
123 Any Street • City, ST 12345 • (555) 555-5555 • *csmith@email.com*

June 1, 200–

Pat Cummings
Employment Representative
Any Employment Agency
456 Any Street
City, ST 12345
FAX (555) 555-5557

Dear Mr. Cummings:

I enjoyed our brief conversation at the New Jersey Sales and Marketing Expo. As you now know, I am actively seeking new, challenging, and rewarding sales or customer service opportunities. I am now formally requesting the assistance of your agency with my search. Attached is a copy of my resume as well as the candidate contract you provided.

As you can see from the resume, I have over seven years' experience in positions including sales assistant, claims investigator, and bank teller. My applicable experience includes the following:

- Acting as liaison between customers, staff, and management.
- Investigating and resolving customer requests and problems.
- Tracking and expediting sales orders; ascertaining order accuracy.
- Processing a wide range of financial transactions; maintaining accuracy and balance.

My current ambitions are to earn more and gain management and supervisory responsibilities. I am willing to travel, and I would be interested in a salary in the $35,000 to $45,000 range. Of course, salary is important, but it is a negotiable issue. Most important, I want enhanced potential to succeed! Performance-based bonuses or other incentives beyond base salary would be welcome for sales or customer service positions.

I would be interested in further discussing my candidacy and identifying any employment opportunities you feel would be applicable to my skills. Please do keep my candidacy confidential. I also respectfully request that you or any prospective employers only contact the references listed on the contract. Thank you for your professionalism, consideration, and assistance. I will call soon to discuss your reactions to this fax (originals to follow by mail) and to begin our association. If needed, you can always reach me via the cell phone number listed above.

Sincerely,

Chris Smith

Chris Smith

Security Guard

Chris Smith
123 Any Street • City, ST 12345 • (555) 555-5555 • *csmith@email.com*

June 1, 200–

Pat Cummings
Director
Any Employment Agency
456 Any Street
City, ST 12345

Dear Mr. Cummings:

First, thank you for speaking with me on the phone. Your advice was much appreciated, and you are correct that most of the major hotels use agencies for their placement efforts. I hope the ad appearing in the *Las Vegas Sun Times* indicates that an opportunity now exists with one of these employers. Having recently moved to the Las Vegas area, I would greatly appreciate your assistance in securing a position as a security guard. After our conversation, I am confident that you can do so.

As described on my resume, I have worked as a security guard in banks, museums, and other settings. At the Willow Mead Art Museum in Wyoming, my duties included patrol, surveillance, and control of facilities and areas. I also maintained reports, records, and documents as required by administration. Prior, I received formal training through Security Guard Company and served in numerous training rotations while serving in full-time capacities for the Big Mall in Cheyenne.

For the past three years as a bank security guard, I have been responsible for ensuring the safety and security of customers, bank employees, and bank assets. My compensation for that position was about $30,000. Clearly, I am an experienced, motivated, and well-trained professional. I do hope that Any Employment Agency has current clients, and related postings, that match my background.

I look forward to finding a great position through your agency. I can begin working immediately, and I would be happy to meet with you, one of your colleagues, or one of your employing clients whenever needed. Again, thank you for your advice and assistance.

Sincerely,

Chris Smith

Chris Smith

Chapter 12

Contacting Headhunters and Search Firms

Search professionals, or "headhunters" as they are called, know about "hidden postings." While they regularly source candidates, like you, they also seek retainer or contingency relationships with potential employers. Once employers post a listing, these professionals screen information from candidates to determine those who match. Most often, search professionals deal with management or executive-level candidates and opportunities or with very specialized fields. Directories of search professionals are easy to locate in a bookstore or library, so use them.

Director of Information Services

Date: June 1, 200–
From: *csmith@email.com*
To: *pcummings@email.com*
Subject: Director of Information Services

Dear Mr. Cummings:

During our meeting at the Minority Professional Recruiting Expo, we discussed opportunities with your client firms that are of great interest to me. As we discussed, I am currently seeking a challenging environment where I can apply my combined technical knowledge, experience, and ability to create and implement innovative concepts for greater information systems efficiency.

My qualifications, all detailed on the resume attached to this e-mail, include the following:

- Thirteen years of experience with MIS corporate information systems.
- Experience in operating and supervising administrative functions of several UNIX systems.
- Skill in communicating with domestic and international networks, mainframes, and network system support.
- Ability to work as a team member, team leader, and/or independent contributor, working offsite via modem and data network, to assist users in sales, finance, manufacturing, and production.
- Ability to generate positive results in a company's information systems and networks by streamlining systems and improving user training and performance.

Relocation is not a problem—my target cities remain Chicago, Boston, and San Francisco, and my compensation requirements are in the low $70,000 range. Please keep my candidacy confidential, and do let's continue our conversations regarding opportunities as they arise. I would welcome your advice regarding interviews when they are arranged, and I do understand your role as an executive search professional. Thank you for your assistance with my efforts to find a new opportunity.

Yours sincerely,
Chris Smith
123 Any Street
City, ST 12345
(555) 555-5555
csmith@email.com

Management Consultant

Chris Smith
123 Any Street • City, ST 12345 • (555) 555-5555 • *csmith@email.com*

June 1, 200–

Pat Cummings
Executive Recruiter
Any Corporation
456 Any Street
City, ST 12345
FAX (555) 555-5557

Dear Mr. Cummings:

To date, I have played a key role in designing, implementing, reorganizing, and managing a variety of functions—including operations, manufacturing, materials, engineering, and quality assurance—for nationally and internationally recognized corporations. The attached resume documents my past achievements. My contact with you reveals my ambitions for future challenges and rewards.

Currently, I am seeking a position in management consulting. I strongly believe that your firm and your clients can benefit from my twenty years of progressively responsible management experience in the above-cited areas. My diverse areas of expertise, and those that can ultimately yield value-added assets within consulting roles, include the following:

- Five years as director of operations for a $60-million manufacturer.
- Over six years as materials manager with a multiplant, multiwarehouse, $10-million manufacturer of industrial rubber products.
- Over nine years as manufacturing coordinator with a toy manufacturer, with responsibilities related to expansion of existing manufacturing and support facilities, setup of new facilities, manpower planning, union relations, and capital equipment investment and materials purchases.

Please review your current contingency and retainer client relationships to determine those that might match my strengths. I would greatly appreciate your consideration and, ultimately, your referrals for interviews with a consulting organization or firm seeking to hire an internal consultant. In advance, thank you for your assistance. I can discuss my candidacy with you further by phone or in person. I can also interview for specific positions whenever needed, but please do keep my candidacy confidential.

Yours sincerely,

Chris Smith

Chris Smith

Operations Manager

Chris Smith
123 Any Street • City, ST 12345 • (555) 555-5555 • *csmith@email.com*

June 1, 200–

Pat Cummings
President
Any Search Firm
456 Any Street
City, ST 12345

Dear Ms. Cummings:

Based on my diverse background and experience with high-end, midrange, and low-end hardware, software, and network products, I feel that I can make a valuable contribution toward new product planning, market development, and expansion for a firm now among your clients. Any Search Firm is well known within the industry, so I am confident that ours will be a positive and mutually beneficial relationship. I am actively seeking a new and challenging position, and I am confident that you will find me a candidate easy to place.

My experience over the last seventeen years, all described on the enclosed resume, has required the ability to develop and market packaged and customized software for many industries in domestic and international markets. It has also required that I oversee the support of these products for end-users at all levels. I am sure I can succeed in the hardware and software marketing and development field. Because of diversity of past achievements, I am able to transfer skills to marketing, manufacturing, distribution, and service of other products. In addition to a strong marketing and sales background, I have also established a record for setting up, staffing, and managing top-producing, profitable district sales and service operations.

Should you be aware of an advanced marketing and development position in the $100,000 to $150,000 range, please consider me an eager and qualified candidate. I would welcome your assistance with my search efforts and I would be happy to discuss my background with you or one of your client firms at any time. I will call to confirm your receipt of this letter and to clarify appropriate next steps.

Thank you for your consideration and assistance.

Sincerely,

Chris Smith

Chris Smith

Plant Manager

Chris Smith

123 Any Street • City, ST 12345 • (555) 555-5555 • *csmith@email.com*

June 1, 200–

Pat Cummings
President
Any Search Firm
456 Any Street
City, ST 12345
Fax (555) 555-5557

Dear Ms. Cummings:

During the past ten years, I have held positions ranging from production supervisor to plant and operations manager with a $16-million manufacturer and importer of electrical products. I am now seeking a new position where I can contribute to the quality and cost-effectiveness of a company's operation and profitability. The attached resume and this fax (originals to follow in the mail) should reveal to you, and to any clients you have on contingency or retainer, my qualifications for challenging and rewarding opportunities.

In my current position as plant manager, I have developed a stable workforce and environment following a restructuring. Under my direction, the company has benefited from efficient supervisory staff and support personnel in all phases of plant operations, including production, purchasing, inventory control, warehousing, distribution, and maintenance of a 325,000-square-foot facility.

I would welcome the opportunity to apply my proven track record to one of your client firms. Relocation is not a problem. While salary and compensation are negotiable, my current salary is in the low $70s, so I would anticipate a new position to offer an increase or the potential to earn more. Please, let's discuss my candidacy and how Any Search might assist me with my search. In advance, thank you for your consideration.

Sincerely,

Chris Smith

Chris Smith

Senior Accountant

Date: June 1, 200–
From: *csmith@email.com*
To: *pcummings@email.com*
Subject: Senior Accountant

TO: Pat Cummings, Executive Recruiter

The varied accounting, finance, and general management experience I have gained over the course of my career should be of interest to you as you conduct current or future client searches. As you may recall, you once contacted me regarding a Senior Accountant position, but at that time I was not ready to seek new opportunities. Well, now I am ready, willing, and eager to do so.

As described on the attached resume (which is uploaded to your web-based candidate application system), I am a certified accountant who has successfully managed general ledger, cash accounting, accounts payable, employee disbursement, and fixed-asset operations. As a manufacturing plant controller, I managed accounting activities of a $35-million manufacturing plant. My accomplishments include:

- Preparing, analyzing, and presenting P&L, balance sheet, departmental expense, manufacturing variance, and other operating reports.
- Preparing $2-million annual departmental operating budgets, analyzing results, initiating required operational improvements, and preparing forecasts.
- Developing annual strategic and operational improvements, resulting in a 15-percent increase in efficiency.
- Overseeing human resources, purchasing, payroll, and other plant administrative functions.
- Maintaining quality accounting operations by implementing internal controls in testing programs.

I also managed the interface between accounting and data centers, directed MIS professionals who supported my applications, and managed an enhancement project that improved day-to-day operations. While my prime interest is in securing a position on the East Coast, I am willing to relocate for the right opportunity and compensation (ideally $85,000 to $95,000 annually). Thank you for your consideration in this matter. I will call to confirm your receipt of this e-mail and to discuss next steps.

Sincerely,
Chris Smith
123 Any Street
City, ST 12345
(555) 555-5555
csmith@email.com

Chapter 13

Networking Letters

Networking letters are solicitations for particular positions or requests for referrals. Most often, these are proactive documents addressed to people who can grant consideration or offer names of others who might also consider candidates for employment. Occasionally, they are reactive documents, when a particular person's name is cited as supporting your candidacy for a specific job. Review of the attached resume is clearly the main purpose of this letter.

Administrative Assistant

Date: June 1, 200–
From: *csmith@email.com*
To: *pcummings@email.com*
Subject: Francis Williams Referral

Pat Cummings
Attorney at Law
Any Firm
456 Any Street
City, ST 12345

Dear Mr. Cummings:

Recently, Francis Williams suggested I contact you regarding my job search. I am currently seeking a position that would use my legal, administrative, and office-management knowledge and experience.

As indicated on my attached resume, for the past twelve years I have supervised records and staff activities within the Any County Registry of Deeds. I have ambitions beyond my current role, but unfortunately I have reached a career plateau within the structure of this position. I am especially interested in a legal administrative, paralegal, or research position, preferably with a private firm or corporation, and I am willing to relocate for the right opportunity.

Should you know of any related openings, or contacts to whom I should forward a resume, I would appreciate your advice and referrals. Of course, if your firm were in need of a person with my background, your consideration would also be much appreciated. I will call to confirm receipt of this resume and to discuss your reactions to my request. A detailed cover letter and resume will be forwarded to any individuals you recommend.

In advance, thank you for your time, assistance, and, if appropriate, your consideration.

Sincerely,

Chris Smith

Chris Smith
123 Any Street
City, ST 12345
(555) 555-5555

Auto Salesperson

Chris Smith
123 Any Street • City, ST 12345 • (555) 555-5555 • *csmith@email.com*

June 1, 200–

Pat Cummings
Regional Manager
Any Auto
456 Any Street
City, ST 12345

Dear Ms. Cummings:

During a recent visit to Rochester, my longtime friend Francis Williams mentioned your name as a contact in the field of auto sales. I understand that your corporation has contracted Francis's agency several times to promote your regional dealerships. I would like to take this opportunity to ask for any assistance or, ideally, consideration you might be able to provide with my job search.

Due to recent downsizing, I am seeking a new, long-term association with an aggressive, fast-paced dealership. As detailed on my attached resume, during the past eight years, my positions have ranged from salesperson to sales manager with a high-volume dealership. My expertise is in developing, training, motivating, and managing top-producing sales teams in highly competitive markets. I have established and continually maintained a record of achievement as Salesperson of the Month and Salesperson of the Year for generated sales and margin of profit.

I will be visiting the Rochester area next week, and I would like to meet with you if your schedule permits. Your insight into the market, as well as any specific advice or contact names, would be very helpful. I will call your office next Monday to see if we can find a convenient time to meet. In advance, thank you for your counsel and, if one of your dealerships would find my candidacy worthy, for your consideration.

Sincerely,

Chris Smith

Chris Smith

Chris Smith

123 Any Street • City, ST 12345 • (555) 555-5555 • *csmith@email.com*

June 1, 200–

Pat Cummings
Vice President, Operations
Any Bank
456 Any Street
City, ST 12345
FAX (555) 555-5557

Dear Mr. Cummings:

Francis Williams, a colleague of mine at United Bank, mentioned your name as an authority in the Midwest banking industry. Francis met you on a visit to your Omaha office last month and was impressed by both the reputation and successful operation of your branches. I now respectfully request advice, consideration, or referrals as I seek banking employment opportunities in the Omaha area, where I will be relocating next month.

As my resume indicates, I am a skilled professional with over ten years of relevant experience. In addition to an MBA degree (Executive Program), I have five years of loan officer experience, and a BA degree in Economics and Finance. Overall, I have more than ten years of comprehensive experience in varied banking roles. My expertise includes all aspects of banking and finance, credit administration, and management, including commercial lending and development, real estate loans, and end-to-end joint-venture management.

I will be conducting a pre-relocation visit to Omaha next week to actively begin my job search. Would your schedule permit a few moments for us to speak? During a brief telephone conversation, or, ideally, in person, I could gain contact names within Any Bank, or within other area financial institutions, as well as any search professionals you think might be of assistance. Of course, if Any Bank were to find my candidacy attractive, I would also welcome your consideration.

If your schedule is too busy for a meeting, you can contact me via the above information, and e-mail me any referrals you deem appropriate, including search professionals.

Thank you.

Sincerely,

Chris Smith

Chris Smith

Chief Financial Officer

Date: June 1, 200–
From: *csmith@email.com*
To: *pcummings@email.com*
Subject: Francis Williams Referral

Dear Ms. Cummings:

I am currently seeking a position as a chief financial officer. Francis Williams, a mutual friend and fellow member of the American Association of Financial Officers, suggested that I contact you regarding my job search. For personal and professional reasons, I am now exploring the Wisconsin and Michigan areas as sites for relocation, and I am eager to expand my list of contacts in the region. Ideally, upon review of my resume, you will feel comfortable identifying a few individuals, perhaps corporate clients of Any Bank, to whom I can present my candidacy, as well as search professionals who specialize in my field.

My sixteen years of progressively responsible experience has encompassed management of all aspects of financial and treasury functions, from cost accounting manager to chief financial officer and vice president, finance. This experience includes managing corporate real estate, human resources, and general operations. In addition to holding an MBA in Finance and a BA in Accounting, I am a Certified Public Accountant.

Are there individuals you would encourage me to contact? Your advice and counsel would also be appreciated. I will follow this e-mail with a phone call, but as I am sensitive to your busy schedule, I understand if an e-mail response is more appropriate.

Thank you for your assistance with my efforts.

Sincerely,
Chris Smith
123 Any Street
City, ST 12345
(555) 555-5555
csmith@email.com

Customer Support Representative

Chris Smith

123 Any Street • City, ST 12345 • (555) 555-5555 • *csmith@email.com*

June 1, 200–

Pat Cummings
Customer Support Manager
Any Corporation
456 Any Street
City, ST 12345

Dear Ms. Cummings:

I am a former college classmate of your son Dennis, and I have, since graduation, worked as a customer-support representative for a manufacturer of high-volume copiers and reprographic equipment. Although my position has been challenging and rewarding, at this point in my career I am seeking a new position where my expertise, motivation, and drive can be more fully applied and compensated.

I had lunch with Dennis last week while on a business trip to Pittsburgh, and he suggested that you might have an opening within the customer-support department of your corporation. He also mentioned that because of your active involvement in the Pennsylvania Association of Customer Service professionals, you might have some suggestions regarding others to whom I can present my candidacy.

As is detailed on my attached resume, during the past three years, I have gained progressively responsible experience providing sales support and training to new hires and end-users of major commercial, institutional, industrial, and government accounts on a national level. I am an effective representative and support professional with the ability to serve as a liaison between sales, service, customers, and corporate personnel.

Could we meet so that I can further outline my qualifications for contributing successfully to your firm? And, if appropriate, could you provide me with a list of additional contacts? I look forward to your advice, referrals, and, ideally, consideration for employment with Any Corporation. I will call to discuss your reactions to this request.

Sincerely,

Chris Smith

Chris Smith

Editor

Chris Smith
123 Any Street • City, ST 12345 • (555) 555-5555 • *csmith@email.com*

June 1, 200–

Pat Cummings
Vice President of Editorial
Any Publishing
456 Any Street
City, ST 12345

Dear Ms. Cummings:

John Curran, whom I saw recently at the ABA convention, spoke highly of your creative, market-sensitive approach to publishing and the tremendous impact you have had on Any Publishing. He also said you might have plans to expand your editorial team and suggested that I write you.

As is described with great pride on the attached resume, I have seven years of experience as a nonfiction editor. For the past two years, I have acquired books for Other Publisher's Professional Book Group, where I work with authors on books that address the wide range of challenges facing today's managers and small-business owners. I also acquire books on personal business topics for the career/self-help market, like Kelly Miller's *Loving Your Job*. This recent release has already received a strong response from book clubs (20,000-copy advance order) and an enthusiastic endorsement from Francis Morin (as quoted on the attached release).

Earlier in my career, I acquired and edited books on health, fitness, recreation, and other nonfiction topics for Stevens & Dunn. Although designed for the academic environment, these books had strong crossover appeal to the trade market. My passion for procuring authors, negotiating contacts, and transforming book ideas into profitable, well-crafted, and popular works remains strong!

Could we meet to discuss the possibility of an opening at Any Publishing? Thank you in advance.

Sincerely,

Chris Smith

Chris Smith

Finance Manager

Chris Smith

123 Any Street • City, ST 12345 • (555) 555-5555 • *csmith@email.com*

June 1, 200–

Pat Cummings
Human Resource Director
Any Bank
456 Any Street
City, ST 12345
FAX (555) 555-5557

Dear Ms. Cummings:

Kelly Monroe, of First Avenue Bank, informed me that Any Bank might be expanding its professional staff. Kelly once worked for me and can attest to my past performance and potential for future success. Based on my comprehensive experience in the field of finance, all detailed in the attached resume, I can offer your bank a broad range of management and technical skills.

To date, I have played a key role in the trust banking industry, in positions ranging from tax officer to my current position as chief trust officer. Because of my ability to adapt strategies to changing conditions, I was able to apply innovative approaches that increased productivity, accuracy, and profits. This substantially improved our customer service, corporate visibility and image, and customer base.

I am confident I could contribute my expertise to the continued success of Any Bank and would welcome the chance to discuss career opportunities. My desire to relocate to the New York City area is strong, as is my willingness to travel, solicit new business, and become an accomplishment-driven professional on the Any Bank team. Please, let's begin our discussions over the phone and, should you judge appropriate, follow with in-person meetings. A trip to New York would be easy to arrange, whenever is convenient for you. In advance, thank you for your time and consideration.

Sincerely,

Chris Smith

Chris Smith

International Controller

Date: June 1, 200–
From: *csmith@email.com*
To: *pcummings@email.com*
Subject: International Controller

It was a pleasure meeting you last month when we were both visiting the Maximillians at their home in Austin. As you may recall, I was then working as international controller of Other Company, a multidivision manufacturer of automatic test equipment. Recent ownership changes have prompted me to seek a new position in finance management. When I recently spoke with Francis Maximillian regarding my search, I was strongly encouraged to request your assistance.

As the attached resume reveals, I possess over sixteen years of experience working with foreign manufacturing entities and sales and service subsidiaries, which has involved corporate financial planning and analysis, international reporting, treasury and tax management, and interactive MIS systems for both corporate and divisional financial operations. Should you know of any corporations in the Austin area in need of someone with my qualifications, would you kindly forward me the names of appropriate contacts? I will, of course, identify you as the referral source in any correspondence with these individuals.

Also, I will be visiting the Maximillians again in two weeks. Should your schedule permit, I would like to meet, perhaps for lunch or dinner. This would allow me to thank you properly and personally for your assistance and provide me the opportunity to gain additional insights you might have regarding my search efforts as they focus on Austin. I will contact you next week to find a time that is convenient for you.

Thank you for your assistance. I hope to see you again soon.

Sincerely,
Chris Smith
123 Any Street
City, ST 12345
(555) 555-5555
csmith@email.com

Marketing Assistant

Chris Smith

123 Any Street • City, ST 12345 • (555) 555-5555 • *csmith@email.com*

June 1, 200–

Pat Cummings
Director of Marketing
Any Corporation
456 Any Street
City, ST 12345
FAX (555) 555-5557

Dear Mr. Cummings:

It was a pleasure talking to you during our flight to Chicago last April. I hope you enjoyed your trip! As you may recall, I was then a senior at Simmons College studying marketing and sales. You were kind enough to give me your business card with instructions to contact you once I was "liberated from the demands of academia." Finally, that day has arrived.

Although I am a recent graduate, I have held several internships at major Boston consumer-product manufacturing and marketing corporations, as well as advertising and public relations agencies. As a result, I am now realistic about my desire to locate a position that will require market research, analysis, promotions, event-planning, and sales-support talents. Enclosed is a copy of my resume for your reference and referral.

Are there Chicago-based individuals you would encourage me to contact? Can I use your name in my correspondence with these persons? Do you particularly know anyone at Leo Burnett or Quaker Oats? Would it be too assertive if I requested consideration for a position with Any Corporation?

Ideally, when I return to Chicago for an interview, I can thank you in person and update you regarding the status of my job search. Soon after I accept an offer and relocate to your amazing city, I would like to buy you dinner and show my appreciation for your assistance. I'll call soon to discuss your thoughts regarding this request. Thank you.

Sincerely,

Chris Smith

Chris Smith

Marketing Specialist

Date: June 1, 200–
From: *csmith@email.com*
To: *pcummings@email.com*
Subject: Marketing Specialist

TO: Pat Cummings, Director of Sales and Marketing
RE: Marketing Position with Any Corporation

Thank you for taking the time to speak with me after your sales presentation last Thursday. As you may recall, I am now actively seeking consideration for a marketing position within Any Corporation. I have applied for a Marketing Specialist position via the online system, but your advice and support would be much appreciated. Are there individuals to whom I should send my resume and cover letter directly?

As detailed on the attached resume, during the past five years, my experience in my present marketing position has focused on product management, strategic planning, marketing, and the sale of equipment, systems, chemicals, and related products and services. I am a strong contributing member of the team responsible for the worldwide marketing of bio-instrument chemicals sold to biotech markets, pharmaceutical markets, and research laboratories. Success in product management, new business and market development, and sales management of national and international markets has developed qualifications I feel would contribute to the growth and profitability of Any Corporation.

At your convenience, I would like to discuss, in detail, the mutual benefit of my joining your management team. I consider myself to be a consistent achiever and feel confident that I can make a significant difference.

I appreciate your advice, consideration, and support of my candidacy, and I look forward to speaking with you regarding appropriate next steps.

Yours sincerely,
Chris Smith
123 Any Street
City, ST 12345
(555) 555-5555
csmith@email.com

Mortgage/Loan Officer

Chris Smith

123 Any Street • City, ST 12345 • (555) 555-5555 • *csmith@email.com*

June 1, 200–

Pat Cummings
Chief Loan Officer
Any Bank
456 Any Street
City, ST 12345
FAX (555) 555-5557

Dear Mr. Cummings:

Francis Williams, one of your branch office managers, and fellow alum of Any University, thought you might be interested in someone with my qualifications. I am currently seeking a new position with a bank or specialty lender as a mortgage loan officer. When I shared my goals with Francis, I was strongly encouraged to contact you immediately.

As the enclosed resume indicates, my extensive loan experience has encompassed office supervision as well as transaction documentation and review within the mortgage, insurance, and banking industries. My concentration has been in credit and collections. In my current position as a senior collections specialist, I have had the opportunity to accomplish and exceed a set objective of reducing delinquent loans from $24 million to $10 million within six months. At this point, I feel I have successfully surpassed both company and personal goals and am searching for new and greater challenges, particularly those that would involve marketing and client relationship-building responsibilities.

After my conversation with Francis, I am quite interested in the opportunities available at Any Bank. Could we meet for a personal interview? I will call to confirm receipt of this fax (originals to follow in the mail) and to arrange a mutually convenient time and date. Thank you for your consideration. Of course, feel free to communicate with Francis or anyone on my reference list regarding my potential to be a performance-driven and very successful loan officer.

Sincerely,

Chris Smith

Chris Smith

Chris Smith

123 Any Street • City, ST 12345 • (555) 555-5555 • *csmith@email.com*

June 1, 200–

Pat Cummings, RN, MSN
Nursing Director
Any Hospital
456 Any Street
City, ST 12345

Dear Nurse Cummings:

Kelly Williams, a nurse in your pediatric unit, suggested I contact you regarding the currently posted senior nursing position at Any Hospital. Kelly believes that I have the qualifications, motivation, and special qualities needed to join her as a member of your care-focused nursing team—or "family," as she calls it.

As detailed on the attached resume, I now have fifteen years' experience in clinical research and direct patient care, with an emphasis on neuroscience intensive care, memory disorders, and brain and cognitive sciences. During the past three years, I have functioned as a staff nurse with duties in a neuro intensive care unit.

I am well qualified to teach, counsel, conduct utilization reviews, or administer programs related to health care, equipment, or related services. I am capable of making presentations to individuals and groups, with the skill to conduct meetings and teach classes. I have the communication skills and sensitivities to demonstrate as well as instruct medical professions and support staffs of varied levels and backgrounds.

I trust you will agree with Kelly's views regarding my candidacy and grant me the opportunity to interview for this position and support my credentials in person. Of course, I have completed your online application, but I wanted to personalize my candidacy via this letter, accompanying resume, and letters of recommendation. Thank you for your consideration.

Sincerely,

Chris Smith

Chris Smith, RN

Payroll Supervisor

Chris Smith
123 Any Street • City, ST 12345 • (555) 555-5555 • *csmith@email.com*

June 1, 200–

Pat Cummings
Human Resource Manager
Any Corporation
456 Any Street
City, ST 12345
FAX (555) 555-5557

Dear Ms. Cummings:

I received your name from a mutual friend, Francis Williams. I was employed at Francis's bank several years ago, and we worked closely on several projects. In a recent conversation, Francis mentioned that you were actively recruiting candidates for the position of payroll specialist. I hope upon review of the attached resume that you will judge my candidacy as worthy of an interview.

As my resume indicates, in addition to a Bachelor of Arts in Economics, my background encompasses eleven years of progressively responsible and sophisticated hands-on experience, including serving as a union benefits coordinator and human resources administrator. Most significant, in my present position as payroll administrator, with its special emphasis on the day-to-day details of related financial and MIS operations, I have gained the particular expertise required of a payroll supervisor. I am confident overseeing the efficiency of this critical function, able to work with third-party vendors, and experienced at addressing the queries and concerns of employees related to payroll.

I look forward to speaking with you in detail about your expectations for the person who becomes Any Corporation's next payroll specialist and regarding my qualifications for this position. Thank you for your consideration.

Sincerely,

Chris Smith

Chris Smith

Production Manager

Chris Smith
123 Any Street • City, ST 12345 • (555) 555-5555 • *csmith@email.com*

June 1, 200–

Pat Cummings
Director of Operations Management
Any Corporation
456 Any Street
City, ST 12345
FAX (555) 555-5557

Dear Ms. Cummings:

As Francis Williams may have informed you, as a result of a dramatic downsizing, my production position has been eliminated, so I am immediately available to interview for the Production Manager position now posted on Any Corporation's website. Francis is familiar with my managerial style and accomplishments, for he started his career in production under my supervision. I am proud that he now encourages me to seek this position and again collaborate successfully with him and his Any Corporation production colleagues.

As you can see from my resume, my production-related experience extends throughout the last two decades. After completing a Bachelor's of Science in Management, I entered the Other Company's management development program and found operations and production to be my greatest strengths. Several titles, progressively responsible positions, and promotions later, I had amassed supervisory and production management experience with the same large, Washington, D.C.–based corporation. While the firm is now downsizing, I remain eager to continue an accomplishment-filled career with Any Corporation.

I will call to confirm your receipt of this fax and, if you judge it appropriate, to arrange an interview. Of course, feel free to contact Francis or others on my reference list regarding my qualifications and potential. Thank you for your consideration.

Sincerely,

Chris Smith

Chris Smith

Publicist

Date: June 1, 200–
From: *csmith@email.com*
To: *pcummings@email.com*
Subject: Publicist Candidate

TO: Pat Cummings, Publicity Director

Francis Williams suggested I write to you in regard to opportunities in advertising, public relations, and promotions. I would appreciate any information, advice, or consideration you could provide as I search for publicist or related positions. The attached resume and writing samples are offered to acquaint you with my background and qualifications.

As you will see upon review of my resume, I possess comprehensive experience supporting the successful direct-mail fundraising effort of a major university. My training and expertise also include publicity and public relations, staff training and supervision, program coordination, budget management, market research, copyediting, and management and administration of related details.

I have excellent writing skills. I also work well under pressure and meet deadlines consistently. Francis was a classmate of mine, and we completed numerous courses together. He and I have maintained a strong relationship since then, so he is quite familiar with my potential to succeed in the role of publicist. Most important, I would like you to assess my potential, ideally offer me an interview, and, if you judge me worthy, offer me the opportunity to achieve at Any Corporation. I will call to confirm your receipt of this e-mail and to discuss next steps. Thank you for your consideration.

Sincerely,
Chris Smith
123 Any Street
City, ST 12345
(555) 555-5555
csmith@email.com

Quality-Control Engineer

Chris Smith

123 Any Street • City, ST 12345 • (555) 555-5555 • *csmith@email.com*

June 1, 200–

Pat Cummings
Production/Operations Manager
Any Corporation
456 Any Street
City, ST 12345

Dear Mr. Cummings:

I enjoyed talking on the plane from Denver. I trust you enjoyed the conference as much as I did. I am sorry we did not meet earlier in the week because we would have had more time to share professional ideas and interests. Enclosed is the resume you asked to see. Yes, I am interested in discussing quality-control opportunities within Any Corporation.

As a quality-control engineer, I played a key role in the growth of Other Company, Inc., where I interfaced with all departments, including sales, purchasing, manufacturing, and inventory. I am knowledgeable about quality functions and have experience bringing product lines through the transitional stages from research and prototype to full production and distribution. During the past seven years I have completed many projects, all cited on my resume, and have held many titles. This breadth of experience should be of interest to you and your Any Corporation colleagues. Most significant to your current circumstances, I recently implemented and audited clean-room contamination control, electrostatic discharge, and internal auditing programs for semiconductor and engineering facilities.

I will be in Chicago for a training conference from April 10 to April 17, and I would enjoy continuing our conversation then. Of course, if you wish to speak before, or if you would like to arrange for face-to-face visits with others on the Any Corporation team, just let me know. I am very serious about wanting to be considered for a position with your company. I do look forward to continued communications and consideration.

Sincerely,

Chris Smith

Chris Smith

Secretary

Date: June 1, 200–
From: *csmith@email.com*
To: *pcummings@email.com*
Subject: Francis Williams Referral

Dear Mr. Cummings:

Francis Williams suggested I apply for the secretarial position (#23B) recently posted on your company's website. As a current employee of Any Corporation, she is well aware of the qualifications and motivations you seek in administrative support professionals. As a past coworker of mine, she is very familiar with my potential to join here on the Any Corporation team. I hope that after reviewing the attached resume, you will find that my abilities and capabilities suit your needs and that I will be invited to interview for this position.

During my last five years with Any Photographers, my responsibilities have included assisting on shoots, handling incoming calls, arranging appointments, and drafting, editing, and word-processing all correspondence. As a service representative for the Other Corporation, I dealt with all customer inquiries and resolved problems in shipping and billing, maintaining all written documentation and electronic information accurately. I am accustomed to working closely with staff and management in a fast-paced environment and enjoy the satisfaction of doing a job well. Summarizing, the skills I now offer Any Corporation include:

- Administrative and customer-service achievements spanning 6 years.
- Abilities to use, support, and teach others Word, Access, PowerPoint, Excel, and Internet applications.
- Bilingual Spanish-English abilities that have been used on the job.
- Awareness of the critical importance of secretarial and administrative staffers.

I look forward to interviewing for the secretarial position now available at Any Corporation. Thank you for your consideration.

Sincerely,
Chris Smith
123 Any Street
City, ST 12345
(555) 555-5555
csmith@email.com

Staff Accountant

Date: June 1, 200–
From: *csmith@email.com*
To: *pcummings@email.com*
Subject: Staff Accountant Position

Dear Mr. Cummings:

It was a pleasure meeting you at the alumni luncheon last Monday, and how kind of you to offer your assistance with my job search for a new and challenging accounting position. As you suggested, by following the instructions on the handout you provided I did register for and now have access to the online posting system and electronic alumni directory. Any additional assistance, advice, or referrals would be most welcomed.

As detailed in my attached resume (now uploaded to the system), during the past three years, I have been employed as a staff accountant with Other Corporation, with responsibility for maintaining financial statements and monthly closings and preparing financial reports using Excel. Prior, while attending college, I held part-time accounting and office-support positions of increasing responsibility, in areas ranging from auditing to accounts payable in corporate and nonprofit environments.

If you know of any corporation in need of an experienced accountant, in addition to those now posting on Any College's online system, I would appreciate your letting me know. Yes, the idea of contacting all past on-campus recruiters was a good one, and I look forward to receiving the listing from you. In addition, I will of course begin to network with other alumni in the accounting field to conduct, as you called it, "a proactive networking blitz." Again, thank you for speaking with me and for offering to assist me with my job search. I look forward to continued phone and e-mail communications.

Sincerely,
Chris Smith
123 Any Street
City, ST 12345
(555) 555-5555
csmith@email.com

Telecommunications Specialist

Chris Smith
123 Any Street • City, ST 12345 • (555) 555-5555 • csmith@email.com

June 1, 200–

Pat Cummings
Telecommunications Consultant
Any Corporation
456 Any Street
City, ST 12345
FAX (555) 555-5557

Dear Ms. Cummings:

A few years ago, I was your son Dan's classmate at the University of Miami. When I bumped into him last week in Billings, Montana, of all places, he informed me that you deal closely with several leading specialists in the telecommunications field and suggested I contact you immediately. At present, I am interested in joining a company where I can contribute strong skills and an education in communications.

My qualifications, all detailed on the enclosed resume, are as follows:

- A Bachelor of Arts in Communications that included courses, projects, and case studies addressing marketing, public relations, web-design, and advertising issues.
- Experience with all planning and implementation areas of marketing, public relations, advertising, and sales.
- Experience as an assistant account executive for a major advertising agency, whose clients include telecommunication firms, and as promotions intern at a radio station.
- Bilingual German-English skills and experience living and studying in Europe.

I would greatly appreciate any advice or referrals you might be able to provide. A listing of firms and contact names would be wonderful, and I would of course cite your referral in any communications with these individuals. I will call you in a few days to follow up. Thank you for your assistance in this matter.

Sincerely,

Chris Smith

Chris Smith

Telemarketer

Date: June 1, 200–
From: *csmith@email.com*
To: *pcummings@email.com*
Subject: Francis Williams Referral

TO: Pat Cummings, Director of Telemarketing

Francis Williams, who I understand has worked with you on several promotional projects, gave me your name. Francis has been very helpful in aiding my efforts to obtain an entry-level position in telemarketing, and he felt that I would benefit from your extensive industry experience.

As detailed on the attached resume, I possess four years of successful part-time and summer employment in sales administration and support. I have worked most recently in telemarketing, direct mail, marketing, and sales for a variety of product and service-oriented companies, including Other Company, one of Any Corporation's competitors. I am proud of all my practical and academic achievements to date, and as a soon-to-be college graduate, I am eager to begin a career in telemarketing.

Any referrals, advice, or consideration you could provide would be greatly appreciated. While I would certainly welcome the opportunity to interview for a position with Any Corporation, other assistance would also be well received. Names of those whom you think I should contact and ask to interview with would be great. I will call to confirm your receipt of this e-mail and the attached resume and to discuss your reactions to my request for consideration. In advance, thank you for your time, consideration, and assistance.

Sincerely,
Chris Smith
csmith@email.com

Chapter 14

Networking Notes

These notes, which are usually e-mailed, should be brief (one or two paragraphs) and personal. They are intended to begin a process that will build momentum with each communication and should not contain detailed summaries of qualifications. Resumes are attached or enclosed to share biographical information quickly, not to solicit consideration formally.

To Faculty Member

Date: June 1, 200–
From: *csmith@email.com*
To: *pcummings@email.edu*
Subject: Your Advice and Assistance

With commencement near, I wanted to gain your insight and referrals regarding potential employers. As you know, my interest in marketing and promotions is quite strong, and I am very proud of my accomplishments in your Marketing Cases and Strategies course. Our final project is prominently detailed on my attached resume, and I hope that someday soon I will describe it to prospective employers during interviews.

Are there particular companies, contacts, or alumni you would encourage me to communicate with? And also, may I use you as a reference? I will call to follow up this e-mail, but as you are so busy, I understand that continuing our communications electronically would probably be easiest. Thank you.

Chris Smith

To Past Employer

Chris Smith
123 Any Street • City, ST 12345 • (555) 555-5555 • *csmith@email.com*

June 1, 200–

Pat Cummings
VP of Finance
Any Corporation
456 Any Street
City, ST 12345
FAX (555) 555-5557

Dear Pat:

I am very proud that my accounting career began as an intern and, after, as an audit trainee with Any Corporation. As you know, when I left Any Corporation to earn my MBA at Any University in Boston, my performance record was strong and my friends within the organization many. While my postgraduate school achievements with Other Company have been strong, and all documented on the attached resume, your assistance with my efforts to relocate "home" to the Rochester area would be most welcomed. Do you know of any companies now seeking someone with my finance, auditing, cash-flow, and strategic-planning expertise? Are there individuals you would encourage me to contact? Are there particular posting sites I should utilize or professional organization members I should network with? Last, and most ideally, would Any Corporation consider my candidacy?

Your answers to these queries would be most welcomed and appreciated. Beyond that, a few minutes of your time when I next visit Rochester for a pre-relocation trip would be wonderful. Please convey my regards to all of my old Any Corporation colleagues. Thank you.

Sincerely,

Chris Smith

Chris Smith

To Professional Society Colleague

Date: June 1, 200–
From: *csmith@email.com*
To: *pcummings@email.com*
Subject: Advice, Assistance, and Referrals

Dear Pat:

It was good seeing you at the Association of Computer Professionals conference. As we discussed briefly, I am now actively seeking new software design opportunities. Would you feel comfortable sharing some contact names with me? Of course, in addition to the attached resume, I will provide each individual a detailed cover letter and cite your referral. You know of my background and abilities, and I am very appreciative of our friendship and respectful of your professional reputation, so I will handle all communications appropriately. Again, the names of contacts, as well as e-mail, fax, or mailing information, would be most well received and appreciated. Thank you.

Chris Smith
csmith@email.com

To Professional Society Officer

Date: June 1, 200–
From: *csmith@email.com*
To: *pcummings@email.com*
Subject: Advice, Assistance, and Referrals

Pat:

As the Vice President of Membership for Women in Advertising, I thought you might be able to assist me with my efforts to begin a post-baccalaureate career in the field of advertising. Does WIA offer any specialized posting or networking services to members? Are there particular members in the San Francisco Bay area whom you would encourage me to contact? Because I will be graduating in June, I would welcome consideration for a full-time, part-time, or internship position.

The attached resume is intended to quickly inform you of my background, not to solicit consideration. Of course I will forward an appropriate and detailed cover letter when I send this document to Women in Advertising members you recommend. Your assistance with my efforts would be most appreciated. Thank you.

Sincerely,
Chris Smith
123 Any Street
City, ST 12345
(555) 555-5555
csmith@email.com

To Friend of the Family

Chris Smith

123 Any Street • City, ST 12345 • (555) 555-5555 • csmith@email.com

June 1, 200–

Pat Cummings
Any Corporation
456 Any Street
City, ST 12345
FAX (555) 555-5557

Dear Pat:

It does seem a bit awkward asking you for assistance with my job search, but Mom and Dad encouraged me to overcome my concerns and do so anyway. As you may know by now through your communications with my family members, I am actively seeking new property management opportunities that will allow me the chance to relocate to the New York City area. Do you know of any companies now seeking someone with my real estate background? Are there individuals you would encourage me to contact with a copy of the attached resume? Are there particular posting sites I should utilize or local professional organizations I should join? Last, and most ideally, would Any Corporation consider my candidacy?

Your answers to these queries would be most welcomed and appreciated. A few minutes of your time over the phone would be great. When I am next in New York, for interviews or pre-relocation visits, please allow me to take you and your family to dinner or lunch. Thank you for your assistance now and, sincerely, for being a great family friend for so long.

Sincerely,

Chris Smith

Chris Smith

To an Alumnus(a)

Date: June 1, 200–
From: *csmith@email.com*
To: *pcummings@email.com*
Subject: Advice, Assistance, and Referrals

Dear Ms. Cummings:

As an alumna of Any College, I thought you might be able to assist me with my efforts to find a public relations position in the Chicago area. Attached is a copy of my resume that clearly projects my qualifications for these positions. Any contacts within your firm, in other firms in the city, or with search firms specializing in public relations and communications would be appreciated. Of course, I would send a more detailed cover letter with my resume to these individuals. While I do hope your firm might consider my candidacy, any referrals to other firms would be welcomed. In advance, thank you for your assistance.

Sincerely,
Chris Smith
123 Any Street
City, ST 12345
(555) 555-5555
csmith@email.com

Chapter 15

Other Letters

Thank-you notes, status checks, and other correspondence are good for keeping the employer's attention on you. E-mails, faxes, written notes, and voice-mail follow-up efforts can reinforce your candidacy, resurrect consideration after rejection or lack of response, and transform network members into job-search advocates. Acceptance letters, resignation letters, and decline-of-offer letters are also included.

Chris Smith

123 Any Street • City, ST 12345 • (555) 555-5555 • *csmith@email.com*

June 1, 200–

Pat Cummings
Director of Human Resources
Any Corporation
456 Any Street
City, ST 12345
FAX (555) 555-5557

Dear Ms. Cummings:

Thank you for taking the time from your schedule to speak with me regarding the available COBOL programmer positions. I look forward to meeting on Friday at 10 A.M. As we discussed, and as is detailed on my resume (additional copy attached for your files), my hardware exposure has included Suzuki and HyTech, and I have had substantial experience in implementing both batch and online computer systems using COBOL. Each position I have held has led to advancement and the assumption of greater responsibilities. Clearly, I hope that this pattern of success will continue at Any Corporation.

I appreciate your time and consideration. I look forward to meeting with you. As I prepare for the interview, are there any particular questions I should think about, or documents or web pages I should review?

Sincerely,

Chris Smith

Chris Smith

Between Phone Conversation and Interview II

Date: June 1, 200–
From: *csmith@email.com*
To: *pcummings@email.com*
Subject: Phone Follow-Up

TO: Pat Cummings, Vice President

Following up on our brief phone conversation, I am forwarding my resume with regard to the opening we discussed in your marketing department.

Although I am currently employed in a management position, I am interested in a career change, especially one that requires a thorough knowledge of boating with sales, marketing, and communication skills. Others describe me as an imaginative, well-organized self-starter with a strong interest in boating, and I am proud of this assessment. As a semiprofessional sailboat racer, I twice won national honors and participated in the races at Cape Cod. In addition, I have made lasting contacts with owners and officials. I am confident that my business background and knowledge of boats would enable me to have a favorable impact on Any Corporation sales and image.

Thank you for your attention. I look forward to speaking with you again and, ideally, to conducting in-person meetings with you and your colleagues. Attached is a resume for all to review. Thank you for your continued consideration. I will call soon to discuss your thoughts regarding next steps.

Sincerely yours,
Chris Smith
123 Any Street
City, ST 12345
(555) 555-5555
csmith@email.com

Date: June 1, 200–
From: *csmith@email.com*
To: *pcummings@email.com*
Subject: Appreciation and Consideration

Pat Cummings
Manager, Billing Department

Thank you for a most enjoyable and informative interview. I do most definitely want to receive an offer for the computer operator position at Any Corporation. It was a pleasure meeting you and Francis Williams and learning more about the operations of your billings department. I am most interested in contributing my experience operating computer systems to the success of your firm. Per your suggestion, I will call your office next week to check the status of the decision-making process. I definitely want this job! Again, thank you for your time and continued consideration.

Sincerely,
Chris Smith
123 Any Street
City, ST 12345
(555) 555-5555
csmith@email.com

Following a Job Interview II

Chris Smith
123 Any Street • City, ST 12345 • (555) 555-5555 • csmith@email.com

June 1, 200–

Pat Cummings
Hiring Manager
Any Corporation
456 Any Street
City, ST 12345
FAX (555) 555-5557

Dear Mr. Cummings:

It was a pleasure meeting you and Francis Williams yesterday. As I learned more about the products and services provided by Any Corporation and the people who truly make up this organization, I hope I was able to convey my sincere desire to be your Executive Assistant. This seems an ideal opportunity to apply my administrative and organizational skills to the overall effectiveness of your efforts.

As mentioned during the interview, and summarized on my resume, qualifications I would bring to the position include the following:

- Nine years' experience handling all office functions, including preparing and generating letters and reports, payroll, accounts payable and receivable, and customer service.
- Organizational proficiency, reflected in my revamping of a records storage system at Quicksilver Metro to reduce records access time by over 60 percent from the previous system.
- Experience working with a variety of software, including Word, WordPerfect, Excel, and Internet applications.

Thank you for considering my candidacy. I look forward to hearing from you regarding your final deliberation. I do want this offer and to someday soon support the efforts of Francis Williams to transform the goals of Any Corporation into achievements. Please share this note with all whom I spoke with.

Sincerely,

Chris Smith

Chris Smith

Thanks for a Great Reference

Date: June 1, 200–
From: *csmith@email.com*
To: *pcummings@email.com*
Subject: Phone Follow-Up

Dear Pat:

Thank you so much for agreeing to be on my list of references. Your support when I recently applied for the bookkeeping position at The Baldwin Company was much appreciated and, frankly, successful. After your e-mail to Francis Williams, I interviewed for the position and have since been offered it. I accepted. I appreciate your efforts on my behalf. My appreciation is strong and sincere. Please, let's do keep in touch and let me know if there is ever anything I can do to reciprocate. I am so thankful that you were not simply a passive name on a sheet of paper but an active advocate and much-needed supporter of my efforts. Again, thank you.

Sincerely,

Chris Smith
Any Corporation
123 Any Street
City, ST 12345
(555) 555-5555
csmith@email.com

Thanks for a Great Recommendation

Chris Smith
123 Any Street • City, ST 12345 • (555) 555-5555 • *csmith@email.com*

June 1, 200–

Pat Cummings
Accounting Supervisor
Any Corporation
456 Any Street
City, ST 12345
FAX (555) 555-5557

Dear Mr. Cummings:

I appreciate the kind letter of recommendation you wrote to support my job-search efforts. Yesterday, I received an offer to begin work as a staff accountant with Williams and Williams. Your description of my internship achievements at Any Corporation definitely contributed to my success. If there is anything I can do in return, please contact me. Thank you again and again.

Sincerely,

Chris Smith

Chris Smith

Thanks for a Great Referral

Date: June 1, 200–
From: *csmith@email.com*
To: *pcummings@email.com*
Subject: Appreciation and Consideration

Pat:

I am happy to inform you that I have just accepted an offer to become the acquisitions editor at Other Publishing Group. I should begin work within the next few weeks.

I would like to thank you for all your help during my job search of the past few months, specifically for putting me in touch with Francis Williams at Other Publishing. If there is ever anything I can do in return, please don't hesitate to contact me. Yours was a favor I shall not soon forget. Your confidence in my abilities will, I trust, be rewarded as I continue an achievement-filled career with this new organization. Again, many thanks and best wishes.

Sincerely,
Chris

After an Informational Interview

Chris Smith
123 Any Street • City, ST 12345 • (555) 555-5555 • *csmith@email.com*

June 1, 200–

Pat Cummings
Occupational Therapist
Any Rehabilitation Center
456 Any Street
City, ST 12345
FAX (555) 555-5557

Dear Ms. Cummings:

Thank you for taking the time to meet with me on Friday. I enjoyed learning about the programs offered at Any Rehabilitation Center and about the roles and responsibilities of being an Occupational Therapist.

Our discussion definitely strengthened my interest in occupational therapy as a career. I am planning to take your advice and apply for enrollment in a graduate program in September. In the interim, I will contact the referrals you provided to inquire about part-time positions and summer internship possibilities. Of course, I will keep you informed of how my job-search and application efforts progress. If you have any other suggestions, referrals, or contact names, please do not hesitate to contact me via the information above.

You are truly an inspiration and a role model. Thank you again for your assistance.

Sincerely,

Chris Smith

Chris Smith

Follow-up Letter

Date: June 1, 200–
From: *csmith@email.com*
To: *pcummings@email.com*
Subject: Business Manager Candidacy

TO: Pat Cummings, President
Any Corporation

In a recent e-mail, Francis Williams, group vice president with your company, indicated that my resume and letter regarding employment with Any Corporation were being forwarded for your review. Not yet having received a response, I am enclosing the attached resume to reinforce my interest in becoming your next Business Manager.

As detailed on the attached resume, I offer seven years of experience and qualifications that could be well applied in the Business Manager position. In addition to a master's degree in Business Administration, I offer experience in relevant positions ranging from product management trainee to clinical service manager of five company-operated outpatient treatment centers. During an interview, I can personally expand upon all qualifications and motivations.

Please interpret continued communications as indicative of the strength of my interest in someday interviewing for and, ideally, serving within the capacities of Business Manager. Should you judge my capabilities as more appropriate for other positions, please, let's discuss those opportunities as well. Thank you for your continued consideration. I look forward to hearing from you sometime soon.

Sincerely,
Chris Smith
123 Any Street
City, ST 12345
(555) 555-5555
csmith@email.com

Response to a Rejection

Chris Smith
123 Any Street • City, ST 12345 • (555) 555-5555 • *csmith@email.com*

June 1, 200–

Pat Cummings
Editor
Any Publication
456 Any Street
City, ST 12345
FAX (555) 555-5557

Dear Mr. Cummings:

I would like to thank you again for the chance to interview for the assistant editor position with Any Publication. Although disappointed I was not chosen, I enjoyed meeting with you and your staff and learning more about your company.

I remain very interested in opportunities with Any Publication, and I would appreciate it if you would keep me in mind for future openings in your magazine or book divisions. Your thoughts regarding my potential to someday join you and your colleagues would be welcomed. I will call to confirm your receipt of this fax and to discuss your reactions to this request for continued consideration. I would also welcome consideration for freelance assignments in support of any special projects that might arise.

Thanks again for past and, I do hope, future consideration.

Sincerely,

Chris Smith

Chris Smith

Withdrawal from Consideration

Chris Smith
123 Any Street • City, ST 12345 • (555) 555-5555 • *csmith@email.com*

June 1, 200–

Pat Cummings
Human Resources Director
Any Corporation
456 Any Street
City, ST 12345
FAX (555) 555-5557

Dear Mr. Cummings:

As you may recall, I spoke with you over the phone several weeks ago regarding the status of my application for the regional sales manager position. While I understand that you are still in the process of screening resumes, I wanted to notify you that I have just accepted an offer for a similar position. Therefore, I respectfully request that you remove my candidacy from consideration.

Thank you for the time you spent to inform me of the hiring process. Perhaps someday I might apply for future opportunities with Any Corporation. Again, thank you for the consideration you granted me.

Sincerely yours,

Chris Smith

Chris Smith

Rejection of an Offer

Date: June 1, 200–
From: *csmith@email.com*
To: *pcummings@email.com*
Subject: Declining Your Offer

Pat Cummings
Senior Editor
Any Publishing Company
456 Any Street
City, ST 12345

Dear Mr. Cummings:

Thank you for your offer of employment and for your confidence in my abilities as an editor. As I explained during our phone conversation, I have re-evaluated my plans to relocate to Miami. After much deliberation, I have decided that I must postpone relocation, stay here in Bartow, and decline your offer.

I apologize for informing you by e-mail, but I wanted to let you know of my decision as soon as I could and formalize my actions. I would be happy to discuss the circumstances that necessitated this decision if you wish. You can expect my call tomorrow in thanks for the consideration you granted me and to elaborate upon any issues.

I regret not being able to accept the opportunity to work at Any Publishing. Again, I appreciate your offer. My interest was most sincere, and it is very difficult to now decline this great opportunity. Please convey my best to all whom I met during the interview process.

Sincerely,
Chris Smith
123 Any Street
City, ST 12345
(555) 555-5555
csmith@email.com

Acceptance Letter

Date: June 1, 200–
From: *csmith@email.com*
To: *pcummings@email.com*
Subject: Appreciation and Consideration

Dear Mr. Cummings:

I received your letter, and I am pleased to accept your employment offer. I look forward to beginning work as an underwriter at Any Insurance. Your offer of $42,000 per year, including all appropriate benefits, is most generous. I would like to confirm my start date of June 21. Notice has been given to my current employer, and I expect a smooth transition to Any Insurance.

Once again, I would like to thank you and Francis Williams for your positive response to my candidacy. I look forward to joining you both on the Any Insurance team. If you wish to communicate with me, for any reason, especially if I need to formally document my acceptance in any way other than this e-mail, please do not hesitate to contact me. Also, I will be in touch with the human resources office to complete all required paperwork. I look forward to seeing you on the morning of June 21. If you need anything before then, just call or e-mail.

Sincerely,
Chris Smith

Address or Phone Number Change

Date: June 1, 200–
From: *csmith@email.com*
To: *pcummings@email.com*
Subject: Laboratory Assistant Position

Pat Cummings
Research Scientist
Any Medical Association
456 Any Street
City, ST 12345

Dear Mr. Cummings:

I am writing to inform you that I have moved to the address and telephone listed below and on the attached revised resume. I offer this updated resume for your information and to affirm that my interest in this position remains strong. Described on the copy of the original cover letter used to support my candidacy, I offer broad and in-depth qualifications, as well as directly related education. I am looking forward to hearing more about the status of the laboratory assistant search and about your assessment of my worthiness for an interview.

Thank you for your continued consideration.

Sincerely,
Chris Smith
123 Any Street
City, ST 12345
(555) 555-5555
csmith@email.com

Resignation Letter

Chris Smith
123 Any Street • City, ST 12345 • (555) 555-5555 • *csmith@email.com*

June 1, 200–

Pat Cummings
President
Any Company
456 Any Street
City, ST 12345

Dear Mr. Cummings:

Regretfully, I must tender my resignation, effective the 1st of next month. Although I have enjoyed working with you and our Any Company colleagues, I have accepted a position with another company that offers the potential for continued professional growth and many tangible and intangible rewards. Please let me know what formal steps should be taken to complete all projects I am now currently involved in and all documentation needed for human resource purposes.

I am grateful for the experience this position has offered me. If there is anything I can do to make my departure a smooth one, please let me know. I also hope that all professional relationships and personal friendships will last beyond my tenure at Any Company. You and my Any Company colleagues have truly been inspirational role models, and I owe you much. Thank you.

Sincerely,

Chris Smith

Chris Smith

Critiquing Checklist

You can use this quick critiquing checklist to review your own resumes and cover letters as well as those of others. Remember, the revision process is an important step in writing great job-search documents!

Identifying Information

- ❐ Is your name in larger font and bolded on both?
- ❐ Is your address, phone, and e-mail information presented on one line?
- ❐ If more than one address or phone appears, is there a reason?

Overall Appearance and First Impression

- ❐ Are both cover letter and resume neat, easy to visually scan, and in quick-glance logical formats?
- ❐ Is font type and size easy to read and professional in appearance?
- ❐ Can you identify a logical pattern of headline placement and highlighting techniques for the resume and paragraph order for the cover letter?
- ❐ Can both resume and cover letter be cut and pasted into e-mail text blocks and still retain logical formatting?

Objective, Qualification Summary, and First Paragraph

- ❐ Does the objective or qualification summary of the resume and first paragraph of the cover letter project knowledge of your desired job, using field-specific phrasing?
- ❐ Does the qualification summary in paragraph or bullet-point form on either resume or cover letter project your desired objective?
- ❐ Does the qualification summary reveal your understanding of selection criteria, specialized terminology, and key words associated with your job-search goals?
- ❐ Do headlines and paragraph order inform readers of key qualification connections?
- ❐ Are most significant goal-related qualification statements first, and those of less importance later?
- ❐ If viewed independently from the resume, or within a cover letter, does the qualification section project focus and an impressive knowledge of your desired field, job function, and target firm?

Educational and Professional Development

☐ Do special headlines in the resume and paragraph order project focus?

☐ Does order of appearance accurately portray significance, with most important information first?

☐ Do the resume and cover letter highlight school(s), degree(s), area(s) of concentration, courses, and honors related to your goals?

☐ Are courses, papers, and projects listed and described in behavioral and outcome terms?

☐ Are specialized goal-focused training seminars presented under headlines in the resume or special paragraphs in the cover letter?

Experience

☐ Do special resume headlines and second and third cover-letter paragraphs reinforce your focus?

☐ Does formatting like bolding, italics, or bullets make it easy to see information?

☐ Are most significant target-specific employment achievements presented under appropriate headlines in the resume and easy-to-identify paragraphs in the cover letter?

☐ Are resume cover-letter entries described using active and accomplishment-oriented phrasing, including facts and figures when possible?

☐ Are goal-specific experiences grouped under appropriate resume headlines and in most significant cover-letter paragraphs?

☐ If entries on the resume are less important, are they simply listed, not described, and left off the cover letter?

Community and Cocurricular Activities and Special Categories

☐ If specifically related to your goals, is a special headline used in the resume, or are these activities listed in early paragraphs of the cover letter?

☐ Do all resume entries and cover-letter references seem relevant to stated goals, and is it logical for them to be included?

☐ If specifically related to your goals, are experiences referred to in a qualification summary?

Overall Presentation, Last Glance, and Final Details

☐ Are most important headlines and paragraphs first, with most significant information appearing?

☐ If you have more than one targeted resume, are the objectives clear? Did you change order of presentation on each? Are summaries of qualifications target-specific?

☐ Do the resume and cover letter each present a professional image, and are summaries of qualifications target-specific?

☐ Would a prospective employer sense goal-specific competence and confidence if the resume and cover letter were reviewed independently of each other?

☐ Can you elaborate upon each document and use both as a guide during the interview?

☐ Are you ready to distribute the resume and cover letter?

E Printed and Web Resources

This appendix offers a comprehensive listing of publications and Web resources that should be used by all job-seekers, no matter the age, stage, or goals. It is truly a "best of the rest" inventory.

Additional Books in the Everything® Series

The Everything® Resume Book, 2nd Edition: In today's competitive job market, resumes have become more important than ever. With hundreds of applicants seeking to interview for the same position, your resume must stand out. This completely revised and updated second edition guide shows you exactly how to focus your skills and tailor your resume to get the job you want. In it, you'll find winning action verbs, helpful hints on format and presentation, and savvy advice for posting online. Most importantly, it contains more than 100 sample resumes for virtually any profession. Many of these samples inspired the sample cover letters appearing in this book.

The Everything® After College Book: If you are a new graduate and you haven't a clue about what to do to get your first job, check out the information in this publication. This is a practical guide to the real world and just happens to contain everything you need to get your post-commencement act together.

The Everything® Get a Job Book: Written in an unintimidating style, this book offers advice for finding your first job or a better job. This comprehensive publication provides guidance on how to find companies that are hiring without even having to pick up the want ads; identifying networking opportunities; performing an Internet job search; writing cover letters and resumes; interviewing; dealing with headhunters and employment services; negotiating salary, bonus, and benefits packages; and much more.

The Everything® Hot Careers Book: Before you begin a job search, you need to know what careers are good choices for you and to set your goals accordingly. Whether you're just entering the job market or considering switching careers, you need to conduct research to help you choose a path and develop effective strategies. This book provides savvy job-seekers with up-to-date information as real people reveal what it's like to work in fifty exciting professions, introducing readers to contemporary careers some may not even know exist.

The Everything® Job Interview Book: This book is perfect for all job-seekers, from recent college grads looking for that first job to seasoned candidates who are looking for new opportunities or are switching careers. It encourages readers to define career goals and develop a job-search plan; maximize interview performance; make memorable first impressions; handle difficult interview questions; and take effective post-interview actions. Also included are sample interviews for a variety of industries and tips on handling job offers and salary negotiations.

The Everything® Online Job Search Book: In today's world, job-seekers must become Internet-literate and "e-ffective." This book informs job-seekers how to access all kinds of information via the Web, including tips on searching thousands of listings on major sites and finding advice on how to write electronic resumes. Readers will learn how to find literally millions of job listings on the Web; use the leading career Web sites effectively; write electronic resumes and cover letters; research companies online; locate online contacts at companies worldwide; conduct a job search while maintaining privacy; and network on the Internet.

The Everything® Writing Well Book: This book encourages readers to maximize the impact of writing for virtually any situation, formal or informal, business or personal. It guides you through all aspects of skills building, including choosing the appropriate tone, building document structure, and communicating a clear and concise message. This publication addresses issues related to electronic writing, such as e-mails and faxes; layperson's journalism, such as "letters to the editor"; copyright matters for research topics; essays, including personal and biographical; academic papers, such as theses and dissertations; as well as business writing, such as job offers, corporate memos, and press releases.

Other Publications

America's Top Internships (The Princeton Review): An extremely valuable annual publication that identifies options for those seeking pre- and post-graduation internships. Used creatively, it can offer insights into potential careers and employers. Indexes by geography, field, and special criteria make it easy to use and, for some, a pre-research as well as job-search tool. In fact, you can use the indexes of this book, combined with its companion piece, *The Internship Bible,* as goal-setting assessment devices. By reviewing the indexes, then identifying and prioritizing your top five fields of interests, you can gain focus and identify potential employers.

The Back-Door Guide to Short-Term Job Adventures (Ten Speed Press): This publication addresses the needs of those seeking pre- or post-graduation internship, externship, and related experiences. Readers can use post-graduation experiences to "bridge" from commencement to first jobs. It includes opportunities that are not precisely business oriented, ranging from the creative and fun to community service and meaningful skill-building opportunities.

Book of Lists (Crain Communication and/or your local business journal): These annual publications list "Top 25" firms in specific cities or regions. The A-through-Z listings of top firms include fields such as the following: Accounting, Advertising, Airlines, Architecture, BioTech, Commercial Banking, Computer Networking, Computer Training, Venture Capital, and Video Production, to name just a few. They often include listings of "fastest growing public and private firms" as well as "highest paid CEOs." Clearly, these are among the best resources to use when seeking up-to-date information needed to create a hit list of potential employers and, of course, when networking.

Career Opportunities In . . . (Checkmark Books/Facts on File): Titles and topics in this series include the following: Health Care, Newspaper, Magazines, Mental Health and Social Work, Marketing and Sales, Medical Technologies and Technicians, Radio and Television, Public Administration, Education, Public Relations, Film and Video, Performing Arts, Therapy and Allied Health Professionals, Environmental, and Physical Sciences. This is one of the best "if you can describe a job, you can get a job" collection of publications. Books contain concise descriptions of field and functional options. Like many books of this kind, appendices list potential employers and professional associations, as well as educational options. These too-often-ignored final sections can be hidden gems for career explorers and job-seekers.

The *Careers For* series (VGM Career Horizons, a division of NTC Publishing Group): This series of intriguing titles includes "Careers for" the following groups: Animal Lovers, Bookworms, Caring People, Computer Buffs, Crafty People, Culture Lovers, Environmental Types, Fashion Plates, Film Buffs, Foreign Language Aficionados, Good Samaritans, Gourmets, Health Nuts, History Buffs, Kids at Heart, Music Lovers, Mystery Buffs, Nature Lovers, Night Owls, Numbers Crunchers, Plant Lovers, Shutterbugs, Sports Nuts, Travel Buffs, and Writers. This is a creative and ever-expanding "What can I do with a set of skills and interest in" collection. Each book expands upon its title to connect readers with career options. Each books contains brief descriptions of fields and functions, intended to stimulate additional pre-research.

The *Careers In* series (VGM Career Horizons, a division of NTC Publishing Group): Titles and topics in this series include "Careers in" the following areas: Accounting, Advertising, Business, Child Care, Communications, Computers, Education, Engineering, Environment, Finance, Government, Health Care, High Tech, Journalism, Law, Marketing, Medicine, Science, and Social and Rehabilitation Services. This is one of the most-used and easiest-to-read series of "jobs-within-fields" publications. Each book contains brief descriptions of functional options within fields noted in the titles. Information regarding fields and employment options should inspire continued pre-research and facilitate development of the career focus required of effective job search. Listings of professional associations are very useful. Reviewing these publications will most definitely instill within readers the vocabulary required to state goals and, later, to direct resume-writing and job-search efforts.

The Directory of Executive Recruiters (Kennedy Information): This comprehensive listing of contingency and retainer firms is indexed by industry and recruiter specialty. This publication is particularly valuable for experienced job-seekers and those with technical and specialized backgrounds.

The Executive Recruiters Almanac (Adams Media): A user-friendly listing of search firms and other third-party organizations. It contains discussions of how to use these organizations most effectively as well as listings of numerous firms indexed by fields, functions, and industries. While exceptionally valuable for experienced candidates, this publication can facilitate the efforts of almost all candidates.

The *Great Jobs For* series (VGM Career Horizons, a division of NTC Publishing Group): Majors included in the series include the following: Psychology, History, English, Communication, Business, Sociology, Foreign Language, and Engineering. This is an excellent "What can I do with a major in" collection of publications. Each easy-to-read book contains recommended fields listed by majors. These books naturally stimulate pre-research efforts that facilitate goal-setting. Even if your particular major does not appear in a title, reading a few of the books in the collection should inspire you to complete field-focused research.

The *Harvard Business School Career Guide* series (Harvard Business School Publishing): Subjects include the following: Management Consulting, Finance, Not-for-Profit, and Marketing. These books are written for MBAs, but if used creatively, they can provide exceptional support for undergraduates and others interested in "Ivy League–caliber jobs." Each begins with general discussions of investment banking, finance, and consulting, followed by comprehensive listings of organizations within these fields, and ending with extremely powerful annotated bibliographies.

Internships (Peterson's): Another annually published book that identifies pre- and post-graduation "internships" that, if used creatively, offers insight into potential externship and post-graduation opportunities. Indexing by geography, field, and special criteria makes it easy to use and, for some, a pre-research as well as job-search tool.

The Internship Bible (Princeton Review/Random House Inc.): Another of the annually published internship directories that, if used creatively, offers insights into post-graduation opportunities. It also offers indexing by geography, field, and special criteria.

The JobBank Guide To series and *The JobBank* series (Adams Media): JobBank guides list companies by industries, including Health Care, Computer, and High Technology. In addition, JobBank books list companies as well as other job-search-related organizations within specific cities and regions. Geography-focused titles cover cities and regions such as the following: Atlanta, Austin/San Antonio, Carolinas, Chicago, Connecticut, Dallas/Fort Worth, Denver, Detroit, Florida, Houston, Indiana, Las Vegas, Los Angeles, Minneapolis/St. Paul, Missouri, Ohio, Greater Philadelphia, Phoenix, Pittsburgh, Portland, San Francisco Bay Area, Seattle, Tennessee, Virginia, and the Washington, D.C., metro area. These publications also contain brief, yet inspirational discussions regarding general job search.

The Knock 'em Dead series (Adams Media): These general job-search, resume, and interview guides target experienced as well as first-time jobseekers. Each is comprehensive in content, yet easy to read and inspirational. They educate and motivate people in all phases of job searching.

Making a Mil-Yen Teaching English in Japan (Stone Bridge Press): This specialty publication highlights an increasingly popular post-graduation option. For those who wish to use opportunities to "Test teaching as a career," "Begin an international career," or "Bridge from commencement to first jobs," this is an excellent resource. Once in Japan, you can explore education, business, travel, tourism, and varied other careers.

Naked at the Interview (John Wiley & Sons): Immodestly speaking, one of the best comprehensive goal-setting, job-search, and interview resources for soon-to-be and recent college grads. Don't let the title fool you. It is not X-rated, nor is it just for those seeking to improve interview skills. This is a humorous and easy-to-use pre-research as well as job-search tool. Many of the resumes and correspondence examples offered illustrate effective approaches applicable to all job-seekers.

The *Opportunities In* series (VGM Career Horizons): Another of the often-used and easy-to-read set of "If you can describe a job, you can get a job" collection of publications. Each book contains brief descriptions of functional options within fields noted in the titles. The information regarding fields and employment options and should inspire continued pre-research and, ultimately, facilitate development of the career focus required to begin an effective job search.

Peterson's Job Opportunities series (Peterson's): Titles include opportunities for the following concentrations: Business Majors, Engineering and Computer Science Majors, and Health and Science. This is an exceptional series of employer directories that, if used effectively, facilitates internship, externship, and post-graduation job-search efforts. Like others, it offers indexes by geography, field, and other special criteria. Indexes refer readers to brief profiles with names, addresses, and basic identifying information for potential employers.

Plunkett's Industry Almanacs (Plunkett Research, Ltd.): Collection of publications including industries such as the following: Biotech and Genetics, Health Care, Retail, and E-Commerce, to name a few. This is an excellent resource for those seeking internships, externships, or entry-level opportunities within any of the fields covered. These books also offer geographic and functional indexes and Web page citations. They are very expensive, so they are best used as library resources.

US Directory of Entertainment Employers (EEJ Publishing): An annual specialized publication that can be used as a comprehensive employer listing for those seeking internships, externships, or entry-level opportunities within the entertainment field. This directory lists advertising agencies, television, and film production houses, lawyers, public relations firms, agents, recording studios, film studios, and many other prospective employers.

Vacation Work's Teaching English Abroad: Talk Your Way Around the World! (Peterson's): This comprehensive guide offers information for those seeking this increasingly popular option. Teaching overseas can be a "wonderful experience," as well as a "springboard to an international career."

The *Vault Guides* series (Vault Reports, Inc.): Another collection of publications that begin with detailed field and functional descriptions and ends with employer listings. In addition to name, address, phone, and URL for each employer, this publication offers good "getting started" and "pre-interview" information. The one-page-for-each-employer format is easy to use and offers quick photocopying options, which facilitates employer research. It is an excellent first resource to use to start developing a "hit list" once goals are focused. Also, more comprehensive industry and employer reports can be ordered as desired.

Wet Feet Press Guides (Wet Feet Press): This is another series of print and Internet publications focusing on specialized fields including Advertising and PR, Biotechnology, Consulting, Entertainment and Sports, Finance Services, and Technology. These publications offer field and function information, as well as firm and industry specific profiles. Specialized resources targeting particular companies and addressing issues related to interviewing are accessible via the Web.

Web Sites

As you progress in your own research, you will find your own valuable sources of information on the Internet. Here are a few places to begin:

www.ipl.org—The Internet Public Library Associations on the Net provides access to professional associations. Resources available through professional associations are often the most valuable. Membership directories facilitate networking for goal-setting as well as job-search efforts. Journals and other publications enhance the vocabulary needed to enhance specialized field-focused vocabulary. By joining associations, attending seminars, reading literature, and networking with members, you will truly talk the talk and walk the walk.

www.yahoo.com—Allows you to navigate your way through plenty of pertinent information, including offerings on information such as the following: Resume Builder, My Career Center, Salary Wizard, Executive Center, Career Communities, and Company Research. The site also provides information about associations, company information, and additional data that can be used for goal-setting, networking, as well as direct job-search efforts.

www.careerbuilder.com—One of many multiple industry and national posting, resume-collection, and job-search information sites. It promotes the capabilities of a "personal search agent" that allows you to identify job-search criteria and then be contacted whenever new postings come up. This site notes "over 400,000 better jobs" posted.

✍*www.careers.wsj.com*—The *Wall Street Journal's* Career Journal is a multifaceted site. It contains articles, postings, resume collections, links to other sites, resume critiquing, and general advice regarding job search and careers. It is a high-tech, online version of what would have been career- and job-search-focused periodicals or newspaper sections just a few years ago. It is an inspirational as well as educational and logistical support site of value for experienced candidates.

✍*www.flipdog.com*—Another multifaceted site that contains articles, postings, resume banks, resume critiquing, and general advice. While the over 300,000 jobs within the system should motivate some, others will find additional resources quite valuable. You can get expert advice from the Resource Center, have employers look for your resume, enhance your career via a semimonthly newsletter, use the search agent, and reach employers through job banks and employer links.

✍*www.hotjobs.com*—This site, a Yahoo! service, boasts over 400,000 jobs, internships, and career-oriented positions. It also offers industry information, job-search advice, and a relocation center.

✍*www.WorkTree.com*—The self-proclaimed largest job-search portal in the world, this site offers access to over 50,000 links to all types of job and career resources. It also boasts user access to 3,000,000-plus jobs. Boasting aside, it is a comprehensive portal that eases access to information that can maximize the efforts of many.

✍*www.monster.com*—Literally and figuratively, the monster of all posting, resume-collection, and career-advice sites. This creatively advertised and most-recognized posting, resume-bank, employer-research, search-agent, and job-search advice site isn't scary at all. It is very user-friendly, and their cute corporate logo is rather inviting. This site promotes with great pride that it contains over 17 million resumes and 1 million postings for job-seekers of all stages and ages, including internship candidates, soon-to-be and recent college grads, and experienced professionals. While too many use this resource passively for reactive efforts only, it can be a very, very powerful proactive tool.

www.wetfeet.com—"Do Research," "Get Advice," and "Find a Job" are the first three major headings you will see when you access this site. Find a Job has two basic links: Job Listings and Internship Listings. As you navigate through the varied links, you will be provided general information and offered opportunities to buy some of the varied and valuable publications created by this group.

www.vault.com—Another great resource for job-seekers. Employers are encouraged to post jobs and internships, access the resume database, and complete surveys so data on the firm might be included in future publications. Community users are granted access to Message Boards, Ask Our Experts, and How's My Resume links. Industry options include Consulting, Finance, Law, TV News, and more, with Career Topics offering information on Career Change, Compensation, Job Search, and other issues. Like other sites, basic information is offered, and you will be given opportunities to purchase publications created by this particular group.

www.fortune.com—Grants you access to information and the annual lists generated by the venerable periodical *Fortune*. Lists include *Fortune* 500, Global 100, 100 Best Companies to Work For, and 100 Fastest Growing Companies. Topical career advice as well as "Q&A" exchanges are also offered. This is a useful resource when developing hit lists of prospective employers.

www.thomasregister.com—A comprehensive resource for finding companies and products manufactured in North America. Simply enter one or more words into the search box after selecting the product, company, or brand name you're looking for to search from over 72,000 product headings and more than 170,000 company listings.

www.net-temps.com—Net-Temps is the self-proclaimed number-one destination of job-seekers looking for contract, temporary, or direct employment through a staffing agency. Employers can post a job, candidates can find a job, gain career advice, post a resume, or create a search agent. This site is unique in that it addresses needs of those seeking part-time, temp, or contract situations, and it highlights various agencies. Over 45,000 total jobs are advertised.

www.rileyguide.com—A directory of employment and career information sources and services on the Internet, this site provides instruction for job-seekers and recruiters on how to use the Internet to their best advantage. Originally a comprehensive printed reference, then a rather passive, yet thorough listing, and now an interactive site, this is an excellent resource.

www.idealist.com—Lists over 29,000 nonprofit and community organizations in 153 countries, which you can search or browse by name, location, or mission. It contains thousands of volunteer opportunities in your community and around the world and a list of organizations that can help you volunteer abroad. It is characterized by many as the best Nonprofit Career Center on the Web, with thousands of job and internship listings.

www.twc.edu—One of the pre-eminent summer and year-round internship program, the Washington Center offers internships and academic seminars for all majors in Washington, D.C. Whatever your major, the program finds a suitable internship and includes housing. When accepted, students are assigned, according to interests, either to the Main Program, to one of approximately a dozen special, thematically organized programs, or to one of two postgraduate programs.

www.uofdreams.com—Another pre-eminent summer internship program, University of Dreams places college students in summer internships in fields including, but not limited to advertising, engineering, entertainment, finance, fashion, investment banking, law, programming, public relations, not-for-profit, and real estate. Programs in New York City, San Francisco/Silicon Valley, and Los Angeles involve guaranteed internships, seminar series, housing at NYU, Stanford, and UCLA, as well as transportation, weekend excursions, and more.

Industry-Specific Sites

- *www.association.org*—Association of Internet Professionals
- *www.adage.com*—Advertising Age
- *www.bio.com*—Biotechnology and Pharmaceutical
- *www.chronicle.com*—Chronicle of Higher Education
- *www.fjn.com*—Financial Job Network
- *www.gamasutra.com*—Gamasutra for Computer Animation and Video Games
- *www.lawjobs.com*—Law Jobs
- *www.medzilla.com*—Biotechnology, Pharmaceutical, and Medical
- *www.pmi.org*—Project Management Institute
- *www.prsa.org*—Public Relations Society of America
- *www.starchefs.com*—Food Services

Ⓔ Special Strategies for Special Groups

The information in this book is presented for readers of varied backgrounds, with diverse goals, and at different stages of career development. As final words of wisdom, each potential target group will be given specialized job-search and cover-letter advice. Think about which group best defines your efforts, and be inspired by these highly focused tips.

High School Students

You are most likely looking for part-time or summer employment or for an internship. When you write your cover letters (e-mailed or even hand-delivered), you can keep them straightforward and short. In fact, most will be brief "cover notes." Don't use fancy words or two sentences when one will do.

Your resume will most likely be a very broad presentation of your background. Include lists of courses, papers, and projects, and use a summary of qualifications that clearly presents your goals.

Your words (in your cover letter as well as during your interview) must present focus and curiosity. At your stage, curiosity in a particular career field can be enough to gain an internship, externship (shadowing experience), or volunteer position. To land a job you must show an understanding of the skills needed, that you possess some, and that you have the potential to quickly learn others. You must show that you know what it takes to succeed. Be courageous, and apply for opportunities that might be a bit beyond your ability level. Contact individuals you have never met. And seek the help of your parents, teachers, counselors, and friends' parents.

College Internship Candidates

Before you begin your search, be sure you understand what an internship is and what kind of experience you are looking for. Are you seeking a paid internship, or are you willing to be unpaid? Do you want to earn academic credit or not? Will it be a formal opportunity, with a step-by-step process and deadlines or an informal one, generated through a number of self-initiated discussions? It can be "all of the above," but whatever your definition, please share it with potential internship employers through your cover letters and networking notes.

Make both reactive and proactive efforts by responding to postings in various newspapers and Internet sites and contacting potential employers and specific people of particular interest. Do not limit yourself to looking at postings, or you may become quickly frustrated and disappointed. When responding to postings, show the reader that you understand what the internship entails and that you have what it takes to succeed. When conducting proactive efforts, always define what you want and, when possible, ask: "Is there a special project I can help with over the next few months?" If the response is "Yes," you've landed an internship!

While many may say "We don't hire interns" or "We don't have any internships," their definition of internship may be different from yours—almost all, when asked properly, will say "Of course we have projects on the horizon." Some creative internship-seekers skip the word "internship" altogether, replacing it with "special projects."

Amazing internship programs, including the University of Dreams (*www.uofdreams.com*) and Washington Center for Internships (*www.twc.edu*) offer challenging and rewarding opportunities. These "package programs" often include housing, seminars, social activities, the opportunity to earn academic credit, and great internship options. In return for your tuition and fees, you get a great experience and the security that professionals have "placed you" in a challenging, yet supportive internship site and living environment. These programs are particularly appropriate for students seeking internships in cities far from home or school.

College Seniors

While the three most important things to know about real estate are location, location, and location, the three most important things for college seniors to know about job search and cover letters are focus, focus, and focus. The ability to articulate goals (multiple objectives) is critical to success. Focus impacts how you plan and implement your search and, most important, the words you choose and use in your cover letters and resumes as well as during your interviews. It's also important to do your research—read up on careers and specific positions, speak with your counselors or advisors, and also be sure to schedule meetings with persons working within your fields of interest.

Within all your letters, from informal notes sent via e-mail to formal letters, make connections for the reader. Reveal that you know how your education, experience, and personal traits connect with your desired job. Show you know what it takes to succeed in a particular job. Don't just offer broad overviews of a well-rounded candidate and hope the reader will "see potential."

You want the reader to perceive you as a match because you have linked past experiences and present skills to your future job.

Reveal your knowledge of field, function, and firm by using language and phrases appropriate for your field of interest. Be aware of key word searches and be sure your letters reflect the field-specific words and phrases that employers are looking for. If you don't have experience specific to a field, state that you have "curiosity about…" or "capabilities to learn…" and finish these statements with a listing of very pertinent and required skills or knowledge.

Stay focused, no matter what. You can have more than one goal, but do not fall into the "I'm going to look for anything" trap. And, of course, use both proactive and reactive techniques and resources. Don't limit yourself to one or the other, or become particularly hypnotized by the allure of on-campus recruiting or career fairs.

Use resources identified in Appendix B, network with as many people as you can, nurture and use job-search advocates, and do visit your school's career center frequently. Keep in touch with these professionals after commencement.

Recent College Grads

Remain persistent, patient, and purposeful. Continually reassess your goals and refine them. Add new ones, but don't drop existing job-search targets unless you are convinced, after three to six months of effort, that they are unrealistic. Do not be overcome by a fear of focus. Looking for "anything" will not speed up the process. Remaining focused on the types of jobs you are seeking is always best.

In fact, magnifying focus by continually enhancing your knowledge of fields of interest (through reading or information conversations) can speed up the process. The more you learn, the more you share this knowledge in letters, notes, and during conversations, the better. Mix a little research with job search, always remaining curious about targeted fields, functions, and firms. Read professional journals or specialized publications that someone now in the field might read. Make reference to your reading when communicating with network members, advocates, or potential employers. Many job-seekers can overcome a lack of experience with increased knowledge. And, one or two courses might be all you need to succeed!

While it's emotionally difficult to think of taking another course after you've finished four (or more) years of college, strategically it might be exactly what you have to do! One course, prominently displayed on a resume, actively discussed in an interview, and clearly presented in a cover letter, might be all you need to get an offer. As you conduct research, you will realize what particular courses might be most logical and most likely to positively impact your efforts. Don't worry about "credits" or about "prestige" when signing up for these educational options. A local community college or state extension program would be fine, and you don't have to earn credits for the experience. It's truly amazing how many who take this option successfully jump-start their search and ultimately land a great job. One, two, or three courses completed during the summer or fall after commencement can be keys to your success.

Don't ignore internship options, either. While conducting your job search, also look for an internship option or, as cited earlier, "a special project to do over the next month or two." In some fields it is common to intern your way in to a paying job. Include internship inquiries at the end of job-search correspondence, both initial contacts and follow-up efforts. Also explore special programs. The dollars invested in these programs, particularly for those seeking to enter special fields and relocate far from home or school, will pay off. Using examples already cited, an internship in Washington, D.C., gained through the Washington Center for Internships, or one in New York, Los Angeles, or Silicon Valley and the San Francisco Bay area, completed through the University of Dreams can, and should, enhance your potential to find a full-time and paid experience. Remember, when all other interns have to return to school, you can stay to complete all of the projects you started, and you are already in your target city. A long-distance job search is challenging, to say the least.

Recent Graduate School Grads

Depending upon your field of interest, your efforts may focus on academics, scientific research, business, law, or any number of fields. Reinforcing the advice given seniors and recent undergraduate degree recipients, become focused and stay focused. Be goal-articulate, make critical connections in all communications, and use language appropriate to fields of interest. Follow the strategies outlined earlier and throughout this publication.

Sometimes graduate study will have enhanced your focus and field-specific language skills, but sometimes not. Magnify your skills through targeted documents. Open efforts are most often the least effective and most frustrating. Readers may not make the connection between a general resume and cover letter and your desire to enter advertising, so you must make it for them. Use targeted documents that show your knowledge and "Careers as a Second Language" talents.

Those Switching Jobs

If you graduated a few years ago and are now ready for that next job, go for it. Follow the steps to job-search success outlined in Chapter 1, and all steps to resume and cover letter writing documented in subsequent chapters. Act on the advice given here for soon-to-be and recent grads, yet realize that your efforts are a bit different. You now have a record of success to build upon. Some may be taking logical and easy-to-identify next steps on a career path begun when they accepted their first job. Others may want to make a transition to another field.

If the next job you desire is related to the one you now have, cover letters and resumes must reveal goal-directed accomplishments and all communications must be written or spoken using language specific to your field. You've already begun to make your way along your career path—now you must continue to move ahead.

Be careful how you present ambitions and goals to your current employer, but do so. Don't put your current position in jeopardy because you are ambitious and qualified to find greater challenges and rewards. Be sensitive to what your supervisors might think if they knew you were actively looking for a new job. Make sure you have used all appropriate means to share your goals for promotion or expanded roles and responsibilities internally. Find an advisor, mentor, or advocate with whom you can discuss strategies and issues. Keep in mind that your college or university may offer alumni career services, so take advantage of these resources.

It is easier to find a job when you have a job, so use your current position as a springboard to your next opportunities and achievements. In most cases, networking and proactive efforts will be very successful, but do not ignore postings and reactive strategies and techniques. As always, become focused and stay focused. Those seeking to make a transition from one field to another must be particularly goal-articulate and goal-directed.

Career Changers

It is essential that you conduct research and reveal your knowledge of your target field in all communications. Too many applicants simply share letters that proudly present broad potential and success in other fields, hoping that readers will make connections needed to grant interviews and, ultimately, make offers. Be proud, yet remain focused. Share with readers of your correspondence and with network members that you know what you want and that you are willing to do whatever it takes to get there.

Start by signing up for one course directly related to the field of interest. One course may be all that is needed to make a transition, but it might take two or three. These academic bridges from one field to another can become foundations of your job search and the beginnings of a new career path. Saying you want to make a transition may not be enough, but by taking initial academic steps your actions are speaking much louder than words. Your class doesn't need to be a semester-long commitment—a well-chosen seminar or weekend workshop may work just as well.

Check to see if the new field you're interested in welcomes volunteers, and if it does, go for it! Volunteering is the best way to help you get onto a new career track. Also remember the power of networking. The more role models you meet, the more advocates you can nurture, the more likely you can make your desired change. It may not be as easy as you think, but if you follow the advice offered in this book, and in other resources identified in Appendix B, it won't be as hard as you think, either. Go for it!

THE EVERYTHING SERIES!

BUSINESS & PERSONAL FINANCE

Everything® Budgeting Book
Everything® Business Planning Book
Everything® Coaching and Mentoring Book
Everything® Fundraising Book
Everything® Get Out of Debt Book
Everything® Grant Writing Book
Everything® Homebuying Book, 2nd Ed.
Everything® Homeselling Book
Everything® Home-Based Business Book
Everything® Investing Book
Everything® Landlording Book
Everything® Leadership Book
Everything® Managing People Book
Everything® Negotiating Book
Everything® Online Business Book
Everything® Personal Finance Book
Everything® Personal Finance in Your 20s and 30s Book
Everything® Project Management Book
Everything® Real Estate Investing Book
Everything® Robert's Rules Book, $7.95
Everything® Selling Book
Everything® Start Your Own Business Book
Everything® Wills & Estate Planning Book

COOKING

Everything® Barbecue Cookbook
Everything® Bartender's Book, $9.95
Everything® Chinese Cookbook
Everything® College Cookbook
Everything® Cookbook
Everything® Diabetes Cookbook
Everything® Easy Gourmet Cookbook
Everything® Fondue Cookbook
Everything® Grilling Cookbook
Everything® Healthy Meals in Minutes Cookbook
Everything® Holiday Cookbook

Everything® Indian Cookbook
Everything® Low-Carb Cookbook
Everything® Low-Fat High-Flavor Cookbook
Everything® Low-Salt Cookbook
Everything® Meals for a Month Cookbook
Everything® Mediterranean Cookbook
Everything® Mexican Cookbook
Everything® One-Pot Cookbook
Everything® Pasta Cookbook
Everything® Quick Meals Cookbook
Everything® Slow Cooker Cookbook
Everything® Soup Cookbook
Everything® Thai Cookbook
Everything® Vegetarian Cookbook
Everything® Wine Book

HEALTH

Everything® Alzheimer's Book
Everything® Diabetes Book
Everything® Hypnosis Book
Everything® Low Cholesterol Book
Everything® Massage Book
Everything® Menopause Book
Everything® Nutrition Book
Everything® Reflexology Book
Everything® Stress Management Book

HISTORY

Everything® American Government Book
Everything® American History Book
Everything® Civil War Book
Everything® Irish History & Heritage Book
Everything® Middle East Book

HOBBIES & GAMES

Everything® Blackjack Strategy Book
Everything® Brain Strain Book, $9.95
Everything® Bridge Book
Everything® Candlemaking Book

Everything® Card Games Book
Everything® Cartooning Book
Everything® Casino Gambling Book, 2nd Ed.
Everything® Chess Basics Book
Everything® Crossword and Puzzle Book
Everything® Crossword Challenge Book
Everything® Cryptograms Book, $9.95
Everything® Digital Photography Book
Everything® Drawing Book
Everything® Easy Crosswords Book
Everything® Family Tree Book
Everything® Games Book, 2nd Ed.
Everything® Knitting Book
Everything® Knots Book
Everything® Motorcycle Book
Everything® Online Genealogy Book
Everything® Photography Book
Everything® Poker Strategy Book
Everything® Pool & Billiards Book
Everything® Quilting Book
Everything® Scrapbooking Book
Everything® Sewing Book
Everything® Woodworking Book
Everything® Word Games Challenge Book

HOME IMPROVEMENT

Everything® Feng Shui Book
Everything® Feng Shui Decluttering Book, $9.95
Everything® Fix-It Book
Everything® Homebuilding Book
Everything® Lawn Care Book
Everything® Organize Your Home Book

EVERYTHING® KIDS' BOOKS

All titles are $6.95

Everything® Kids' Animal Puzzle & Activity Book
Everything® Kids' Baseball Book, 3rd Ed.

All Everything® books are priced at $12.95 or $14.95, unless otherwise stated. Prices subject to change without notice.